D0360251

$ 650

TRAVELING WITH FLY ROD AND REEL

Also by Gary Soucie

*Hook, Line, and Sinker: The Complete Angler's
Guide to Terminal Tackle*   (1994)

Home Waters: A Fly-Fishing Anthology   (1992)

Soucie's Field Guide of Fishing Facts   (1988)

Gary Soucie

TRAVELING WITH
FLY ROD AND REEL

An Owl Book

Henry Holt and Company
New York

Henry Holt and Company, Inc.
Publishers since 1866
115 West 18th Street
New York, New York 10011

Henry Holt® is a registered
trademark of Henry Holt and Company, Inc.

Copyright © 1995 by Gary A. Soucie
All rights reserved.
Published in Canada by Fitzhenry & Whiteside Ltd.,
195 Allstate Parkway, Markham, Ontario L3R 4T8.

"*Yolky Palky!*" was first published in different form
as "The Great Scientific Siberian Salmonid Search"
in *Fly Rod & Reel*, March 1992.

"Junior, Charlie, and the Whale" was first published
in different form as "Beginner's Luck?" in *The Atlantic
Salmon Journal*, Autumn 1989.

"Lord of the Winds" was commissioned for publication
in *West of Key West*, edited by John N. Cole, to be
published by Serendipity Press in 1995.

Library of Congress Cataloging-in-Publication Data
Soucie, Gary.
Traveling with fly rod and reel / Gary Soucie—1st ed.
p.   cm.
"An Owl book."
Includes index.
1. Fly fishing.   2. Soucie, Gary—Journeys.   I. Title.
SH456.S62   1995   95-4198
799.1'2—dc20   CIP

ISBN 0-8050-3651-2

Henry Holt books are available for special promotions
and premiums. For details contact: Director, Special Markets.

First Edition—1995

Designed by Amy Hill

Printed in the United States of America
All first editions are printed on acid-free paper. ∞

10 9 8 7 6 5 4 3 2 1

Cover photos: Art Lee nets a Patagonian trout in Argentina
(Frontiers); Atlantic salmon from Russia's Ponoy (Frontiers);
Russia's first airliner, the *Antonov 2*, still widely in use.

Like its author,
this book is dedicated
to Marina,
the catch of a lifetime.

It is not worth the while to go round the world to count the cats in Zanzibar.

We are acquainted with a mere pellicle of the globe on which we live. Most have not delved six feet beneath the surface, nor leaped as many above it. We know not where we are. Beside, we are sound asleep nearly half our time.

—Henry David Thoreau,
Walden; or, Life in the Woods

The world is a country which nobody ever yet knew by description; one must travel through it one's self to be acquainted with it.

—Lord Chesterfield,
Letter to his son

CONTENTS

ACKNOWLEDGMENTS

This book and I owe a great deal to:

Marina Brodskaya, who traveled thousands of miles to a strange country to join a man who paid her far too little attention because he had a book to finish, and who cheerfully went without a honeymoon for the same reason.

Bill Davies and Kola Salmon, Inc.; Dick Burdick and Northland Adventures; Silvio Calabi and *Fly Rod & Reel;* Jan Nordström and Intersky of Scandinavia; Alan Scott and the Highlands and Islands Development Board; Morris Silver and M. Silver and Associates; Louis Brousseau and Pourvoyeurs Inuit & Indiens du Québec; Morrie Israel and the Alaska Sport Fishing Lodge Association; René Paul de la Varre and Dejan Zivojnovic of the former Yugoslav National Tourist Office; Steve Shimek and Travel Montana; Johnny May and Punnik Camp; Jean Dupuis and the Whale River Salmon Camp; Ed Conradson and Annika Goldfarb and the Swedish Tourist Board; Lars Georgsson and Ambassador Magnus Faxén of the Swedish Foreign Service; Alec Turner, Carl-Wilhelm Braun, Björn Everman, and Abu Garcia; Stojan Rus and Alpetours; Monty Lewis of the former Soviet Sports Connection; the Tourist Association of Slovenia; Gerry Emond and the Quebec Department of Indian Affairs and Northern Development; the late Dwight Rockwell and Grumman Manufacturing; Jack and Elaine London of Summerland Key, Florida; Ray Madeo of Key West and Cudjoe Gardens, Florida; Captain Marshall Cutchin of Key xvi Acknowledgments

West; Magnus Herou, Willi Utter, and Johnny Albertsson of Stockholm; Carl Safina of Islip, New York; George Reiger and Roger Matthews of the Eastern Shore of Virginia; Jack Casey and the National Marine Fisheries Service; Captain Steven V. Connett of the *Geronimo* and St. George's School in Newport, Rhode Island; Les Line (formerly my boss at *Audubon* magazine); and all the others who in one way or another made my far-flung fishing adventures possible or better.

Mike Fitzgerald, Sr. and Jr., and Frontiers for furnishing photographs from their fishing destinations around the globe.

Ted Williams, for taking time out of his busy schedule to write the foreword.

All the others who contributed invaluable information or Traveler's Tips.

This is a book for people who travel and fish and for people who travel to fish. It is brimming with valuable, ingenious tips for making potentially average fishing trips good and salvaging potentially horrible ones. In his usual crisp, entertaining prose Gary Soucie delivers his own solid, practical advice, then builds on it with equally fine how-to info garnered from some of the nation's most experienced, most traveled fishermen.

That's the intended message, and it come through loud and clear. But there is also an *unintended* message in *Traveling with Fly Rod and Reel*, and it is this that makes the book extra special for me. Careful readers will learn what it takes to become a master angler. Pay close attention because virtually everything written intentionally on this subject has been bad advice.

Gary Soucie strongly suggests in this text that he is less than a master angler. Don't believe him. By "master angler" I am not talking about prettiness of technique, especially not fly-casting technique. If I ran a fly-fishing school, I would arrange for students to be instructed mainly in *fishing*, not casting. Either you cast proficiently enough to fish, or you do not. Almost all the fish writers I know, including Soucie, cast plenty well enough to fish.

What I have learned from Gary Soucie on many occasions, including while reading a review copy of *Traveling with Fly Rod and Reel*, is that there's only one prerequisite for becoming a master angler, and that is a large supply of enthusiasm or, as Rachel Carson called it, "a sense of wonder." Carson was writing about noticing and rejoicing in nature, which happens to be the best definition I know for fishing. This is why fishing has enormous appeal for people who aren't old enough to have had their sense of wonder fried out of them by their pompous, myopic elders, who think "news" happens in places like Washington, D.C., instead of in places like rivers, lakes, and oceans. Gary Soucie is among the very few people I have ever known to have escaped into adulthood with his sense of wonder perfectly intact.

I first noticed this in 1979 when he lunched with me in New York City, the better to line up some story ideas for *Audubon* magazine, where he worked as Executive Editor. (Of all Soucie's accomplishments at *Audubon*, the most impressive to me was that he never allowed the filth, noise, mobs, and depravity of New York City to dispirit him or distract him from serious piscatorial thought.) Somehow I emerged from our session with an assignment to do an eighteen-thousand-word critique of fishing tournaments—the first item on both our wish lists. Instead of devoting our lunch to a discussion of story ideas, we talked about terminal tackle—a subject that had always bored me and bores me still, except when Soucie is expounding on it. Soucie loves fishing gear of all sort; he loves to talk and write about fishing gear; he loves the *idea* of fishing gear. And such is his enthusiasm that even people like me enjoy his pontificating. For instance, he wrote a thick book on terminal tackle called *Hook, Line, and Sinker*, and as I was reading it I found myself chuckling at the witty writing and asking myself why I hadn't tried this rig or that. The answer was that, previously, no one had been able to hold my interest long enough to teach me.

The more enthusiastic people are about fishing, the more they notice things happening around them—how nervous water forms over Atlantic salmon moving up a channel, for instance, or how over-fed, fly-spurning trout will fall all over your offering if they think another fish will get it first, or how selective salmonids sometimes forget what they're supposed to do and swill deer-hair beetles during Trico hatches. It is this ability to notice things that breeds "fish sense," and it is fish sense—not the way your fly line turns over or the distance it travels—that makes a master angler. "A fisherman," wrote Roderick Haig-Brown, "is good in proportion to the satisfaction he gets out of his sport. [Thus] a merry duffer is better than a dour master." I'll presume to take this one step further and suggest that if a fisherman is dour, he cannot be a master. Dour fishermen miss things because they are not excited enough by nature to always notice what is happening around them.

I'll confess now that I am not altogether innocent of dourness. In Alaska I toured with the same tortured soul who hosted Soucie's party a year later, and at times I was tempted to break his legs myself. (Ultimately, I came to recognize some of the demons that possessed him, and we parted amiably.) I am dourest of all when, as so frequently happens, I go on an outdoor writers' trip and learn that the lodge has booked us during a time of no fish because, as the proprietor unsmilingly explains, that's when he had free space; and, by the way, could we please write something nice. It is difficult for me to extricate myself from the emotional slumps induced by such disasters, but knowing Soucie and reading his book has helped. I am getting better.

For example, I'm writing this from a private club now mired in the urban sprawl connecting Miami and Fort Lauderdale. I am here not by choice, but by filial duty and guilt. The club represents much of what I most detest. One may not loosen one's tie at dinner, even at ten thirty and after four rum punches. And today I was evicted from the tennis court because the white dress shirt I was wearing (the whitest I had) had a faint checked pattern to it. The boat traffic is hideous, and the dirty sea has been stripped of fish. The minor slump I'm in would have been a lot worse without Soucie's book. It persuaded me to bring a 6-weight fly rod, and I am catching little lance-finned fish with the vaguely ominous-sounding name "leatherjackets." Whatever leatherjacket fishing is not, it is better than sitting on the beach and doing nothing.

Leatherjackets are very strong for their size (six or eight inches), and they have beautiful yellow tails. I may well be the first person ever to seriously fish for them; and that, exactly, is what this book is all about: meeting nature and fish on their own terms, and making the very best out of every fishing minute this short life allows us. Last night I phoned Gary Soucie and told him about my leatherjacket fishing. He sounded proud of me.

—Ted Williams,
Grafton, Massachusetts

TRAVELING WITH
FLY ROD AND REEL

BEGINNING AT BAKER'S CREEK

My first angling expedition would seem not to belong in a book like this. It wasn't a fly-fishing trip abroad, it was a hometown hike to hand-line marshmallows and Velveeta cheese. Let me beg your indulgence by invoking the shade of Thoreau: "It takes a man of genius to travel in his own country, in his native village; to make any progress between his door and his gate." I wasn't even a man, just an eleven- or twelve-year-old boy, and it was the first time I'd ever skipped school or gone fishing without adult supervision.

I don't remember how we got the idea to cut classes that fine May day, or whose idea it was. In fact, I don't even recall for certain who "we" all were. Probably Tom Bates and Larry Godin, for we were fast friends then and used to walk to and from school together. Or maybe it was the Paulissen brothers, Jim and Ronnie, who lived next door. No matter. I do recall that none of us had ever been to Baker's Creek, but that we'd heard about it from older kids and that it loomed large in our geographical iconography.

To avoid being seen by parents or nosy neighbors, we must have traveled through the woods north of Waterman Park, across the field of truck gardens from Larry's house and right next to the Paulissens'. Except for a quick dash across Justine Drive, we could have kept to the woods until we got to the country club. Then it would have been catty-corner across the fairways, or perhaps we crawled through the tunnel in the privet hedge to get to the pump house. Either way, once we hit the river, we'd have been safe.

On the upstream edge of the golf course was another little patch of woods, interrupted only by the Ambergs' yard. But Pete, Tony, and Pam would have been in school and Mr. Amberg at his office. We wouldn't have worried about Mrs. Amberg, because I don't think she knew any of us by name back then—only later, when academic and athletic achievements in school tended to erode socioeconomic boundaries. On the other side of the Amberg yard the woods were lower and muddier, a tiny bottomland forest.

And suddenly we were there: Baker's Creek.

It was everything we'd imagined, and more. The creek flowed through a hardwood forest that was as thick as it was small. Probably second or third growth, but mature, with lots of fallen trees moldering on the ground, some of them just long lumps in the broadleaf carpet of the forest floor. Just before it joined the river, the creek made a sharp left-hand bend. It might as well have been flowing out of the north woods wilderness, so mysteriously unknown it seemed. We didn't explore upstream that day, because the creek mouth was all we could handle.

Baker's widened to maybe twenty-five or thirty feet at its mouth, and the water looked deep. It was almost clear enough to see the bottom, yet dark enough to harbor who knows what watery secrets. A big, old tree—a maple, I think, but it might have been a cottonwood or sycamore, perhaps even an oak—leaned out over the widest and deepest part of the creek. It was a perfect fishing platform.

My memory of that first fishing trip is incomplete, fragmentary, disjointed. But what I remember I remember vividly, some of it as clearly as if it had happened last week.

First, I remember the high drama and excitement of catching those scrappy little sunfish. We must have caught bullheads too, but I don't recall them. I do recall the brilliant rainbow colors in the pumpkinseeds and bluegills, the sedate formality of the crappies, the imperious, bright-red eyes of the somber rock bass. And I recall the extraordinary beauty of the mystery fish.

It was the biggest fish anyone hooked that day, even though it writhed its way off the hook in midair. But it was the most beautiful creature I'd ever beheld. As it flipped back into the water, it flashed like a living lodestone in the streaks of filtered light—mostly gold, but also burnt red and dark green, and it was stunningly lovely. We were all so excited we nearly fell off the tree trunk we were straddling.

(A couple years later I would pore through my new copy of A. J. McClane's *Wise Fisherman's Encyclopedia,* looking for the fish portrait that most closely matched my memory of that fish. The picture that bridged the synapses, unfortunately, was the golden trout's. Of course it couldn't have been *aguabonita.* The Kankakee River is too warm and turbid and sluggish as it slides through the cornfields and cow pastures of Illinois, more than a thousand miles removed from the golden's easternmost habitat. I still can't tell you what species it might have been. Whatever it was, that little fish burns brightly in my memory, a viable contender for the most beautiful fish in my personal experience.)

At some point that day we discovered the crawdad burrows in the bank below the base of our tree. For a while at least, we turned our attention away from fishing and dangled our cheese baits before those lilliputian lobsters. Whether we used any of the crayfish, or their tail meats, for bait, I can't say. But I can still hear the shrieking and whooping as we tried to capture the hard-shelled crustaceans without getting pinched.

The biggest excitement of the day involved another lost fish, and it came when all but one of us were still on the bank, playing with the crawdads. Just as whoever was fishing was hauling a fish up from the depths, he shouted something like "Holy cow! Look at that turtle!" I remember looking up and seeing the turtle going for the fish. Then I realized that what I had taken to be the turtle's carapace was only its head. The hooked fish disappeared in its great jaws and the monster sank back to the bottom. It was far and away the biggest turtle I've ever seen in fresh water. Still is, and I've seen some pretty decent alligator snappers down in Florida. I have no idea how big that turtle was. Things look bigger when you're eleven or twelve, and it simply couldn't have been as big as it seemed, but it was enormous. When I shut my eyes and conjure up that scene, the turtle seems almost as big as some of the sea turtles I've seen since. Whatever its size, that monstrous chelonian made us aware of the passage of time, and we decided to head for home soon thereafter.

How much trouble that outing caused us at home or school is lost to memory. How much good came out of it isn't. The road hasn't been straight, or without many a detour and interruption, but that day was the first step on a long journey. For the next half-dozen or so years, we spent a lot of time on Baker's Creek, fishing and exploring and getting into trouble with the Schneiders, who owned a lot of the land. From there it was on to the stripmine pits near Braidwood and the harbor breakwater at Michigan City, on to Montauk, Key West, Lake Nicaragua, the Julian Alps, and the Barents Sea coast. It has been a long and wonderful trip, and it all began at Baker's Creek.

1

REASONABLE EXPECTATIONS

When a trip comes apart on somebody, it's always, *always* because of false expectations," Silvio Calabi said recently. "People arrive at a destination with a mindset—not just about the size and quantity of fish, but about the food, the amount of game animals they're going to see, how crowded the fishery is." An experienced traveler and expert fly-fisherman as well as editor in chief and associate publisher of *Fly Rod & Reel* and *Fly Tackle Dealer* magazines, Calabi knows what he's talking about. My experience certainly corroborates his.

After reading the outfitter's or booking agent's promotional hype about the place (not to mention the breathless prose in the outdoor magazines, almost certainly written by nonpaying junketeers), it's hard not to arrive at a fishing destination with pumped-up expectations. I mean, if you didn't expect great fishing, why would you have spent so much time and money on the trip?

It's okay to be optimistic about a fishing trip; just be a realistic optimist. Unless you're a real piscatorial shut-in, one who's experienced little variety and a lot of shutouts in your fly-fishing, you can't realistically expect that a trip to some angling mecca halfway around the world will provide the *fishing* of a lifetime. The *trip* of a lifetime, maybe. But the fishing? There are simply too many variables to count on having great fishing, no matter where you are heading: weather, timing, your abilities and skills under the conditions at hand, even luck.

Art Lee nets a Patagonian trout in Argentina. *(Frontiers)*

☞ **TRAVELER'S TIP**

Hang loose and be flexible. Everything may not always go as hoped or planned, but you should make the best of all situations and keep a smile on your face. After all, you are having fun!

—Randall Kaufmann
president, Kaufmann's Streamborn, Inc.,
and author of *Bonefishing with a Fly*
Portland, Oregon

Yes, luck. After we've tucked a few seasons under our belt, we like to think that luck no longer plays a role in our fishing, but it does. The first time I went fishing abroad—on a writers' junket to the Scottish Highlands and the Orkney Islands—luck conspired with the calendar. Mid-May in such high latitudes, we expected the water to be cold and the salmon run to be spotty. And they were. But who could have predicted weather too hot and sunny for good fishing, two days out of three, that early, that far north? To make a long story short, nobody caught a salmon. But at least we all caught trout. All but one of us, that is. The one who went completely fishless the whole trip was probably the most experienced person among us, insofar as fly-fishing and trout fishing are concerned. You'd recognize the byline for sure, but I won't embarrass him further. Lady Luck can be fickle and perfidious. Or she can smile on those least deserving. I hadn't yet learned to fly-cast but somehow managed to catch the first fish of the trip, a brown trout from Loch Swannay that turned out to be half the first day's total catch. Believe me, it was dumb luck. Skill had nothing to do with it. Nothing.

Summing up the Scottish Highlands and Islands experience: The weather had been perverse (as it so often is when fishing is involved), we got there before most of the fish did, my fly-fishing skills (virtually nonexistent) were not up to the challenges, and luck dealt out some pretty strange hands. As I would come to learn with more fishing-travel experience, it was a pretty typical fly-fishing trip.

The least experienced fly-fisherman on that trip to Scotland, I was the least disappointed. My expectations were vague and, except for the one about catching a salmon, mostly exceeded by the particulars of the experience: seeing the Scottish countryside, watching birds,

---

☞ **TRAVELER'S TIP**

More than a quarter century ago when I began writing the "Wood, Field and Stream" column for The New York Times, *I was, for nearly two years, greeted with success wherever I went with my fly rod. After that delightful start, I began striking out or managing a few infield singles at least half the time. Bad weather was responsible for most of this, but changes in my quarry's habits were also relevant.*

This leads me to suggest that he who sallies forth—whether for tarpon or Atlantic salmon or brook trout—with the notion that he is going to have the best fishing of his life, is probably going to be disappointed much of the time. Better to revel in the place and in the freedom you had to visit it. Also be wary of putting too much hope in encountering the same success and the same delights in old spots revisited.

What you should do is pick the ideal time and hope for the best, and no matter what happens, you will certainly learn something.

—Nelson Bryant
formerly "Wood, Field and Stream"
columnist, *The New York Times,*
and author of *Outdoors*
West Tisbury, Massachusetts

---

learning about flies, meeting a lot of interesting people, discovering single-malt Scotches. But I think some of the others were disappointed. Expectations and disappointment are closely related, and mostly mirrored: High expectations beget high disappointment, unreasonable expectations result in unreasonable disappointment.

Go anywhere in the world expecting to shoot fish in a barrel, and you are setting yourself up for a major disappointment. Odds are the fishing won't be that good at any given time and place. If it is, it'll be too easy to be much fun.

From hard-won experience, I can tell you that *no* fishing trip ever turns out exactly the way you thought it would. Sometimes the fishing is better than expected, but usually it's worse. Every famous fishing mecca has its off days and weeks, weather can turn the fishing on its ear in a minute, and both people and machinery sometimes fail at the tasks assigned them. As the Scottish poet Robert Burns so memorably put it, "The best laid schemes o' mice and men/Gang aft a-gley." If the fishing isn't off or the weather uncooperative, you almost certainly can count on something else going wrong at some point during the trip. Sometimes a lot of somethings else. I've learned that "no problem" is the last thing you want to hear before or during a fishing trip, because it usually means the person you are talking to (a) doesn't understand the question, (b) doesn't know the answer, or (c) is pretty sure you don't want to hear the answer.

Historic Drought and Hysterical Disappointment

Very recently, on Russia's Kola Peninsula, I had the misfortune to spend a bad week on a great salmon river with a bunch of rich,

---

☞ **TRAVELER'S TIP**

Try to go on a trip with an open mind, not expecting to catch every fish in the ocean or in the river, but to go with learning about a new place and a new style of fishing and a new thing. I think a lot of people go to places with high expectations and expect to catch way more fish than what they end up with, and I don't care whether you go to Alaska or the best place in the world, it doesn't always work that way. Reduce your expectations by half, and know that you're going to have a wonderful time and a different experience. If the fish are there, it's an extra, a bonus.

I've been more often pleasantly surprised on trips by surroundings, whether it's the scenery, the mountains, the wildlife, the birds, whatever it is visually that I see—that's always been a surprise. I guided out in Alaska, Bristol Bay, for a lot of years, but a few years ago I went up to the coastline of Alaska—southeast, the Sitka area—and to see the glaciers and the abundance of birds and ocean life. . . . I mean, I was overwhelmed with the beauty of the place and I really thought the fishing almost became secondary. From my perspective, having caught a number of fish in years gone by, the fish-catching aspect becomes less and less critical, but the surroundings and the beauty of the trip are important to me.

— Steve Rajeff
director of research and development, G. Loomis, Inc.,
twenty-two-time national and eleven-time world casting champion
Woodland, Washington

spoiled American fishermen. Granted, a heavy May snowfall followed by midsummer-like temperatures and the worst drought in four hundred years had put the fishing off. Way off. When the salmon finally arrived at camp, a bit later than expected, there weren't many of them. The water had fallen quickly from its preseason high levels. By the last week of June, the river was low enough and warm enough for August. The fish were almost certainly holding in the deep, lakelike sections lower down, waiting for the water to rise, then start falling again. The fishing was tough. Not quite as tough as it had been the previous three weeks, but tough enough, thank you.

There we all were, on what should have been one of the two or three best weeks of the season, on what is perhaps the most prolific salmon river in the world, and the fishing was downright disappointing. You had to work hard for every fish, as hard as if you were fishing the well-flogged salmon streams of eastern Canada or the U.K., not a lightly fished wilderness river north of the Arctic Circle in Russia.

It's hard not to be downcast when a world-class fishing spot fails to live up to its reputation or your expectations. But that's fishing, as the saying goes. To cite another cliché, that's why it's called fishing, not catching.

Instead of trying to make the most of the weak hand they'd been dealt by fate, the Californians bitched and moaned. They didn't even give the river a fair trial. They caught a few fish their first afternoon and evening in camp, and another before breakfast the next morning. But by dinner that first full day, their chorus was in full whine. They said the booking agent who'd sold them the trip had told them he'd caught 162 fish in one week the year before. It's a good thing no one had offered them a good deal on a certain bridge in New York.

Where did these guys think they were going, Fantasy Island? Even giving them the benefit of the doubt—that they were lied to by someone overhyping an expensive fishing trip (naturally, the booking agent tells a slightly different story)—their disappointment was still out of proportion. It has been a long, long time since a single rod has caught 162 Atlantic salmon in a single week, anywhere. Even commercial netters don't do that well. The last year I fished the Whale River up in northern Quebec, the allowable commercial catch on the river for the whole season was just 500 fish.

In his *New Standard Fishing Encyclopedia and International Angling Guide*, surely the best-known, most often cited angling refer-

☞ **TRAVELER'S TIP**

Always be prepared for the worst to happen. You should always have reading material. One paperback book is as much as I want to carry. I don't want to carry heavy books, or lots of them, on a trip when I'm going fishing. And then if things go bad you just make the best of it. I've been in Boca Paila for six days of wind, when the fishing just wasn't any good. So you enjoy the company and you play cards or you read or you walk the beaches. You know, the places that we go to fly-fish are usually wonderful places, so just because you can't fish, or the fishing is not so good, doesn't mean you can't enjoy it.

We have too many people coming in who think you can buy fly-fishing. That's the whole thing that's happening with this explosion. We're going to get lots of people in there who don't belong. And so they do get their noses out of joint.

You do need to know that where you're going will produce the services that they say they will. You should always have a recommendation, one way or another. Either from your travel agent, who should know, or from someone who's been there. Ask for a previous client's name and number, so you can get firsthand information.

> — Joan Salvato Wulff
> fly-casting champion and president of
> Royal Wulff, Inc., and the Wulff Casting School
> Lew Beach, New York

ence book in the English-speaking world, the late A. J. McClane wrote that "money spent in pursuit of Atlantic salmon ranks midway between money invested in backing a Broadway show and money invested in an Irish Sweepstakes ticket" and that "par for the course, the world over, is a fish a day, but very rare is the salmon angler who consistently breaks par." Any fisherman ought to have done at least that much easy, armchair research before plunking down $5,500 for a week's fishing and maybe another $2,500 or more for airfare, tips, booze, and nights on the town in Moscow.

Admittedly, these guys were new to salmon fishing. But they weren't inexperienced anglers, yuppies who'd only recently taken up fly-fishing, or duffers used to put-and-take casting overstocked hatchery trout. Most of them were seasoned steelheaders. Now, if anyone should know about putting in long hours and hundreds, maybe thousands, of casts between fish, it's a California steelheader. In *Pavlov's Trout, the Incompleat Psychology of Everyday Fishing*, the fly-fisherman and clinical psychologist Paul Quinnett—who lives outside Spokane, Washington, "near some of the best steelhead fishing in the world"—says, "Red hot steelhead fishing means the average angler will catch one fish for every seven to ten hours of fishing. Slow steelheading means one fish every 25 or 30 hours. Even if you fish hard all day when the fishing is hot, chances are you will *not* catch a steelhead." By those standards, the salmon fishing on that Russian river that June was at least middling warm. In six and a half days of fishing, the eight whiners caught something like thirty fish, for a per-rod average of about one fish every fourteen or fifteen hours. Not up to their unreasonable expectations, certainly, nor even to Kola Peninsula standards, but hardly a shutout.

Traveling to Fish, or Fishing to Travel?

If catching fish—lots of fish or big fish—is your main objective, you have few good reasons to leave the continent. Our fifty states, Canada, and Mexico offer North American anglers a staggering variety of world-class fishing opportunities. Geographic nitpickers might want to exclude Hawaii from a strict-constructionist definition of North America, but that still leaves us way ahead of anyone else. On the other hand, geographic liberals might want to cede the Bahamas, Cuba, Puerto Rico, and the Virgin Islands to North America, all significant piscatorial enhancements of Florida's already considerable subtropical attractions. Either way, no other continent comes close. Put them all together, and we still give the world a run for its money.

You won't get far into your toes counting the number of places around the world that offer better fishing than you can find in North America: humongous brown trout in New Zealand and Patagonia, sea trout in Argentina and Sweden and on the Barents Sea coast of Russia, plentiful steelheading on Kamchatka, enormous pike in the Baltic, billfishing in the Azores, sails and bills off the Pacific coast of Panama and Costa Rica, two-hundred-plus-pound tarpon on the west coast of Africa, easy bonefish in the Bahamas and Los Rocques and on Christmas Island, and, yes, Atlantic salmon on Russia's Kola Peninsula. That's about it.

Is that any reason to stay home? Far from it. If exotica is your game, then the world is indeed your oyster: taimen in Siberia and Mongolia, peacock bass and payara in Venezuela, dorado in Paraguay, Nile perch in Lake Victoria, kahawai and kawakawa in Australia and New Zealand, giant trevally on Christmas Island, barramundi in Australia and Papua New Guinea (plus niugini bass in the latter), tigerfish in Zambia and Zimbabwe, mahseer in the Himalayas, huchen in the Danube, snoek in South Africa, machacas in Central America, cherry (masu) salmon and suzuki in Japan. I could go on, but I think you get the point.

But even if you aren't into casting flies at exotic species, consider the spectrum of opportunities affording to fly-fish for *Salmo trutta* in, say, the braided channels of Montana's Madison, the Ulvsparre water on Sweden's Em, the little Carmans on Long Island, Bhutan's Mochu, the Test and Itchen and other storied English streams, the Atlas Mountains of North Africa, Tierra del Fuego's Río Grande, the eastern slopes of the Urals, the Transvaal streams of South Africa's Drakens-

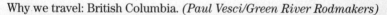

Why we travel: British Columbia. *(Paul Vesci/Green River Rodmakers)*

berg, the Norfork in the Ozarks, Iceland's Stadara, the Carpathian Mountains of Slovakia, the Mataura on New Zealand's South Island, Connemara's Ballynahinch water or Lough Corrib, the Karup Å in Denmark, Bulgaria's Stara Planina, the high Pyrenees of Andorra, the Firehole during an October snowfall, the Transylvanian Alps of Romania, the San Carlos on East Falkland, the Stockholm and Åland archipelagoes in the Baltic, the Tarsus Mountains of Turkey, the Vale of Kashmir. All just brown trout fishing? I think not.

What the rest of the world has to offer, and which North America can't match, is just that: the rest of the world.

Know Thyself

Unless you enjoy suffering expensive disappointment, you need to prepare yourself adequately for a trip. And that begins by looking inward. Don't spend so much time lusting over the images in the magazine ads and travel brochures. First, know what it is you hope to get out of a trip.

Datus Proper, the author of *What the Trout Said*, saw a lot of fishing in his career as a U.S. State Department foreign service officer. His third overseas posting (following assignments in Angola, where he caught a two-hundred-pound tarpon, and in Brazil, "where there was at the time some pretty good trout fishing") was to Ireland. Proper says the Irish assignment was "wonderful: very difficult fishing for very wild brown trout, big ones, and all waiting-for-the-hatch. It was the kind of fishing I like best." Now, if matching the hatch and "very difficult fishing" are not your cup of tea, you might find the same experience other than wonderful. You might be better served heading for Alaska, Labrador, Argentina, or Chile rather than Ireland. The way *you* like to fish is more important than how "wonderful" the fishing is supposed to be in some far-flung fly-fishing Valhalla.

"The most important thing is that fishing destinations are very different," says Don Causey, the editor and publisher of *The Angling Report*. "People's tastes, desires, and special interests in fishing are very different as well, and you simply have to find the right fishing opportunity for yourself."

I've fished three different salmon operations in Alaska, all members of the same cooperative, and they were as different as morning, noon, and night. Except for a heavy run of humpies, the fishing was way off, and the kings had developed lockjaw at the lodge I wound up liking best because it was so well run and the setting was so wild and lovely. I caught the most fish (lots of silvers between eight and twelve pounds) at a poorly run lodge on a wide, muddy river I doubt I'd return to. You might have ranked them in a different order. Different strokes, as they say. That's why asking when the "best" time to fish a given place is not necessarily a good question. I want to know when they're hitting Hendricksons, say, not when every fish in the stream will take Woolly Buggers. You may prefer something different: the caddis hatches or the rusty spinner fall.

My good friend and sometime fishing and traveling companion George Reiger, conservation editor of *Field & Stream*, contributor to numerous other fishing and outdoor magazines, and the author of several thoughtful books on the outdoor life, recently dropped me a line I'd like to share:

> What traveling anglers must realize is that if they make a commitment to five days of fishing in some remote place, that's *it!* There's seldom anything else to do. For me, dawn-to-dusk fishing along one short stretch of river, or even a patch of flats, gets boring awfully fast. Especially when just one species is involved, and all the fish are pretty much the same size.
>
> *Know thyself.* Before you commit to a week at some remote camp, be sure you and your companions have the temperament for such isolation. Some anglers are quite content to go to a Labrador lodge and fish all day, every day, for a week, catching 4- and 5-pound brook trout, or to Christmas Island to catch 4- and 5-pound bonefish for days on end.
>
> For me, that's like sitting down with a 10-pound bag of Hershey's chocolates until they're all gone. I'm a Whitman's Sampler man, myself. Ninety percent of what makes fishing fun is the travel, the people, and the land—the geography and the history. It's the bird life as much as the fish life. It's the serendipity of discovering something new and trying something different every day.
>
> I think you've got to have a certain curiosity, a certain perspective, to get the most out of a fishing trip.

Now, if you're not a Whitman's Sampler kind of guy, you just might relish the idea of catching three-pound rainbow after three-pound rainbow, ten-pound coho after ten-pound coho, day in, day out. As George says, Know thyself. Before heading off on a megabuck, megamile fishing trip, be sure you know what it is *you* are after. Is catching big fish, or a lot of fish, important to you? It isn't for everyone, not even some of the big names whose published exploits feed your angling wanderlust.

"I don't like *not* catching fish," Datus Proper says, "but I don't need to catch a lot of trout. I keep hearing people talk about fifty-trout days and one-hundred-trout days, which is not the kind of talk I like to hear. I can't imagine still wanting to run up big scores on trout after you've been fly-fishing a few years."

So much for numbers. What about size? Ted Kerasote, the camping editor for *Sports Afield* and a well-traveled fisherman who has been to all four corners of the globe, says, "You don't travel halfway around the world just to haul eight pounds of fish out of a river." He goes on to put fishing travel in proper perspective: "My best trout fishing experience was in Kashmir. The fishing was so totally wrapped up with hiking in big mountains without a map—or a pretty insufficient map—just going on the directions of local nomadic herders, and coming up to these incredible glacial lakes and going over passes and looking for exotic Himalayan wildlife. It was a whole environmental experience that had much greater ramifications than just the fishing. But you know, we caught ten-inch fish in these high glacial lakes and met some wonderful people and went through the whole Indian bureaucracy to get a fishing license and permission to visit this place. It turned into one of the most memorable fishing trips in my life."

That—to me as well as to Ted Kerasote—is what fishing travel is all about. The experience is the thing, not the number of fish or the aggregate weight of the catch.

Know Thy Skills

Knowing thyself also means knowing whether your skills are up to the demands of a place or species. If you can't make long, fast, accurate casts (most likely into the wind), flats fishing for bonefish may not be your métier. (It certainly hasn't been mine.) You might be better off casting flies into a chum slick for tarpon—*if* you are up to a long, hard fight with a heavy, athletic fish.

Your expectations ought to be based in part upon a realistic appraisal of your own angling and fly-fishing skills. There's an old angling axiom to the effect that 10 percent of the fishermen catch 90 percent of the fish. The saying's sound the world around. Good fishermen will always outfish mediocre fishermen, no matter where they are fishing. Bob Nauheim, president of Fishing International, says:

> I'll tell you something that's really, really true, and should be in your book in big, bold, black letters: If you can't catch fish here in the United States, don't expect to catch them someplace else. I mean, it's simple as that. You might have more opportunity to catch a bonefish, let us say, at Christmas Island—you will have more opportunity than in the Florida Keys, but the guy that can catch them in the Florida Keys is going to catch ten to your one. You know, that's simple truth.

When it comes to assessing our own casting skills, fishing ability, physical strength, stamina, and temperament, most of us tend to be, well, kind. Bob Nauheim has sent a lot of people fishing over the past two decades (the majority of them trollers, plug-casters, and spin-fishermen), and he doesn't like a lot of what he has seen: "I've got to tell you, the biggest number of traveling fly-fishermen are rank amateurs. . . . It's something they like the idea of, but they just don't spend enough time at it. . . . Most of them can't perform. Some of them are good enough to say, 'I know I wasn't up to it.' Others will find fault with the place, the lodge, the guide, us, you know, whatever."

Be sure you choose a trip you can handle. Nowhere in the world will the fishing be much better than you are. If you can't cut the fishing, you won't like the trip. Period. It's downright difficult to appreciate the glories of a place or the amenities of an operation when you are facing hour after hour of frustration on the water. There's a saying in the fishing travel business: When the fishing is poor, the soup is cold.

Caveat Lector, Caveat Piscator

Unfortunately, a lot of travel writing is more promotional hype than journalistic reporting. And that includes a lot of fishing-travel writing. Rosy reports of the fishing give rise to even rosier expectations on the part of the fisherman itching for that trip of a lifetime.

You have to read between the lines, even when the writer is trying to tell it like it is. A writer's experience may make for good reading, but it may also be irrelevant to your expectations. For one thing, writers are often accorded opportunities and experiences that aren't available at any price to the traveling public. The result is honest, but distorted reporting. Ted Kerasote describes another source of misunderstanding:

> Most of us go traveling because we've read that great things are happening on the other side of the world. But the people who've written those things we've read have probably been back to those spots half a dozen times or spent a month there. They've put in a lot more time than the average traveler can. So, if you're going on one of these flash trips of a week or two, ratchet down your expectations and don't expect all the things that happened to the people who are writing about those places.
>
> You know, I went to New Zealand and had a wonderful time, but I spent almost two and a half months there. And there were fishless days. A lot of fishless days. If I had gone for a week—actually I would have had a very good time on rainbows, because the first week was exceptional, but the brown trout fishing took a lot of work.
>
> I spent five months in South America and had a wonderful time, but I had a lot of fishless days once again.
>
> In Bhutan, where I went for a week, I had a piscatorial disaster. Nothing happened. Terrible fishing. It was raining the entire time. The rivers were high and muddy. Landslides everyplace. We couldn't get to where we wanted to go. Spent a lot of money, and a year of preparation and anticipation, and because we were only there for a week it was nothing like what previous visitors had written.

Take everything you read, no matter the source, with a grain of salt. Still, however much dishonest or distorted reporting contributes to raising unreasonable expectations, the traveler's attitude counts as much as, or more than, anything else in getting the most out of a trip. Mike Fitzgerald is president of Frontiers, the biggest, best-known, and one of the oldest booking agents in fishing travel, and here's how he sees it:

> With the evolution of international fishing, which has basically been a phenomenon of the last twenty-five years, we see people's values getting all out of sync. People who grew up with a good sense of fishing values within the context of where they were doing it will get on the international fast track and somehow, even with the most sophisticated, things get all out of sync. For example, they'll try to compare a week in Patagonia with their last week in Alaska or they'll try to compare an Atlantic salmon week with their last experience with chum salmon. They will be invited to a good Caribbean bonefishing destination and be comparing that with their last trip to Christmas Island.
>
> I find that people so often are going into something without adequate points of reference or really good perspective, and therefore can get wrapped up in numbers, competing with themselves, much less other people, and miss a large quotient of what is really valuable in international travel: the ambience, the history, the cultural experience, the amenities, all the things that to me add so much and are so valuable compared to just the fishing itself.

Amen.

Resources

It's probably safe to say that most anglers get their information on far-flung destinations from three sources: (1) word-of-mouth reports from friends and acquaintances, (2) articles in fishing and outdoor magazines, and (3) advertisements by and direct-mail solicitations from camps, lodges, outfitters, and booking agents. Word-of-mouth is probably trustworthy, but hardly comprehensive; you won't hear about most fly-fishing destinations this way. Because the hook-and-bullet press is so cheap, most of the articles are written by editors on junkets paid for by the camps, lodges, outfitters, airlines, and government tourist offices and so are suspect at best. (Most magazines won't publish negative reports, anyway.) Some direct-mail solicitations are informative, but as for the rest: They don't call it junk mail for nothing. Still, taken with a grain of salt, all the information you can gather is important, and you shouldn't make any major fishing-travel decisions without first wading through the chaff.

Most of the tackle catalogs listed in Chapter 4 carry books and videos, which can be excellent sources of trip-planning information on destinations, species, techniques, and other things you need to know. Most fly-fishing shops offer classes, clinics, courses, seminars, and schools in fly-casting and fishing, which can help you get the most out of a trip. So do the fly-fishing shows around the country. If you live near their stores, some of the big boys in the field also provide instructional help: Orvis, L.L. Bean, Kaufmann's Streamborn, Marriott's, Dan Bailey's, International Angler, and Madison River Fishing Company, for example.

You know the magazines—*American Angler, Atlantic Salmon Journal, Field & Stream, Fishing World, Fly Fisherman, Fly Fishing Saltwater, Fly Rod & Reel, Outdoor Life, Saltwater Flyfishing, Saltwater Sportsman, Sportfishing, Sports Afield, Wild Steelhead & Atlantic Salmon*, and a few others—but you may not know how to lay your hands on other kinds of information.

FISHING TRAVEL NEWSLETTERS

The following newsletters provide information on fishing in the U.S., Canada, Mexico, and abroad, but the first is independent while the second is published by a booking agent. However, Jim C. Chapralis, president of PanAngling Travel Service and editor of *The PanAngler,* insists his newsletter isn't just a sales-promotion organ. He points out that it was the first newsletter on international fishing and that he feels "it is the watchdog on many issues confronting international fishing." Don Causey, editor and publisher of *The Angling Report,* says, "I try to do a real kind of *Consumer Reports* of international fishing."

The Angling Report, 9300 S. Dadeland Boulevard, Suite 605, Miami, FL 33156; phone 1-305-670-1361; fax 1-305-670-1376; independent, consumer-oriented, monthly newsletter, $39 a year; $5 and up for Angler Network (reader-originated) reports on destinations.

The PanAngler, PanAngling Travel Service, 180 N. Michigan Avenue, Chicago, IL 60601, phone 1-312-263-0328. Monthly newsletter, $20 a year.

FISHING TRAVEL BOOKS (MOSTLY PLACE-ORIENTED)

In addition to the country descriptions (now largely out of date but still invaluable) in *McClane's New Standard Fishing Encyclopedia and International Angling Guide* (New York: Henry Holt and Co., 1974), useful trip-planning information may be found in the following books:

Mike Baughman, **The Perfect Fishing Trip** (Englewood Cliffs, NJ: Prentice-Hall, 1985).

Göran Cederberg, ed., **World's Greatest Flyfishing Locations** (New York: Crescent Books, 1991).

Jim C. Chapralis, **PanAngling's World Guide to Fly Fishing** (Chicago: PanAngling Publishing Co., 1987).

Tony Pawson, **Flyfishing Around the World** (London: Unwin Hyman, 1987).

Ernest Schwiebert, **The Traveling Angler: 20 Five-Star Angling Vacations** (New York: Doubleday, 1991).

VARZINA

Try here," Sergey said, waving his hand vaguely at the water. An overgrown kid full of high spirits and low comedy when the banquet table glitters and tinkles with bottles and glasses of vodka, Sergey Demyentyev is the very picture of Russian stoicism when he's guiding: logo cap tipped up and off center above his weary blue eyes, a cigarette dangling from his pouting lips, his posture permanently suggesting a shrug, unused hand stuffed into the top of his neoprene chest waders. I surveyed the scene: We were standing on the edge of a little half-moon cove at the bottom right-hand corner of a huge, wide pool, at the top of a long, fast riffle that bowed out right against a steep bank and then swept hard left before disappearing around a rocky promontory to the right.

"Hey, weren't we here yesterday?" I asked, recalling the complete lack of action the day before.

Sergey raised his shoulders in a full-blown shrug. "We were here the day before that too," he said, "and the first day too." Both hands were tucked into the waders now. My eyes began picking up the visual cues: the big rock in the middle, that tall birch in the alders directly across, the confluence of channels above and along the upper edges of the pool. Until that moment, I hadn't realized we'd fished the same water every day.

We've got thirty miles of river, I thought, and he takes us to the same place four days in a row? He must like this spot, even though we'd not yet raised a fish. "So you think this is a good place to fish?"

"Why not?" Sergey said, apparently forgetting or rejecting my comment that the expression means "Who gives a shit?" to American ears. As I stripped line off the rod, Sergey announced that he'd make lunch on the vegetated point just above us.

Ted Williams, my roommate and fishing partner on the Varzina, said he'd wade out across the big pool to work some water where he'd caught a seventeen-pound salmon the day before. He'd taken the fish on his first cast, on a hairwing Blue Charm. Sergey had started wading out to Ted with the big, long-handled landing net, but Ted had waved him off. Just as Ted tailed the fish, the rod tip snapped in protest. As no one fishing the Varzina River in its first season the year before had named the pool, we did: Broken Rod.

While Sergey built a smoky fire of alder twigs and driftwood to heat the soup, Ted and I worked our respective waters without any success.

After a leisurely lunch, Ted said he wanted to go back to the other side of Broken Rod Pool. I thought I might join him, but was dissuaded by the depth and speed of the channel between our alder-clad point and the waist-deep water in midriver. My right knee had been bothering me since twisting it several weeks earlier on the Shenandoah, so I decided I'd stay on the right bank and try the riffle again.

I'd raised only one fish in four goes at this water, so I decided I'd better study the water carefully before casting. I swept my eyes slowly across the bottom of the pool and down the long riffle. I was still standing there gazing down the broken water when Sergey reappeared behind me. "What do you see?"

"I don't know," I muttered while staring at the bottom of the riffle. "It looks like—" The water seemed whiter, busier, more broken than I had remembered it. Could it be fish? I wondered. *"My God,"* I shouted, *"it looks like Alaska!"* I'd never seen anything like this in Atlantic salmon rivers: dorsal fins and tails moving in the disturbed water and whole, shiny backs of bigger fish thrashing their way up through the shallow water. I hadn't yet tied on a new fly, so while sloshing my way into casting position I gave a cursory glance at the knot and point of the Hairy Mary I'd been fishing before the lunch break. They seemed okay. Now I could see fish everywhere in the run.

There seemed to be more of them than rocks breaking the water. I shouted at Ted, but he couldn't hear me over the water.

My first cast fell into the water in front of me like a plate of spaghetti. When I get excited, I cast like that. The rushing water pulled the line straight and I lifted the line into a back cast. This time the fly went where I wanted it to: on the far side of the riffle, where it could get a full swing across the lanes. *Bang!* a fish struck, I struck back. Too soon, too fast. I lost it. I cast again. Another strike. This time I wrested control of my muscles away from my adrenal gland. The fish was on. Down the riffle he went, then into a pool of pocket water on the other wide. Back out into the riffle and in the deep, fast water beneath an undercut bank on my side. After a lot more seesawing across the current, the fish tired. I slipped him into the calm, shallow water of the little cove and Sergey scooped him up in the net. Now the boy broke through as Sergey's blue eyes lighted up with life and his lips broke into a wide grin. "Good job," he said, but in vulgar Russian: "*Pizdyets*, Gary!"

As Sergey worked the fly loose, muttering a flood of four-letter English words, I admired the fish: a bright, shiny male of maybe five or six pounds. A grilse, fresh in from the Barents Sea. A few sea lice clung to its glistening, iridescent scales. Sergey held the fish up high, so Ted could see it. As Sergey and I released the fish, Ted came sloshing through the chest-deep water of the main pool.

For the next twenty to twenty-five minutes or so, we had the fastest salmon fishing either of us had ever experienced. On the same, increasingly bedraggled Hairy Mary, I stuck a couple of fish, hooked but lost two, and landed one that was a bit bigger than the first. Ted caught four—of five, ten, twelve, and twenty pounds—and lost what looked like a thirty-pounder. (Ted, working harder than I, caught each fish on a different fly: Green-Butt Black Bear, Samson, Squirrel Tail, and Blue Charm, respectively.) Then, as suddenly as the action began, it ended.

Between us, we raised twenty fish and had thirteen hookups in that half-hour of furious fishing. Ted had more luck than I did, both kinds of luck. After his fourth fish caught and released, he went into a long slide that would end two days later, after hooking and losing twelve or thirteen fish in a row. This champion of fish and wildlife conservation, *Fly Rod & Reel* magazine's "Conservation" columnist, began muttering and complaining about the senseless requirement of barbless hooks. I snapped a picture of him in the midst of one of his tirades, saying I would call it "Portrait of a Conservationist Reconsidering Barbless Hooks." I nominated that long, fast, sweeping riffle below Broken Rod Pool as Barbless Run, and after due consideration over vodka and wine, the others concurred. Neither Ted nor I would score again in the run, but it produced fish after each high tide for Roy Richards, Harm Saville, John Gregori, and Gary Anderson.

(Ted's right, you know, about barbless hooks. Like many another conservation-minded fisherman, I like to think my fishing barbless is good for the fish. Common sense and human logic convince us, as well as many regulatory agencies, that barbless hooks do less damage to fish and decrease the mortality of catch-and-release fishing. Unfortunately, there is no science to support the notion. In study after study, ichthyologists and fish managers have failed to find statistically valid evidence that fishing barbless makes a difference. Any evidence of any difference. I still fish barbless most of the time, but I now know I'm doing it for my convenience in unhooking fish, not for the sake of the fish.)

The Varzina is arguably the most fascinating of all the salmon rivers on Russia's Kola Peninsula, which makes it just about the most fascinating salmon river in the world. It isn't an easy river to read, and in the six days we fished it, the Varzina yielded its secrets but slowly. John Gregori and Gary Anderson hike faster and fish harder than anyone else I've ever seen, and the two Canadians covered most of the thirty miles of the Varzina below the big lakes inland, fishing most places two or more times. They fished a lot of the Varzina's Pyenka tributary as well. But most of the fish were taken from the four easily accessible places the guides kept taking us back to: Broken Rod Pool, Barbless Run, and Picnic Pool on the Varzina, and Brown Bug Pool (so named because, save for one taken on a Green Machine, all its fish fell for brown Bombers, Buck Bugs, and Muddler Minnows) on the Pyenka.

No matter where we were dropped, usually in twos with a guide, and sometimes a rubber raft, we always congregated by day's end at the Picnic Pool. Named for the picnic table located in a little hollow out of the wind, Picnic is the lowest fishable pool on the Varzina, at the confluence of the Pyenka. A gravelly estuarine pool maybe three hundred yards long and one hundred yards wide, it is completely wadeable—but for its narrow main channel—and can be fished from all sides. Every evening at seven, the helicopter would land there to take us back to camp. Thinking it was merely a place of logistical convenience, we didn't fish Picnic all that hard in the beginning, despite its having produced a monstrous, 57½-inch fish three weeks earlier. Slowly but surely it dawned on us that, during our week at least, it was the most productive spot in the whole river.

Picnic Pool yielded up fish every day—seventeen of them, from four to forty pounds, on the last day alone. That Friday morning, while six of us were off fruitlessly exploring the Kamenka River at the easternmost tip of the Kola Peninsula, Ernie Schwiebert caught nine fish in the Picnic Pool, including the big one. Ted Bellingrath, a Princeton classmate of Ernie's and a fellow architect, also had taken two salmon from Picnic that morning. For a brief while that afternoon, all eight of us were fishing Picnic Pool at the same time, without ever getting in each other's way.

I had been designated killer of the day—we needed a fish for the farewell dinner that night—and I sent Sergey hiking back to camp with a pretty, silver-fresh cock fish that measured 76.4 cm from tip of nose to fork of tail and 40 cm in girth, and weighed 4.8 kg (30⅛ in, 16 in, and 10.56 lb, respectively, for the metrically challenged). It had rolled once at a black Marabou Muddler, so I kept working on it until it finally took a Hairy Mary. (I had most of my pulls that trip on just four flies: Hairy Mary, Muddler Minnow, Buck Bug, and Electric Blue Whitlock Leech.) Palming the essentially dragless Cortland LTD 100 like mad, I kept the fish on a short leash, because six of us were fishing Picnic at the time—Gregori and Anderson having left us to go catch five salmon up at Barbless Run—and I didn't want to get tangled with anyone or keep the others from fishing while I was playing with my fish. The salmon ran straight at me twice (once swimming between my legs) and rolled itself up in the leader. Finally, after the usual thrashing and splashing that always threatens to arrest my heart, Sasha Tretyakov managed to tail the fish. Twice in that one pool salmon wrapped the tippet around their noses and through their toothy mouths, but I landed both fish. (Salmon-fishing tip: Always use Maxima tippets. I'll probably rue flaunting Lady Luck this way, but I haven't lost a single fish to a broken tippet since I switched to Maxima.)

Even though most of us had missed the morning's great fishing, we were all in high spirits at the party that night. The Kamenka had been a bust (mostly frog water and lots of small brown trout, no salmon), but the excursion had been great—the highlight of the whole trip, really. Our Mi-8 helicopter had flown directly over, and I mean *directly* over, a SAM antiaircraft missile battery at low altitude— maybe five hundred feet. Moments later we'd flown within a few hundred yards of two ten-tube batteries of much larger, probably antiship, missiles. And we had flown within a mile of what the missiles were defending: the submarine base at Gremikha. Several sub tenders rode at anchor in the fiord (one of them sunk at the stern), and hunkered down ominously in the pens were several *podvodnye lodky:* sleek attack subs and big, ICBM-bearing boomers. When we first put down at the Kamenka, a menacing-looking military chopper, still bearing a Soviet red star on its dark-green fuselage, was scrambled from the radar base at the river's mouth to give us a low-altitude look-see. I was vaguely disappointed we hadn't even rated any warning fire.

The farewell dinner featured my fresh salmon—fish and angler both being duly toasted—and at least a dozen Russian delicacies and dishes put on the camp's remarkable menu by the Kremlin's former

Salmon fishing in Russia: Reindeer and Mi-8. *(Frontiers)*

head chef. We drank as well as we ate, which was very well indeed. We had excellent Russian vodkas, good Dutch and German beers, and quite drinkable Georgian wines (especially the red Kindzmaraúli, reportedly Stalin's favorite, everyone is quick to point out). While palates were still reasonably functional, we also drank the last of the bottles Ted Bellingrath had so generously brought from his wine cellar in Connecticut: a fine 1970 Taylor Fladgate vintage port and a superb 1976 Château d'Yquem. (Earlier in the week Ted had blessed us with bottles of 1985 Échézeaux and Grands Échézeaux, a 1983 Château Margaux *premier grand cru classé*, and a 1983 Château Lafite-Rothschild!)

Thus lubricated, several of us fell into maudlin confession that we had been vaguely disappointed earlier in the week. The fishing hadn't lived up to all the hype we'd heard, and by Kola Salmon's own statistics, ours had been only a middling-fair week. Still, most of us had caught more Atlantic salmon than we'd ever caught on previous trips. So we raised a toast to the best salmon fishing of our lives and to even finer fishing in the future.

The camp manager, Igor Bartyenyev, brought out his guitar, I played beer-can bongos, and we all sang into the wee, small hours of the morrow: romping Russian and Ukrainian folk songs and dances, bleak ballads of lost and unrequited love, and stirring tales of bloody battles lost and won. Never mind that the Americans were just lah-lah-lahing and hey-hey-heying along. The two Teds and I were the last Americans to turn in, and I'm not sure some of the Russians ever hit the sack.

As we were packing in furious haste the next morning, having overslept the seven-thirty alarm, Ted paused, grinned goofily at me, and said, "This is the finest, most worthwhile hangover I've ever had."

Despite having made my customary, morning-after pledge never to touch another drop, I said, "I'll drink to that."

2

SEASONABLE PREPARATIONS

Okay, you're raring to go, you've got your head back down out of the clouds and your feet on solid ground. Dream therapy is over. Now it's time to start planning. Continue the reading and research you began in Chapter 1. Only now the drill is:

Know Thine Area

Glom onto as many brochures as you can. Don't pick a general area and then rely on just one agent's or operator's catalog. You can, for example, buy Russian salmon or Belizean bonefish trips from a variety of sources. There's a world of difference between them. So, let's say you've settled on Alaska, specifically on salmon fishing, and more specifically on sockeye salmon. That's only the beginning. Perhaps you've read a lot of exciting, glamorous things about fly-out lodges. But have you heard the down side? Listen to Ted Williams: "I'll never go to another fly-out lodge. You go to these fly-out lodges and you're there for five days and have three days of horrible, unflyable weather and you sit in the camp." Before you book with a fly-out camp, ask whether it has fishable home water that's reasonably accessible on foot or by boat. Would you be happy fishing in a crowd, or do you prefer wilderness solitude? Should the facilities be sybaritic, or can you happily go native for a week? It's extremely important that you and

A fly-out lodge in Alaska. *(Frontiers)*

the place you choose to fish be compatible. And that means doing a lot of careful research.

One thing you will discover quickly in your research, if you read critically, is that there are seasons and seasons. Prime fishing almost anywhere in the world spans but a fraction of the time that's on the market. A lodge may be booking weeks from mid-April to late October, but the fish usually hold their annual convention there each September. Sure, there will be *some* fishing across the season, but if you book that first available week in April, or the last one in October, don't count on fast fishing.

In addition to the hidden-hype problem earlier discussed, magazine articles about fishing trips and destinations often suffer from the shoulder-season syndrome. "Shoulder season" is a travel-industry euphemism for too early or too late. (In Anglish it translates as "Heck, last year at this time we had a foot of snow on the ground," and "You shoulda been here last month.") Naturally, everyone in the

> ☞ **TRAVELER'S TIP**
>
> *Some of my favorite destinations are in tropical waters for bonefish. Before finalizing the dates for these trips, I try to determine the timing of the tides in the area I will be fishing. Ideally, I like low tide during the late morning to allow fishing the moving tides during midday when the light is best for stalking and sighting fish. I also try to avoid periods of the full moon when planning bonefishing trips.*
>
> —Leon Chandler
> retired vice president, Cortland Line Co.
> Cortland, New York

travel business wants to extend the season to make more money. To get some free publicity for their shoulder seasons, lodges, camps, airlines, and tourist-promotion agencies will give outdoor writers a free trip at a time when empty spaces are going begging. Few of them are foolish enough to give away prime-time trips they can sell. So a great many of the accounts you read are written by writers on shoulder-season junkets.

Not surprisingly, the globe-trotting writer sometimes has a mediocre or so-so trip. When he gets home he milks it for all he can, repaying his host for the freebie, trying to recover his investment in time and money, hoping to pump up his reputation as a super fisherman, and knowing that hook-and-bullet editors won't buy an article about a lousy trip, anyway. It's only human nature for writers to seek the path of least resistance. As is often the case, the path of least resistance traverses a morally slippery slope. (It's also human nature to believe what you see in print. So you plunk down your hard-earned cash and take a trip at time when the fishing is hard. If you're an adventurous sort, you might have a grand time anyway. Then again, you might not.)

When you read an article, don't place too much stock in the timing of the writer's trip. Just because he made the trip early in June and claims to have had great fishing doesn't mean you should plan a late-spring trip. Especially not if the rest of your reading and research suggests the really hot fishing is in early September.

Because editors want their articles to appeal to as many readers as possible, crucial distinctions between angling opportunities are too often blurred. "A lot of mischief is created by outdoor writers doing promotional pieces as if every place in the world were perfect for everybody," *The Angling Report*'s Don Causey says, perhaps failing to recall the kind of carving and steering he did when he was executive editor of *Outdoor Life*:

> And very simply, nowhere is like that. I mean, you take someone who goes to Christmas Island and stays at the Captain Cook Hotel with the rusty bedsprings and so forth, and some people are going to be furious over the accommodations. And yet, I found it a perfectly delightful place, and would go back any opportunity I get. It's the same all over the world. Things are very different, and people are very different, and you need to really scratch beneath the surface and figure out whether any given place is right for *you*.
>
> You probably have some kind of fishing you like. Maybe you don't like to do anything except sight-fishing. Then you shouldn't go to the east coast of Costa Rica, where you catch those tarpon, 95 percent of the time, in 35 feet of water. You know, it's just not any fun for somebody who likes to sight-fish.
>
> That's the most important thing, to dig beneath the surface and realize that most of what you read is promotional in nature, either because the guy in his own literature is trying to sell you the trip or the outdoor writer is kind of in the business of paying for his free trip by selling the reading public on how wonderful it was.

Now, I don't want to sound as if I'm dumping on outdoor writers (after all, I am one), but I do want you to know why you've got to do more than read a few brochures and magazine articles before deciding on a fishing trip. Because travel is expensive and "glamorous," publishers expect all travel writing to come on the cheap. And not just outdoor travel writing. Describing the shortcomings of most travel guidebooks in *Modern Maturity* magazine, Bill Marsano (himself an award-winning travel writer) wrote, "Comps (a.k.a. 'freebies') are common in the [travel publishing] industry and openly permitted, but it's tricky to write objectively about the airline providing your flight or the hotel providing your room."

☞ TRAVELER'S TIP

My recommendation, when somebody wants to go somewhere or fish with a guide, is to get a word-of-mouth from somebody who's already been there. I think that's the single most important way to learn about a place or a guide or a person or whatever.

I'd have to go a little bit further and say that if you don't have that and are in a place—for example, the Florida Keys—and you want to go out fishing with a guide, I would walk down to the dock and I would look over the boats, the guides' equipment, and such at the end of the day when they come in and see how they've taken care of their equipment and so on. If in fact all of them were the same, then you've got a problem. If one boat seems to be in better condition than the rest of them, and the equipment seems to be better, that's probably—with everything else being equal—the person that I would choose.

—Stuart Apte
author and world-record fly-fisherman
Gallatin Gateway, Montana

I've said it before, and I'll say it again, it's so important: At some point you will want to talk to someone who has fished the area you are considering, preferably at the same camp or lodge and at the same time of year. If you don't know anyone who has (or who knows someone who has):

▶ Ask the booking agent or operator for references
▶ Order an Angler Network Report from *The Angling Report*

However you go about it, you will learn more valuable information from word-of-mouth sources than from any promotional copy or magazine story. But you must start with the published material, so you will know what to ask and how to interpret what you are told.

Remember, too, that each of us speaks with the bias of our own personality. When you talk to someone who has been there and done that, do a little gentle probing. It helps to know whether your informant has a lot more or a lot less relevant fly-fishing or traveling experience than you do. How did he like his roommate or the angler with whom he shared a guide? (That can color one's whole experience.) And if he liked the trip, ask him about one he didn't (or vice versa). You need context to understand what's being said about a trip or a place.

The Two-Way Fit

No reputable booking agent or outfitter, no camp or lodge operator who hopes to be in business very long, wants to sell you a bad trip. They live or die by repeat business and word-of-mouth advertising. If it were in their power to do so, they'd make sure every client had the fishing trip of a lifetime. So let them help you in your search for the right time and the right place. Tell them precisely what you are look-ing for, and they'll let you know whether they've got what you need.

A few years back, PanAngling Travel Service published a booklet called "How to Plan a Successful International Fishing Trip" (cur-rently in revision for future reissue). Among the many good tips on trip planning, it explains the sorts of things you should say when you write, fax, or call a camp, outfitter, or booking agent:

> Our party of four—men in their mid-fifties—is interested in a week's fishing for bonefish. We are flexible, thus we would appreciate your suggestions as to the best time. Two mem-bers of our party are good fly-fishermen, the other two pre-fer spinning gear. We'd be interested in other species if available, but primarily we wish to concentrate on bonefish. We like to fish hard and have no dietary problems. We've all caught bonefish before during two trips to the Bahamas and consider ourselves skilled anglers. . . .

Having received such a letter, the operator or booker would know how closely he can match your requirements. A letter that said just "I'm interested in a bonefishing trip, send me your brochure and all other details" would be answered, but you and the agent would be backing-and-forthing over several weeks to nail down some sort of match between what you want to buy and what he has to sell. By let-ting the supplier know up front what you are looking for, you stand a much better chance of getting it and having a grand trip.

☞ TRAVELER'S TIP

I would always recommend that anglers contact the lodge directly to see what is the fly of choice, and what tackle they can expect to require to bring with them. Many anglers have prior experience fishing somewhere else in the world or in their local area and bring what they have, and come to find out when they get there they don't really have the right flies or the right line and so forth.

—Steve Rajeff
    director of research and development, G. Loomis, Inc.,
    and twenty-two-time national and eleven-time world casting champion
    Woodland, Washington

(Conversely, if the booking agent asks you how well you cast, or whether you are a strong wader, answer honestly. If you fudge even a little, you could be setting yourself up for a fall. Or worse.)

Don't be afraid to ask questions after you've received and studied the brochures. Especially if you think they are dumb questions (a clear tip-off that you need help). Some brochures aren't very clear as to whether camps or lodges are fly-fishing only. If you care, ask. You'd be surprised what camp and lodge operators sometimes forget to mention in their packing lists. If something isn't mentioned in the literature, ask. From my own sad experience, here are some "dumb" questions worth asking:

▶ Are sheets and blankets provided, or should I bring a sleeping bag?
▶ Are towels furnished, or should I bring my own?
▶ Is laundry service available? If so, at what cost? If not, will there be opportunities to wash my own socks and underwear and hang it out to dry?
▶ Are hotels and meals included on any stopovers en route?
▶ Are airport transfers furnished?
▶ What's a reasonable range of tips, and are tips pooled or handed directly to guides and staff?
▶ How much money should I bring for license or other fees?
▶ Should I bring a wading staff? Landing net?
▶ Are beer, wine, and liquor available, or should I bring my own?

▶ Do you offer vegetarian (low-fat, low-sodium, kosher, whatever) meals?
▶ What are the fishing opportunities when the weather gets really lousy?
▶ Is there a two-way radio in the camp?
▶ How do you handle medical emergencies?
▶ Is it possible to buy flies, spools of tippet material, or other tackle in camp?
▶ Can I bring fish home? Fresh, frozen, or smoked?
▶ May I release any fish I catch? (Ask before you book or charter, especially for saltwater destinations. In some parts of the world, anglers are encouraged to kill their fish to help feed the local population. Incredibly, in some northeastern U.S. ports, any tuna caught belong to the boat and will be killed and sold to a buyer for the Japanese fish markets. If this offends you as much as it does me, shop around some more.)

Booking Trips

Whether you book a fly-fishing trip through a booking agent or directly with a lodge or camp, you need to check them out in advance, dig out the same information, and get at least two references of past cus-

---

☞ TRAVELER'S TIP

If I'm flying into a camp and I'm going to be there for a week, and everything goes sour on what I planned to do, I want to have backup. Make contingency plans in case the weather goes bad or an particular species isn't hitting you can switch to something else. I call ahead to talk to the guide or outfitter, or local anglers, to see whether there are any ancillary fishing opportunities. If your principal goal is northern pike up north, is there any chance on an off day to try for some grayling, and should you bring along equipment for that?

—Ron Spomer
professional photographer
and outdoor writer
Troy, Idaho

---

tomers, preferably anglers who made the same trip at the same time last year. And contact them. It's surprising how many travelers ask for references and then don't check them out.

The accompanying list of booking agents is by no means complete. For one thing, I've chosen to list only the most well established agencies, the ones that have been around awhile and earned good reputations. (That does not mean the ones not listed are shady, fly-by-night johnnies-come-lately.) For another, I've decided to omit the people who book only camps or lodges they themselves own or operate—there are just too many of them. As a result, outfits such as Kola Salmon, Inc. (P.O. Box 27662, Tempe, AZ 85285; phone 1-602-902-0887, fax 1-602-902-0888), and the similarly named but independent Kola Salmon Ltd. (25 High Street, Hungerford, Bershire RG17 0NF, England; phone 011-44-488-683222, fax 011-44-488-682977) have been omitted, even though both operate some of the finest salmon camps on Russia's Kola Peninsula.

A few omitted agents meet my criteria and would have been listed except they failed to reply to my request for information—not a good sign.

If you decide to book directly with an operator, use a good travel agency to handle your airline ticketing and any hotel reservations en route. As soon as you are given your flight information, call the first carrier on your itinerary to:

▶ Confirm your reservations.
▶ Find out whether any change-of-date or other travel restrictions apply.
▶ It's also a good idea to check on your hotel, car-rental, and other reservations, even if you have to make what seem like expensive long-distance calls.

I've been burned several times by reservations that never made it into the computer, impossible connections, severe change-of-date penalties, and nonrefundable, nonalterable restrictions. It can cost you several hundred dollars in penalties and upgrades, lots of hassle, and hours of standing by in airports.

▶ As for visas and other travel documents, be sure you know who's taking care of them: you, the operator, or the agent.

Cash on the Barrel Head

At some point rather early on, you will have to send the operator or agent a deposit. The deposit is a two-sided commitment. On your part, it's earnest money that you will show up when you say you will. Acceptance of your deposit is a promise from the operator that he'll have a place waiting for you.

Before sending that deposit, make sure you know what sort of deal it is. In most cases, the deposit is refundable if you find you must cancel out by some specified time before departure—usually ninety, sixty, or thirty days. In some cases, the operator keeps part of the deposit as a handling charge. In rare cases, the deposit is nonrefundable from the day you send it in. You'd better know what the deal is before you write the check. It isn't always clear in the promotional literature.

If you must cancel at the last minute, you usually forfeit the deposit. A rare few operators will refund some portion of the deposit anyway. A larger minority will give you full or partial credit toward another slot, usually during the same year.

Prepayment is the norm these days, so count on being asked for the balance of the cost maybe a month before departure. If you cancel out after that, you will almost certainly forfeit the deposit, and some operators will keep at least a portion of the full payment. (After all, they might have turned away other customers, especially if you booked during prime time.)

If these deposit, payment, forfeiture, refund, and trip-credit policies aren't clear in the literature, get them clarified—and get it in writing.

Bother and Baggage

Before your booking or travel agent tickets you, be sure you know what you are getting into.

▶ Asking for the cheapest possible fare could be asking for trouble. The cheapest fares often involve nonrefundable or nonchangeable tickets. Given the vagaries of weather or social structure in the kinds of places fish still congregate in numbers, the chances of your missing the first leg of your return flight are pretty good.

If you do miss a flight, you may be liable for a hefty change-of-date penalty. You also might have to stand by or be wait-listed on some of the return legs. During a busy travel time, you might have to pay for upgrades to business or first class. The last time I was burned, it cost me—in addition to considerable aggravation, agitation, and heartburn—$350 in change-of-date penalties and upgrade fees, standing by for the transatlantic leg, $60 in taxi fares to overnight in New York, $17 in overnight-storage fees for baggage, and $85 to replace the no-change ticket from JFK to BWI. It could have been worse.

On my first trip to Russia, I ran into some anglers who'd missed their transatlantic return flight. When informed they'd simply have to purchase new tickets, one flustered, red-faced fisherman waved his old, worthless, nonchangeable, discount ticket in the Aeroflot agent's face and demanded to know just what he was supposed to do with this. Without any discernible levity, the agent said, "Perhaps you could keep it as a souvenir of your visit to the Soviet Union."

▶ Ask the booking or travel agent to give you plenty of time between connecting flights. Flight delays are all too common these days, and airlines are not very sympathetic about missed connections. Also, you want to be sure your baggage and you get on the same flights. And if you are flying to a remote destination, you simply can't afford to miss a flight. There might not be another for days. Even if there is a next flight fairly soon, you can almost bet that your charter to the camp will leave before that next flight arrives with you or your baggage.

▶ Find out about the baggage allowances, regulations, and restrictions *for each leg* of the trip—prior to ticketing, if possible. Once, when I was packing for a two-week fishing trip abroad, I had to juggle the conflicting baggage restrictions of two international airlines. One didn't care how many pieces you checked, as long as they fit within the weight allowance; the other didn't care how much your baggage weighed, as long as you checked only two pieces. Overweight baggage charges can be very high. I've heard of people having to pay four-figure penalties. Before forking over the dough for an extra piece of checked baggage, ask the counter agent to check the airline's policy on fishing rods and skis. (Some airlines exempt skis from the baggage allowance, letting them travel free as an extra piece. Far fewer extend the same courtesy to fishing rods.) If skis are exempt but fishing rods aren't, ask if the agent might not consider your rod case to be a smaller, lighter pair of skis. If you're pleasant, you *might* succeed. If you're imperious or demanding, you'll pay.

▶ Don't check your baggage all the way through to your final destination. Yes, it's plenty inconvenient to claim and recheck your luggage every time you change planes or carriers. But your baggage will have a better chance of arriving when you do. If, God forbid, it doesn't, at least you'll know where it went astray, making it easier to trace. If there is one airport through which you cannot afford to change planes without laying hands on your luggage, it is New York's John F. Kennedy International. JFK is infamous for missed baggage connections.

Practice, Man, Practice

Remember the old joke about the tourist who asked the jazz musician how to get to Carnegie Hall? Once you've decided to invest a week or two of your time and several thousand of your dollars in a fishing trip, it's no joking matter. Practice, man, practice! You can't get the most out of the trip if you aren't prepared for the demands that will be imposed upon you.

☞ TRAVELER'S TIP

Take an extra flashlight and some Band-Aids and some booze and whatever else—those are important too—but, Jesus!, be prepared for these trips. Don't go down half assed.

I think if a guy is going to take up the sport, damn it, try to do it as well as you can. You're not going to do it as well as some, you're going to do it better than others. But try to do it as best as you can, for your ability. Fly-fishing is something you just don't see a movie and then take a few lessons and go do it.

—Bob Nauheim
president, Fishing International
Santa Rosa, California

▶ Casting practice: Before my first fishing trip abroad, I had intended to practice a lot. I lived half a block from New York's Central Park then, I hadn't had a fly rod in my hands for more than twenty-five years, and I was heading for trout lochs and a salmon river in Scotland. My intentions were good, but I let editorial deadlines and other demands eat up my time. I wound up heading for JFK with a new rod that had never been cast. Not once. Was I embarrassed abroad? Humiliated is a better word. The only thing that saved me from *hara-kiri* was that my gillie took pity on me after one day and lent me his two-handed Spey rod. Even a complete duffer like me could throw thirty or forty feet of line with a fifteen-foot rod.

Many a traveling fly-fisher has been humbled by not being able to cast a salmon fly into the wind or quickly lay a cast in front of a feeding bonefish. The spooky brown trout and clear streams of New Zealand have frustrated a lot of North American anglers who've made the long trip down there for little more than naught. Bob Nauheim of Fishing International has advice for such clients:

> So the guy that's going to New Zealand, I tell him, "Go out on the lawn—and I want you to do this at least three times a week before you go down—throw out a bunch of dinner plates at random, all around you. At thirty to forty feet, fifty feet, not long casts, just easy casts. But get the fly into them upwind, downwind, crosswind. Every time you throw, you want that fly near or in those plates. Once you've done that, you're ready to stalk trout in New Zealand. But don't go over there without practicing."

▶ Shaping up: If you'll be fishing for heavyweights—salmon, tarpon, sailfish, or peacock bass, say—train as for an athletic contest, for that is what it will be. Check with your doctor, then head for the gym. Work on building your stamina as well as the muscles you'll need to use (arms, stomach, back, legs). If there will be a lot of hiking involved, take long, brisk walks every day to condition your heart and lungs as well as your legs. You may be fishing ten or twelve hours and walking several miles a day, day after day. Since taking up traveling with a fly rod, I've suffered more injuries (ribs, shoulders, elbow, forearm, thumbs, knees) than ever I did playing football. This fly-fishing travel is pretty rough stuff, man.

Packing and Planning

Before you can start packing, you need to make lists. Not only of the things you need to take, but also of all the things that must be done before you leave: buying film and flies, checking on your fly lines, stopping the newspaper delivery, holding the mail, making the mortgage payment, alerting the police or the neighbors, arranging to have the plants watered or the lawn mowed—that sort of thing. Give yourself a couple of weeks within which to get all these things done, but start working on them right away.

Tony Dawson, the Alaskan writer and photographer, suggests making another kind of lists, not mandates of things to do but "repositories for things I want out of mind." Here's what he does:

> I make notes of projects, goals, domestic tasks—anything that's a source of worry or feelings of obligation. On the surface, I'm creating a standard visual reminder, but my real

---

☞ TRAVELER'S TIP

I have fished in many places around the world, and I believe that preparation ensures a good trip—even if the fish don't cooperate.

I double- and triple-check with friends who have fished the rivers, lakes, or flats which I plan to visit. I assemble all the information and prepare a list. I have all my flies, lures, rods, reels, and outdoor clothing carefully stored and ready in my fishing room, which I take far better care of than any other room in our home.

I can't believe it when friends spend thousands of dollars to fish remote corners of the world without first checking and rebuilding their gear, their waders, everything.

My wife thinks I am a bit nutty on the subject, but to me preparation is a vital part of every fishing adventure, and great fun in itself.

—Nathaniel Pryor Reed
Assistant Secretary of the Interior for Fish and Wildlife
and Parks in the Nixon and Ford administrations,
National Geographic Society trustee, and an officer or director
of several conservation and environmental organizations
Hobe Sound, Florida

objective is to drop a lot of mental baggage I don't want to drag along on the trip.

One sheet tabulates work projects or goals, and stages of completion or upcoming major deadlines. Another inventories personal conflicts, goals, and reminders of things to take care of in the future. I keep it simple, like David Letterman's "Top Ten": just a few words per item and just ten items per page.

Finally, the completed lists are tucked away, awaiting my return.

"Many travelers find it hard to clear their minds of all that clutter," he says. "Worrying about things to do has been the undoing of many a fishing vacation."

Modular packing helps: T-shirts in one plastic bag, shorts in another, socks in a third, and so on. (Just make sure they are transparent bags so you won't have to remember whether the clean socks or the dirty underwear is in the yellow Tower Records bag.)

If you are carrying things that must be declared to customs, pack them near the top, center of the bag, so you won't have to rummage through everything to find them.

Resources

Besides doing a lot of reading on your own, you will want to get brochures and other literature from camps, lodges, and agents. Pore over the ads in the fishing magazines to find the operators who do their own booking; some of them have booths at the various fishing and outdoor shows around the country during the off season. It's easier and more efficient to deal with agents.

A few full-service travel agencies also sell fishing trips. Some of them know a good bit about fishing, others don't. Check them out carefully. The other side of the high-risk coin is the fisherman or fishing writer who has decided to go into the booking business. Some of them know what they are doing, others don't. Check them out thoroughly too.

Booking agents who specialize in fishing and outdoor travel know both sides of the business: fishing and travel. You'll likely be satisfied if you deal with any of the ones listed below.

BOOKING AGENTS

This short list includes only well-established agents who have earned good reputations. An agent's absence from this list should not be interpreted as a warning. It was impossible to check everyone out. If an agent made it to this short list, you can bet you will get your money's worth. I have not included those agencies that book only camps or lodges they themselves own and operate.

The **Best of New Zealand Fly Fishing,** 2817 Wilshire Boulevard, Santa Monica, CA 90403; phone 1-800-528-6129 and 1-310-998-5880; fax 1-310-829-9221

Fishing International Inc., 4010 Montecito Avenue, Santa Rosa, CA 95405; phone 1-800-950-4242 and 1-707-542-4242; fax 1-707-542-1804

Frontiers International Travel/Fish and Game Frontiers Inc., P.O. Box 959, Wexford, PA 15090; phone 1-800-245-1950 and 1-412-935-1577; fax 1-412-935-5388

PanAngling Travel Service, 180 N. Michigan Avenue, Chicago, IL 60601; phone 1-800-533-4353 and 1-312-263-0328; fax 1-312-263-5246

World Wide Sportsman Inc., P.O. Drawer 787, Islamorada, FL 33036; phone 1-800-327-2880 and 1-305-664-4615; fax 1-305-664-3692

TACKLE CATALOGS THAT ALSO OFFER FLY-FISHING TRIPS

Cabela's Outdoor Adventures, 812 13th Avenue, Sidney, NE 69160; phone 1-800-346-8747; fax 1-308-254-7376 *(Most trips are for spin-fishermen.)*

Dan Bailey's Fly Shop/Destinations, 422 S. Main Street, Livingston, MT 59047; phone 1-800-626-3526; fax 1-406-585-3526

The **Fly Shop,** 4140 Churn Creek Road, Redding, CA 96002; phone 1-800-669-FISH (3474); fax 1-916-222-3572

The **Global Flyfisher,** 2849 W. Dundee Road, Suite 132, Northbrook, IL 60062; phone 1-800-457-7026 and 1-800-531-1106; fax 1-708-291-3486

International Angler, 503 Freeport Road, Pittsburgh, PA 15215; phone 1-800-782-4222 and 1-412-782-2222; fax 1-412-782-1315

Kaufmann's Streamborn/Fly Fishing Expeditions, Inc., P.O. Box 23032, Portland, OR 97223-3032; phone 1-800-442-4359 and 1-503-639-6400; fax 1-503-684-7025

Bob **Marriott's** Flyfishing Store and Travel Center, 2700 W. Orangethorpe Avenue, Fullerton, CA 92633; phone 1-800-535-6633 and 1-714-525-5801; fax 1-714-525-5783

Tag Offshore Tackle/South Fishing Adventures, P.O. Box 2538, Edgartown, MA 02539; phone 1-800-FISH-TAG (347-4824) and 1-508-627-8780; fax 1-508-627-8383

Urban Angler Ltd., 118 E. 25th Street, New York, NY 10010; phone 1-800-255-5488 and 1-212-979-7600; fax 1-212-473-4020

WRONG TIME, RIGHT PLACE

The sun was still several ticks above the western horizon when we arrived at Ličko Lešče, but it was already too late to bother fishing, we were told. We had just crossed the Atlantic Ocean to get to what was then Yugoslavia's (now Croatia's) and still one of Europe's most renowned chalk stream, the Gacka (pronounced gots-ka) River, but we were all too jet-lagged to much care about this delay in getting started.

So far, it hadn't been the easiest or best trip any of us had ever been on. The flight had been bad enough (the JAT plane had left the gate at JFK more than two hours late, with every seat filled by passengers taken off a bomb-threatened Olympus Airways flight), even before Dave Finkelstein got into a verbal altercation with the chief steward over people smoking in the no-smoking section and threatening to invoke some rule that would require the pilot to land in Boston and put the puffing violators off the plane. (That little scene had pitched Jack London into a muttering funk from which he never fully emerged during the trip.) After landing in Zagreb, it had begun to look as if Ed Ricciuti's luggage had been left in the States, but it finally appeared on the baggage carousel some half hour after all the other bags and boxes from the flight had been claimed. The driver of our van was ticketed (and very nearly arrested, until our pretty and charming interpreter, Dunja Marjan, assured the cop it was only because the driver had become flustered by the presence of such important American journalists) for having serially driven (a) the wrong way on a one-way street in downtown Zagreb and (b) through a pedestrian mall crowded with tables and chairs and gaily colored umbrellas, not to mention scores of strolling, coffee-drinking pedestrians. Then we had spent five hours careening over narrow, winding mountain roads much in need of repaving.

Anyway, we hadn't yet unpacked or reorganized our gear, dinner would be served within the hour, and the hotel manager was already waiting for us in the bar with a welcoming glass of slivovic. So, atypically, fishing wasn't foremost in our minds.

But imagine our surprise and consternation when we were apprised of the morrow's plan: We should sleep late and have a leisurely breakfast, we were told, because we wouldn't begin fishing until sometime after ten!

Now, it's always worth listening to local advice when you are about to fish new water, and our local advisor was none other than Milan Stepanac, superintendent of the Gacka River, fish and game warden of the Lika District and one of Croatia's most respected authorities on trout and fly-fishing. Milan Stepanac is to the Gacka what Lee Wulff was to the Beaverkill or Charlie Brooks to the Yellowstone. They talked, you listened; they said, you did. Still, the advice was hard to swallow. And, for some of us at least, impossible to follow.

By the time Milan joined us in the hotel lounge the next morning at ten, Ed Ricciuti and I had been flailing away at the river for a couple of hours and had nothing—zero, zip, zilch, *nada*, *ništa*—to show for the effort. Not even a rise or a follow, let alone a strike. We hadn't moved a fish. And there were trout everywhere we looked. Big ones. Both native browns and naturalized rainbows. So much for early birds getting the worms.

Before leading us out to the river, Milan told us a little about it. My notes on his talk are a bit garbled, because Milan speaks no English, none of us spoke any Serbo-Croatian, and Dunja spoke no fishing. But this is what I think he told us:

Unlike other trout streams, the Gacka doesn't fish well in the mornings and evenings. No one who knows the river ever fishes it before nine, and the prime time is between eleven in the morning and two in the afternoon. The Gacka is so rich in natural food, Milan explained, that no fly, no matter how cleverly tied, could hope to compete with the banquet of authentic trout foods. But why would trout take artificial flies in midday, if they won't take them when they're feeding? someone asked. "Perhaps they look for dessert," Milan said through Dunja, his lined, weathered face breaking into an impish grin.

The Gacka is an incredibly rich, stenothermal chalk stream. Its biomass is something on the order of 700 kilograms per hectare, or about 625 pounds per acre, on a par with other spring-fed limestone creeks. As a result, the Gacka's trout grow fast, really fast: as much as 800 grams (twenty-eight ounces, or a pound and three-quarters) a year for browns and 1,200 grams (forty-two ounces, nearly three pounds) a year for rainbows. (In America, only oceangoing steelhead and trout living in big, forage-rich lakes grow that fast. Our stream-dwelling trout add about a pound a year—and usually less than that.)

Briefed to a salivating frenzy of fish lust, we were taken upstream and introduced to the Gacka. Another odd thing about the Gacka is that it's not a wading river. Where it runs through Ličko Lešče, it slopes down quickly from the banks to an average depth of about nine to ten feet. Milan strung us out along a wide stretch of the river where the water was a little cloudy. So it was blind-casting, atypical Gacka fishing. Apparently Milan didn't want our anticipation dulled by the frustration of sight-casting to fish that simply weren't having any of what we had to offer. But we created plenty of frustrations of our own, working through the dufferdom that always seems to strike at the beginning of an early-season trip.

My ganglia were suddenly seized by one of the many bad habits of my youth: the overwhelming urge to cast as far as one can when confronted by a lot of open water. Trying too hard for distance I didn't need, I kept dropping my back casts in the weeds or hanging them in the trees. Finally, my supply of pheasant-tail and GRHE nymphs rapidly dwindling, I gave up on the main stem and waded into a little tributary stream. Success. I started catching trout. Little, young-of-the-year fish, for sure, but beautiful creatures nonetheless, their writhing bodies gleaming and glinting like gem-cut crystals. I don't think I caught anything much over eight inches long, but I was happy just to have broken the ice.

A few bigger fish were caught that late morning in the main stream, mostly by Milan while demonstrating casting technique or showing how to present the flies.

Too soon, it was time for lunch, and Milan assembled us on the little bridge where a gravel road crossed the tributary I'd been fishing. On the far side of a pool where the brook bent under the bridge, I saw the moving shadows of some pretty impressive fish. "Look at those big trout," I said to no one in particular.

"Lipjen," Milan corrected. *"Thymallus thymallus."* Grayling? That big? Apparently the forty-five-centimeter (nearly eighteen-inch) minimum size limit on grayling wasn't the joke we'd thought someone was playing on us.

After a late lunch, we fished the river right in front of the Gacka Hotel. Now, we all know that chalkstream trout can be pretty picky, but these Gacka fish are ridiculous. Because of all the heavy cover available, the fish weren't at all spooky. They'd let you walk right up over them on the bank. In a hundred or so feet of river (which was only twenty to thirty feet across here), you could see maybe seventy-five to one hundred fish. Maybe more. And there were others hiding in the dark-green weeds waving like banners in the crystalline current.

May is the prime dry-fly season here, and there were no signs of hatching insects on this June day. Use nymphs, Milan told us, and he plucked 12s and 14s and 16s out of our boxes. (His fingers had paused momentarily over some 18s, but apparently he'd decided we weren't up to it—having watched us earlier.) Every now and then we'd see the flash of a fish turning on its side to pick a nymph off the grassy bottom, or see the brief, white grin of its open mouth. Otherwise, you couldn't prove it by us they were nymphing. We'd drift nymphs right by fish we could see were feeding, and they'd pay no attention. Oh, we caught a few fish—nice fourteen- to fifteen-inchers, rainbows, mostly—but because we were so aware of the fish we *weren't* catching, it seemed pretty slow.

I asked Milan why the trout wouldn't take our nymphs, when we could see that a lot of them were feeding. He motioned me to follow him across the footbridge to a little tributary that entered the Gacka right in front of the hotel. The brook was only a couple of feet deep, so Milan and I waded out into it in our hip boots. He bent over and scooped both hands through the weeds. When he held his cupped hands out for me to see, I could hardly believe the writhing mass of insect nymphs and tiny freshwater crustaceans: scuds, ostracods, copepods, and who knows what else. Hundreds of them. According to one biological researcher, the bottom of the Gacka *averages* 5,200 food organisms per square meter. One writer says that individual samples have yielded densities close to 20,000 creepy-crawlies per square meter. No wonder our pathetic little fakes failed to draw much interest. Talk about your jaded, sated fish.

The next day I spent the early morning watching birds in the trees and on the wing (dabchicks, swallows and martins, wheatears, coal tits, wagtails, lapwings, magpies, collared doves, hooded and carrion crows, goldfinches, and a lone red-backed shrike) and fish in the river. I didn't fish for them, just studied the way they'd alternate between feeding and resting, the way they'd hold one position for a while and then take up another station or disappear into the weeds. Gosh, but there were some nice fish right here by the hotel.

We spent the midday prime time picnicking and fishing the headwaters, where the water emerged from the porous limestone karst and spilled into a weedy pond, the ruins of a former trout hatchery, before sluicing speedily down a narrow channel to merge with other rivulets and become the Gacka of European trout legend.

The river had once been noted for its monster fish (which weren't all that old), and still yields a few of them, but now the average fish is less than a kilogram. A few German, Austrian, and Italian fly-fishers—along with the odd Brit or Swiss, almost never Americans—still come with hope of meeting one of those Gacka giants. They seldom do. Even under angling pressure that would be considered light by our standards, especially when compared to its productivity, the tiny little Gacka gets fished out pretty fast. This strange river, only twenty-two kilometers (fourteen miles) long, once ended in a pair of natural lakes before disappearing back underground, seeping into the same karst whence it came. (Sort of a riverine ashes to ashes and dust to dust.) Those lakes were where the really big trout lived, rainbows up to ten kilograms (twenty-two to twenty-three pounds). Today the Gacka ends at a dam, where it disappears into tunnels that flush it past hydroelectric turbines on its way to the Adriatic Sea. The fluctuating hydropower lake just doesn't produce the monster trout those natural lakes once did. Now, as elsewhere, a five-pound trout from the Gacka is memorable and a seven-pounder is a bragging fish.

It's a lovely river to fish: flat, swift, clear, winding its way through flowered meadows and cattled pastures. No chemical insecticides are used here, so the air is abuzz with cicadas and aflutter with butterflies. If only mayflies and caddises were more prevalent. Caddises don't come on strong until September, and the big mayfly hatch comes in May—although hatches of *Baetis rhodani* occur in August and, to a lesser extent, in April. In May, I'm told, the river is crowded, or what passes for crowded in Croatia.

We saw only three other anglers while we were at the Gacka, and I never saw where the two Swiss fished. The lone German fly-fisher took pity on us and showed us a neat trick. "You can't trick them into feeding," he said in a thickly accented English I won't even try to replicate. "You must interest them in something else. But first you must get their attention." He showed us how to select a pod of fish and then false-cast just beyond them, letting the fly touch the surface each time. After three to five such flickings, you would cast the fly (nymph, wet, dry, it didn't much matter) maybe two or three feet farther. "One meter, no more. Better, less." The idea was to make the fish aware of the fly and to get them looking away from you. If you did it just right—letting the fly line touch the surface or letting the fly make too much noise while you were flicking simply wouldn't do—one fish would move to get a better look at the thing that had roused its attention, then other fish would race to beat him to it.

The first time I tried it, a twenty-inch brown trout I hadn't even seen roared out of the weeds and smacked the fly so hard I almost dropped the rod. Now we were catching fish with some regularity, even on dries. For ten or fifteen minutes the fishing would be excellent, then taper off to almost nothing. I don't know whether it was returning so many sadder but wiser fish to the river, or whether they just became bored with the game or got used to the commotion. But you could hike up or down the river and enjoy the same flurry of activity before moving on to another green pool or deep glide.

If all rivers fished like the Gacka, I suppose I might miss the long, lazy lunches and the midday siestas under the shade trees when things got slow, but I sure could get used to sleeping late and fishing without mosquitoes.

3
FLY RODS FOR FREQUENT FLIERS

Of course you can travel with your favorite fly rods, as long as they are adequate to the fishing that lies ahead. The weight of the tackle will be determined by the winds you will likely be facing and the wind resistance or weight of the flies you will be casting as well as the size and strength of the fish you will be catching. Most important, your tackle must be balanced, and you must be able to use it well.

So what do you do if 10-weight lines are recommended, you have a good 9-weight rod you love, and your finances have already been sapped by paying for the trip? Your choices are: (1) Buy the 10-weight rod anyway and hope your spouse doesn't see the credit-card slip; (2) beg or borrow a 10-weight outfit from someone who won't sue if you ruin it; (3) stick with the 9-weight tackle, after getting expert advice to confirm that it's up to the task. In many cases, it's better to take not-quite-ideal tackle you are used to and can handle, rather than going with untested tackle acquired through a last-minute loan or purchase.

If you've learned to love that 9-weight outfit while casting smaller flies than you will be using on the trip, or under less windy conditions than you will be facing, you'd better get out there and practice casting bigger flies, or casting against, across, and with stiff winds. Several years ago I bought a fast-action, reserve-power, high-modulus Sage 896RP rod for salmon and saltwater fishing. What I have finally discovered is that, despite the rod's 8-weight rating, it's really a 10-weight rod in my hands, not the 9-weight I thought it would be. I've also discovered it's a good saltwater sight-fishing rod, but it's just too tiring in my hands to use for salmon fishing, where you make hundreds (which will feel like thousands) of casts each day. If only it were a newer and lighter RPL.

But traveling with two-piece rods is, at best, a pain in the neck (usually, the neck of the person seated on the aisle you are struggling to navigate with your carry-ons). Some airlines won't let you carry long rod cases on board, and rods checked as baggage have a way of disappearing or being damaged. Even if you do manage to talk your way past the uniformed gatekeepers at the baggage check-in counter, the departure gate, and the cabin door, struggling through crowded airports with those long cases and tubes is one miserable experience. Most of the dents in my rod cases were picked up in airports, as the tubes rolled off chairs and countertops, were tripped over by fellow passengers, or got whacked by baggage carts in the stampede to customs.

Multipiece Travel Rods

We've come a long way, bubba, from those days not so very long ago when experts would never think of carrying a four-piece fly rod, except perhaps as a spare, in case the checked baggage was sent to the wrong

---

☞ TRAVELER'S TIP

Over the years I have learned that if you travel by air, a four-piece rod that fits into a duffel bag is absolutely essential. I have had two- and three-piece rods in their aluminum tubes smashed by airlines, and the same thing happened when I used heavy, custom-made plastic-pipe cases to hold the rods and their tubes. What happens is that, despite all requests and markings to the contrary, long tubes are put on conveyor belts and when they come to a turn on the belt they create a logjam. To be sure, you get your money back if a rod is broken, but often you'll be where you can't replace your rod in a hurry.

—Nelson Bryant
formerly "Wood, Field and Stream"
columnist, *The New York Times,*
author, *Outdoors*
West Tisbury, Massachusetts

continent or something. Those early fiberglass travel rods—relegated to wilderness-survival status as "pack" rods back then—were deemed too heavy, too weak, too stiff, or just plain uncastable. Even rod manufacturers showed their disdain for multipiece pack rods by making most of them combination rods that could (or couldn't, to be perfectly frank) handle either a fly line or spinning tackle. The combo pack rods were mostly dreadful, barely better than a hand line.

Hardy's Smuggler Rod (available in five, six, seven, or eight sections) was a notable exception to the travel-rod-as-practical-joke theme. Most of us couldn't afford to own one, but the Smuggler enjoyed a certain vogue among the well heeled. I knew corporate lawyers in New York who liked to carry their eight-piece Smugglers in the breast pockets of their three-piece Brooks Brothers suits, brandishing them as conversation pieces during three-martini power lunches. But I also know people, real fly-fishermen, who fish with their Smugglers and love them. Lars Georgsson, with whom I fished regularly when he was the Swedish government's press officer in New York City, always brought his Smuggler when we drove out to the Connetquot River on Long Island. It was his rod of choice for trout fishing, he said, whether traveling or not. He liked it for the way it worked, not just for its portability.

(Incidentally, lest angling Anglophiles attribute the Smuggler's standout performance to natural British superiority in things trouty, I'm told that Hardy Brothers has always used blanks manufactured by J. Kennedy Fisher, Inc., of Carson City, Nevada, to build the Smuggler.)

Naturally, as rod materials and designs evolved, so did the thinking about pack-and-travel rods. As the rods got better and more people began traveling to fish, marketplace acceptance of multipiece rods grew, and manufacturers responded with research and development and a frenzied output of new models. With advertisers to attract or keep happy, the hook-and-bullet magazines reversed gears and jumped on the bandwagon. Four-piece rods were not merely acceptable, the bosky books opined editorially, they were essential. "You can't tell the difference between two-piece and four-piece rods," the lockstep litany goes.

In truth, some of us *can't* tell the difference, except in traveling ease, where the difference is great, and perhaps in weight, where the difference is small and shrinking. I don't cast well enough to discern subtle differences in rod performance, and I suspect one or two others

A two-handed, three-piece salmon rod's portability compared with that of a shorter, one-handed, two-piece rod. *(Sage)* out there can't either. The most I can say about a rod is that it casts as well as I do, faint praise indeed. But good casters and bench testers can tell the difference.

All other things being equal, here are the comparative advantages for rods of similar line-weight rating:

▶ two-piece rod: lighter, smoother, stronger, more flexible, faster tip, less expensive
▶ four-piece rod: easier to carry

But all other things almost never being equal, beware such generalizations. Comparing one rod maker's two-piece rod with another's four-piece stick is, at the very best, comparing apples and oranges. Among the same company's rods, even within the same model series, direct comparisons between two- and four-piece rods are futile. No rod designer is going to make two- and four-piece rods that differ only in the number of sections. Taper of the blank, wall thickness or modulus of the graphite used, ferrule design, wrapping and positioning of the line guides—these and other differences may show up in supposedly equivalent rods. And they can affect a rod's performance more than the number of its sections.

A rod builder, corporate or custom, making a four-piece travel rod can match a two-piece rod's weight *or* strength, for example, but not both. As for action, flexibility, and "feel," perfect matches probably aren't possible, but the good builders can come pretty darned close.

Robert Gorman of Green River Rodmakers has this to say about the differences:

> The ideal rod—an ideal based on a fluid transfer of load from tip to butt, delicacy of presentation, and accuracy— would be of one continuous piece. When you wiggle a fly rod it makes a sine wave, and no matter where you interrupt the rod with a ferrule (peak or trough) you've interrupted that wave. So, one-piece rods are the least compromised and four-, five-, and six-piece rods, in order, the most. The new graphites, enabling us to make very thin-walled sections, help this transfer of energy, but the cost, of course, is usually a rod that is relatively fragile. If ever I get that stretch limo, I'll build a one-piece rod for myself.

A few one-piece fly rods are made, but not many. Gorman's own Green River Rodmakers builds one-piece bamboo rods; at six to six and a half feet and $750, the rods aren't even limited to the stretch-limo crowd. However piscatorially praiseworthy one-piece rods may be, they make lousy traveling companions. Definitely not for the angling jet set. Anyway, if even rodbuilders don't use one-piece rods to fish their own home waters, you can bet the superiority of one-piece rods over two-piecers can't be all *that* great. Convenience counts, even among those who really know the difference and are in a position to do something about it.

That said, convenience and performance are always to some degree in conflict when it comes to fly rods.

In the spring 1994 issue of the newsletter he sends to customers and prospective customers, Dave Lewis of Performance Fly Rods said of fly-rod ferrules that their

> only redeeming quality is to join rod sections; everything else that can be said about them is a negative. They are expensive, they come loose, they weaken the rod, they cause stiff spots, they're heavy, they're ugly, but they are a necessity. Obviously, the more of them you have, the more of those negatives your new fly rod is likely to have. Two-piece fly rods have always been the best performers because the middle of the fly rod is the best place to have a ferrule. It is the least noticeable there.

In that same newsletter, however, Lewis admitted he owns and uses several four-piece rods himself and that he never travels with anything else. "Careful design of ferrules and the use of high-modulus materials in the ferrule area have greatly minimized the effect of the additional ferrules and led to very good performance in multisection rods," he wrote.

(In case you've been sleeping through all the graphite rod hype of recent years, "modulus" is technical jargon for stiffness. Modulus is measured in the force required to bend or deflect a material a given distance. Fly rods made of high-modulus graphite can get the same action by using less material, hence the rod will be lighter, thinner, and more fragile than a rod made of lower-modulus graphite. It will also be "faster" because the same casting effort can move the thinner

☞ **TRAVELER'S TIP**

Due to the callousness of most airlines, I sure as hell wouldn't use two-piece fly rods anymore. If you check your rods as baggage, they'll break or lose them. And the airlines have this quaint attitude that whenever they lose a fly rod they'll reimburse you a hundred dollars. How very nice of them. The fact that most good fly rods today cost about four hundred doesn't seem to have dawned on them yet. I use nothing but four-piece rods. I use two different ones: Fisher and Thomas & Thomas.

When you go into hot, tropical areas for saltwater fishing, fly rods tend to stick together. They expand in the heat because most of them are black, made of black graphite. And when they're out in the hot sun for four or five days, you can't get them apart. I've had them expand so much that it took two or three guys to pull them apart. If you take along either beeswax or a piece of candle, and rub those ferrules and joints before you put the rods together, you can get them apart at the end of the trip. This really makes a difference.

—Jack Samson
saltwater columnist, *Fly Rod & Reel*,
formerly editor of *Field & Stream*
Santa Fe, New Mexico

rod through the air faster and because the stiff material will rebound from being flexed faster than softer material.)

In building his custom Performance rods, Dave Lewis uses blanks made by Diamondback, Fisher, Lamiglas, Loomis, Sage, St. Croix, Talon, and others. So he isn't committed to any particular notions as to graphite material, taper design, or ferrule system. Recently I visited his rodbuilding shop in the Shenandoah Valley outside Harrisonburg, Virginia, to ask him about travel rods. I learned a lot.

About Ferrules

"The closer the ferrules are to either end," Lewis says, "the more you feel their effects." They cause stiffness in both butt and tip, and they also make the tip section heavier and slower.

Lewis thinks "the tip-over-butt ferrule that everybody uses is a poor system," because it's inherently weak. Nearly all his warranty

Spigot, or plug, ferrule on a "flattened-circle" Nicholas Whipp fly rod. *(Castle Arms)*

breakage occurs in the top or bottom ferrules of four-piece rods. Reinforcing the ferrule to make it stronger (he double-wraps with thread) adds weight to the rod and increases the ferrule's negative effect on casting action.

In Lewis's judgment, the plug, or spigot, ferrule is stronger and better. (It is also, in my experience, much less likely than a tip-over-butt ferrule to work loose during a day of casting.) Why, then, do so many rod companies use the tip-over-butt ferrule? "The fishing public demands it. They think it's the only correct system, because it looks right." Plug-ferruled rods "always look wrong to the uneducated. As a result, they don't buy them. They think there's something wrong, because the sections don't go together." When a plug-ferruled rod is put together, there is nearly always a gap between the sections, exposing the ferrule plug. It looks weak, but it's stronger than the neater-looking tip-over-butt ferrule. Lewis also likes plug ferrules because "the plug can be made of a lower-modulus material and interject less of a stiff spot in the rod." He always uses plug-ferruled blanks to build six-piece travel rods. "I don't think you could ever build a six-piece rod with tip-over-butt ferrules. Because it takes so much space to reinforce them, the whole rod would be reinforcement."

Dave Lewis also likes the Orvis ferrule system, which simply uses a glued-on sleeve to attach the sections. "That's an extremely good system for a company like Orvis that wants to save on costs and wants to be able to offer all kinds of different, weird lengths," he says. "They use one-piece blanks, whack them off in the middle, and put a sleeve over the outside. They can chop their blanks into any lengths they want. It's ugly, but it's functional and it's cheap."

About Inherent Differences Between Two- and Four-piece Rod Blanks

"There's so much good two-piece stuff out there, you just don't have to look very closely. The two-piece rods are state of the art. They're just superb. Practically everybody's two-piece rod is great now. There's a lot of dogs in four-piece rods. I think it just takes a lot more skill to manufacture a four-piece blank."

About Graphite Modulus

High-modulus graphite is both stiffer and more fragile than intermediate-modulus graphite, so why are multipiece fly rods (which can be criticized on grounds of being too stiff and too weak) so often made of high-modulus graphite? "Weight," he says. "It's a definite advantage. The light weight doesn't tire you out as much. The weight advantage to high-modulus materials is probably more noticeable in a day's fishing with multipiece rods than two-piece rods, because you can save a lot of weight in multipiece rods by using high-modulus materials."

About the Higher Price Tags on Four-piece Rods

Because of the difficulty in manufacturing four-piece rods, and the material wastage in getting the sections all the same length, he says, "there's not a lot of reasonably priced stuff" in multipiece blanks. (However, if you've put off buying a travel rod because you don't want to spend $400, know that Dave Lewis builds really nice four-piecers on LCI Talon IM6 graphite blanks for $219 and on St. Croix standard graphite blanks for $199—1994 price.) Of St. Croix's inexpensive four-piece blanks, he says,

> Their low-end stuff is excellent. They're standard graphite blanks, and they're easy to cast. They're more like Winston rods than, say, Sage or Loomis. A lot of guys are much more comfortable with that. The high-modulus, fast-action blanks demand much more of you; the timing is more critical. I'm a good caster and I use and enjoy them. But a lot of guys don't want to focus on that. They want to focus on the fishing. The St. Croix rods are more comfortable for them. And they're a good-performance blank.

Given that traveling convenience is the only advantage offered by four-piece rods, do I think you should travel with two-piece rods? Not at all. Convenience is a mighty important consideration when you are traveling. So important, I think it's decisive. Over the years I have added eight multipiece rods to my fly-rod collection (the most recent being a four-piece, nine-foot, 8-weight Green River Enso that will enable me to more or less retire my old Sage two-piece salmon rod to saltwater duty), and I wouldn't think of traveling without them.

Four-piece rods are so handy, and so *nearly* equal to two-piece rods in performance, I find myself using them almost all the time, even when just driving to nearby streams. Although I bought it for traveling ease, my nine-foot, four-piece Powell for 5-, 6-, and 7-weight lines has become my favorite all-around rod for trout, smallmouth bass, and panfish. It's the first rod that goes in the car when I fish local waters.

The most unusual and versatile of my traveling rods are all from Dave Sylvester's Deerfield Rod Company. My first Deerfield—a four-piece, nine-foot, three-tip Over-and-Under Power-Pak GT-40 for 5/6, 7/8, and 9/10—has been a perfect traveling companion, and I can use it for almost everything: trout, bass, salmon, bonefish, stripers, blues. Where I go, it goes, usually as a backup. My other Deerfields include a six-piece, twelve-foot, two-handed rod for 6/7; a three-piece rod that

One of the author's favorite travel rods. *(Green River Rodmakers)*

can be fished as a seven-foot fly rod for 12- and 13-weight lines (a great offshore fly rod for dolphin and sailfish) or as a seven-and-a-half-foot plug-casting rod for lures of ⅜ to ¾ ounces (excellent for bluefish, stripers, and tarpon); and a four-piece, eight-and-a-half-foot, three-tip rod for 2/3, 4/5, or 6/7 (a foot-long butt-section extender makes it a five-piece, nine-and-a-half-footer for 3/4, 5/6, or 7/8). Given all the configurations available, those four Deerfields can be fished as a dozen different rods.

Dave Sylvester uses intermediate-modulus (IM) graphite in his Deerfield travelers; Dave Lewis uses standard, IM, *and* high-modulus (HM) graphites in his various Performance Fours; and Green River uses HM graphites but sometimes "blends" materials. As Green River's Robert Gorman puts it, "I don't hesitate to use two or even occasionally three different graphites (including IM graphites) to get the action I'm after." The four-piece factory rods use a wide variety of graphites, so the careful shopper ought to be able to find just the rod he's looking for. Fin-Nor's eight-foot, three-piece Blue Water rods for 20-pound tippets and 12- to 15-weight lines (which have more than eighty world records to their credit) use graphite-fiberglass composite blanks for maximum strength in battling really big fish. Ultimate casting performance isn't very important offshore.

Even tweedy traditionalists who dote on the soft, slow action of bamboo rods can find a reasonable selection of three-, four-, and even five-piece cane whips—if the budget will bear a price tag that begins at $550 (the price of a four-piece Partridge Poacher) and may run to more than three times that. The hopelessly tweedy can indulge their most retro fantasies with a three-piece Partridge Greenheart (yes, *greenheart!*) rod for 5- or 6-weight line. Neo-traditionalists who appreciate the look and action of bamboo and the strength and durability of graphite can investigate three-piece rods from Hexagraph. The material is graphite, but it's built in hexagonal-strip cross-section, like bamboo. Naturally, Hexagraphs can't duplicate the nuances of cane, but the look and feel are close enough that they were used in the filming of *A River Runs Through It*. And at around $600, they're cheaper than most bamboo rods.

These days, you can find a multipiece travel rod for almost any kind of fishing, one suited to your particular skills or tastes. You no longer have to put up with the clumsiness of long rod cases on the one hand or with heavy, stiff, fragile pack rods on the other. If you are

A brawny, three-piece offshore fly compared to a lighter, two-piece bonefish rod. *(Fin-Nor)*

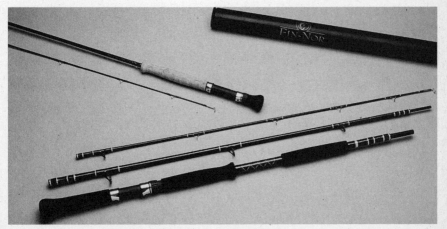

☞ TRAVELER'S TIP

I always take multipiece rods. I always take more than one size, and I take a backup for the all-purpose rod I always travel with. You should have coverage of at least a couple different kinds of conditions. I carry my rods on the plane, which I think is the best thing to do. I have a case that will carry four four-piece rods (unless one of them happens to be very heavy) and two reels. I know that I can fish with what I carry on my back, and I think that's the most important thing to me when I travel. No matter what happens to the baggage, I will have something to fish with. I put my rod-and-reel bag over my shoulder, so they won't notice I have two carry-on bags.

—Joan Salvato Wulff
president, Royal Wulff, Inc., and
the Wulff School of Fly Fishing
Lew Beach, New York

---

like me, you probably will wind up with several multipiece travel rods and even find yourself fishing them close to home. Phil Castleman of Castle Arms (U.S. seller of the unusual, Kevlar-clad Nicolas Whipp rods with the "flattened-circle" cross section) predicts that "in ten years the two-piece rod will be a thing of the past as the four-piece rod casts as well as the two-piece and is easier to carry both in the car and on a plane." Stranger things have happened.

Even if you decide to stick with your two-piece rods, consider getting a three- or four-piece travel rod as a carry-on backup. That way, if your two-piece rods go astray, you'll have the multipiece rod to fish with. Here are some all-around multipiece rods to consider:

▶ For trout: an eight-and-a-half- or nine-footer for 5- or 6-weight lines
▶ For large trout or bass: a nine-footer for 7- or 8-weight lines
▶ For salmon, steelhead, pike, peacock bass, bonefish, barracuda, and baby tarpon: a nine- or nine-and-a-half-footer for 9-weight
▶ For tarpon, sailfish, dolphin, small tunas, and large salmon and peacock bass: a strong, nine-and-a-half- or ten-foot rod with a long foregrip, for 10- or 11-weight line (also good for surf fishing)
▶ For big-game fishing offshore: a seven- to eight-footer with lots of backbone and a long foregrip, for 12- to 15-weight lines

Rod Cases

Writer Ted Williams, ever the iconoclast, does the reverse of what I do: He carries two-piece rods on board and checks a four-piece backup rod (securely housed in a case made of heavy PVC pipe) in his duffel. He says he never experiences trouble carrying the long tubes on board. (I sometimes do.) Just make sure they are slender tubes, he says, so they can't be mistaken for gun cases, bazookas, or rocket launchers. You may be able to fit two rods in a single, thin-walled aluminum tube, if you remove the cloth bag from one them.

If you want to travel with a bunch of two-piece rods, you will have to check them as baggage. Ted advises that you "make a big, heavy rod case out of large-diameter, thick PVC pipe. You can carry four or five rods in one case. Put bags on all the rods, and one of them in an aluminum tube, so you can take an extra rod on the boat."

Ted's advice on rugged PVC pipe is well taken. Thin-walled aluminum tubes are a lot easier to bend or break. Alternatively, tape three aluminum rod tubes together. Even if you are carrying just one or two rods, tape *three* rod tubes together. The triangular cross section is stronger and will keep them from rolling into dark corners of the cargo bay where they may be overlooked.

If you get one of those large-diameter, thin-walled, adjustable-length, tubular plastic rod cases that you see in all the catalogs and Kmarts, be sure your longest rod is first housed in an aluminum (or small-diameter PVC) rod tube within the outer case. At the very least, enclose a broomstick or heavy dowel that is longer than that longest rod section. Either way, if the length-adjuster fails (and sooner or later it will), your rod tips *might* survive traumatic truncation of the case.

I used to mark my rod tubes and cases FRAGILE and DO NOT PLACE ON BELT, but I no longer do. The latter was routinely ignored, and the former sometimes caused the airline to make me waive their responsibility for damage to fragile goods they haven't packed. Anyway, I've never seen a FRAGILE sticker deter a baggage handler from tossing anything. Most airlines and airports are pretty good about special-handling long or bulky objects that might get jammed on the baggage conveyors and carousels. What they aren't good about is handling

MAKING A ROD CASE OUT OF PVC PIPE

Making a PVC rod case is easy. Purchase the following at a hardware or plumbing-supply store:

▶ *Schedule 40 PVC pipe of the appropriate length and diameter (1½-in.-diameter pipe for trout rods, 1½- or 2-in. pipe for salmon and salt-water rods, 3- or 4-in. pipe to carry several rods. The length should be slightly longer than the longest rod section). If you buy a long section of pipe to make several cases, use a hacksaw to cut the pipe.*

▶ *An end cap of matching diameter.*

▶ *A threaded adapter and cap of the same diameter.*

▶ *A small can of PVC cement.*

PVC CEMENT

THREADED CAP   THREADED ADAPTER   SCH. 40 PVC PIPE   END CAP

Following the instructions on the can, glue the end cap and the threaded adapter onto the ends of the section of pipe. Drill a small vent hole in one or both end caps, so the air pressure can equalize itself if ever you put the case in an unpressurized airplane cargo hold. You're done. I always push a small piece of plastic foam down to the bottom of the tube, to help cushion the rod or rods.

If you want a handle (not very important on short, carry-on rod cases), you can use a piece of heavy-duty webbing or nylon strap and two self-locking cable ties or flexible-duct clamps. (You could also use stainless-steel hose clamps, but I think the recommended nylon fixtures are easier and safer to use.) To make the strap handle secure in the clamps, sew loops in each end, fold the ends over, and tape the double-thick sections with good strong tape, or use heat to melt the ends and make them knobby.

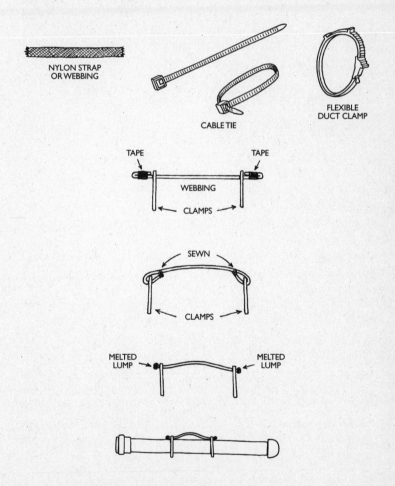

anything gingerly. I recall watching the face of a nattily dressed fly-fisher—the sort of chap who looked as if he might be traveling with a pair of Paynes or Garrisons—go dead white as his hand-tooled leather rod case disappeared on the conveyor belt in Stockholm, followed immediately by a loud WHAM! as it was tossed onto a baggage cart like so much garbage.

Like the rest of your luggage when traveling abroad, rod cases that are checked as baggage should be locked. The locks mustn't be dime-store toys; they can be broken with a pair of pliers or opened with a toothpick. If your rod cases can't be locked, wrap the caps heavily with tape, so tampering will be apparent immediately.

Preventing and Coping with Rod Wreckage

Whether you carry two- or four-piece rods or both, always carry a backup rod or two and a little rod-repair kit. The repair kit should include the following:

- ▶ tiptops (for each rod), snake guides in assorted sizes, and two or three ring guides
- ▶ electrician's or fiberglass tape (for attaching guides and making other emergency repairs)
- ▶ ferrule cement (or hot-melt glue), five-minute epoxy, and Krazy Glue
- ▶ beeswax and a pair of rubber jar openers (for sticky ferrules)
- ▶ dental tape or floss
- ▶ sandpaper (fine and medium)

Finally, to minimize your use of that rod repair kit, let your guide or another angler net, gaff, or tail your fish for you, and use a straight

---

 TRAVELER'S TIP

Always take extra rods, in case anything goes wrong.

—Ron Spomer
professional photographer and outdoor writer
Troy, Idaho

hand pull on the fly line to free a fly that has been snagged. Not counting car doors, capsizings, spills, and misplaced footfalls, most rod breakage occurs while an angler is trying to lift a fish out of the water with the rod or while trying to net or tail a fish at his feet. In both cases, the rod tip gets bent beyond its design capability and snaps.

Another source of angler-induced rod breakage is using the rod to free a fly that has been snagged in vegetation or on some floating or underwater obstruction. Especially when the fly is snagged at the end of a long cast over flowing water. No matter that you are fishing a 6X tippet; the water drag on forty or fifty feet of fly line is a tremendous load. Whip that weight with a fly rod, and the tip will break long before the energy gets down to the leader. A straight pull on the line with your hands may break the tippet or hook but will protect your rod.

Resources

TRAVEL ROD CATALOGS

Many of the mail-order tackle catalogs listed in the next chapter offer a wide variety of travel rods, but you might want to get catalogs from the following builders and manufacturers of first-rate multipiece rods. And I'd sure appreciate your mentioning you heard about them in *Traveling with Fly Rod and Reel*. A few other prominent manufacturers will be conspicuous by their absence in the list that follows; they failed to reply to my request for a catalog, so I can't conscionably recommend that you submit yourself to the same shabby treatment.

Bass Pro Shops, 1935 S. Campbell, Springfield, MO 65898; phone 1-800-403-6000, 1-800-227-7776, 1-417-887-3567; fax 1-417-887-2531

L. L. Bean, Inc., Freeport, ME 04033; phone 1-800-221-4221, 1-800-341-4341, 1-207-865-3111, 1-207-865-3161; fax 1-207-797-8867

Belvoirdale, P.O. Box 176, Wyncote, PA 19095; phone 1-215-886-7211; fax 1-215-886-1804

Blue Ridge Rod Company, 7930 Cryden Way, Suite 201, Forestville, MD 20747; phone 1-301-627-1164; fax 1-301-420-1502 *(rod blanks)*

Cabela's, Inc., 812-13th Avenue, Sidney, NE 69160; phone 1-800-237-4444, 1-800-237-8888; fax 1-800-496-6329, 1-308-254-2200

Clemens Custom Tackle, Inc., 444 Schantz Spring Road, Allentown, PA 18104; phone 1-610-395-5119; fax 1-610-398-2580 *(rod blanks)*

Cortland Line Company, Inc., P.O. Box 5588, Cortland, NY 13045; phone 1-607-756-2851; fax 1-607-753-8835

Deerfield Rod Co., 70-A Arcadia Road, Hackensack, NJ 07601; phone 1-201-343-6044

Fenwick, 5242 Argosy Drive, Huntington Beach, CA 92649; phone 1-714-897-1066; fax 1-714-891-9610

Fin-Nor Corporation, 2021 S.W. 31st Avenue, Hallandale, FL 33009; phone 1-305-966-5507; fax 1-305-966-5509

J. Kennedy **Fisher,** Inc., P.O. Box 3147, Carson City, NV 89702; phone 1-800-334-3474, 1-702-246-5220; fax 1-702-246-5143

Hardy (USA) Inc., 10 Godwin Plaza, Midland Park, NJ 07432; phone 1-201-481-7557; fax 1-201-670-7190

Hexagraph Rod Company, 2703 Rocky Woods, Kingwood, TX 77339; phone 1-800-870-4211

Kane Klassics Cane Fly Rods, P.O. Box 8124, Fremont, CA 94537; phone 1-510-487-8545; fax 1-510-487-6448

Lamiglas Incorporated, P.O. Box U, Woodland, WA 98674; phone 1-206-225-9436; fax 1-206-225-5050

G. **Loomis,** P.O. Box E, Woodland, WA 98674; phone 1-206-225-6516; fax 1-206-225-7169

Offshore Angler, Inc., 1935 S. Campbell, Springfield, MO 65898; phone 1-800-463-3746, 1-417-863-2499; fax 1-417-873-5060

Orvis Services, Inc., P.O. Box 798, Manchester, VT 05254; phone 1-800-548-9548, 1-802-362-3622, 1-703-345-4606; fax 1-802-362-3525, 1-703-343-7053

Penn Fishing Tackle Mfg. Co., 3028 W. Hunting Park Avenue, Philadelphia, PA 19132; phone 1-215-229-9415; fax 1-215-223-3017

Performance Fly Rods, Route 4, Box 440, Harrisonburg, VA 22801; phone 1-703-867-0856; summer phone 1-406-646-7424; fax 1-703-867-0951

Powell Rod Co., P.O. Box 4000, Chico, CA 95927; phone 1-800-228-0615, 1-916-345-3393; fax 1-916-345-0567

RST-Angelgeräte GmbH, Schwaninger Strasse 31, D-89352 Ellzee/Stoffenried, Germany; phone 011-49-8283-2074; fax 011-49-8283-2054

Sage, 8500 N.E. Day Road, Bainbridge Island, WA 98110; phone 1-206-842-6608; fax 1-206-842-6830

Scott Powr-Ply, 707-B Heinz Street, Berkeley, CA 94710; phone 1-501-841-2444; fax 1-501-841-2448

St. Croix of Park Falls, Ltd., P.O. Box 279, Park Falls, WI 54552; phone 1-800-826-7042, 1-715-762-3226; fax 1-715-762-3293

Nicolas **Whipp** Fly Rods/Castle Arms, P.O. Box 30070, Springfield, MA 01103; phone 1-800-525-4866, 1-413-567-8268; fax 1-413-731-1292

R. L. **Winston** Rod Co., Drawer T, Twin Bridges, MT 59754; phone 1-406-684-5674; fax 1-406-684-5533

Interlude ⌒◦

STEAMING WITH
THE ELDERS

Morry had an eternally worried look about him, even when he was smiling. Now he looked downright tormented. Later we learned why. As soon as we'd disembarked on the gravel runway at Ekwok, on the Nushagak River in Alaska's Bristol Bay Watershed, somebody had told Morry that Luki Akelkok said he was going to break Morry's legs, he was so mad. Luki Akelkok was the president of Ekwok Native, Ltd., the village corporation. Morry was the president of the Alaska Sport Fishing Lodge Association and the fellow who booked and promoted the fishing lodge the village owned.

When we got to the lodge, we discovered that, midway through the season, the manager had quit, one of the guides, an Arizonan named Jeff West, had become acting manager, and now that the cook had quit, Jeff was doing the cooking as well.

"See, I told you it could get worse," John Jenkins said. John was then an editor at *Salt Water Sportsman* in Boston, one of the three writers being carted around from lodge to lodge so Morry could show his clients he was working hard for them. The other was Nick Karas, the outdoor columnist for *New York Newsday* on Long Island. At both of the places we'd been previously, it had been obvious that relations between Morry and the operators were strained and that he was taking us around not to his best fishing opportunities but to places where he needed to show the flag. But this was the first time physical violence had been put on the menu. We couldn't wait to see what was next. Ekwok means "end of the bluff" in the Yupik Eskimo language, which in the context seemed ominous.

We had arrived too late to do any fishing that first day, and as soon as dinner was over, Morry disappeared into his room. John, who was rooming with him, reported at breakfast that Morry had gotten up several times during the night to sit in a chair and chain-smoke.

After breakfast the next morning, while John, Nick, and I clambered into our fishing gear, Morry stewed and fretted, fretted and stewed. First he said he wasn't going out with us. He needed to prepare for that evening's village council meeting. At the last minute, he decided he would go fishing after all. He forgot to take his rod.

Bo Olsen, the head guide, took us upstream to a little tributary called Klutuk. The creek looked great, but Bo wouldn't take us up. "Too many bears," he said. "Too dangerous." So we fished the mouth of Klutuk, where it flowed into the Nushagak, a big, deep, wide, muddy river with banks that dropped away fast into water that was too deep to wade.

Fortunately, the Nushagak seemed to be full of coho salmon—silvers, in Alaska sport-fishing parlance—and they came by our position in wave after wave. Unfortunately, they weren't very interested in flies. Nick and John took up ultralight spinning rods. I stubbornly stuck with the fly rod. Unable to fish, Morry waded across the creek and spotted individual fish in the mouth of the creek that were within easy (read "my") fly-casting range. "A little to the left," he'd say, or "Let it sink a little deeper" after each cast. Soon it was "I don't know what's wrong, you're putting the fly right in front of their noses." Soon enough, I put down the fly rod and took up a spinning rod so I could join in the catching.

We caught fish after fish, coho salmon in different stages of spawning color from dark silver to dusky brick red. They ranged from five to fourteen pounds, and most of them went seven to ten. One wave seemed to contain nothing but twelve-pound fish. We caught them on Mepps spinners and Pixee spoons, mostly, but also on T-Spoons, Super Dupers, and Gooey Bobs. Bo kept trying to talk us into putting gobs of salmon eggs on the treble hooks. Occasionally a rainbow trout would take the lure. Most were in the one- to two-pound range, some were smaller and a few were bigger. Richie Acuvak, one of the Yupik guides, caught one that weighed seven and a half pounds, a very nice fish. He caught it on a fiberglass spinning rod that had lost a good foot of its tip and a reel that had less than fifty yards of monofil- ament. (At trip's end, I gave him the graphite rod and skirted-spool spinning reel Orvis had lent me to test.)

Now and again, grayling would take our lures. The biggest only went one and a half to two pounds, and most of them were under a pound. What they were doing, attacking lures almost half their length, I couldn't figure out. I'd never caught grayling before, but a friend in Montana had said he always used size 28 Tricos for them. If they'll take big, number 5 Mepps spinners, I reasoned, they'll take salmon flies. So I limbered up the fly rod and played with grayling while the others kept plugging away at the salmon.

After lunch (coho salmon cooked with vegetables in foil over a driftwood fire, home-fried potatoes, freshly baked bread, cold beer, and a nice California wine), John and I went with Bo to try a few dif- ferent spots on the other side of the river. Nick stayed at the Klutuk with Morry and Richie and had faster fishing.

(During the three days we spent at Ekwok, the fishing never changed: seven- to twelve-pound coho after coho, mostly on spinners and spoons. John and I got so tired of it, we had Bo take us downriver to a slough he'd been telling us about, to catch big pike. We had no wire leaders, so we lost all the big ones, but we caught plenty of pike from three to six pounds. We caught them on Spin-n-Glo spin bob- bers, a steelhead and salmon lure, with bucktail hooks. I was fishing with 6-pound-test line and lost a lot of fish, managing to land seven or eight of them. John, fishing 12-pound-test line, landed seventeen of them, including one we estimated at nine pounds.)

After dinner, Morry reluctantly headed upstream to face the music. While he was still within earshot, John and Nick and I began mock- wagering over whether they'd break one or both legs, and in how many places. (Yeah, it was mean, but he deserved it, bringing three of us all the way across the country for purposes other than showing us good fishing we could write about.) Whatever his fate, Morry was gone for hours. Then Richie showed up with a message that we were to go up to the village to steam with the council elders.

None of us was particularly interested in making a late-night trip through what by daylight seemed tricky rapids, to steam-bathe with people we didn't know, especially with angry people we didn't know. Laura Schroeder, the accountant and business advisor to the lodge and village, said it was an invitation we shouldn't refuse. Steaming is an important Yupik tradition, she said, and it wasn't often the council elders invited outsiders to steam with them. Morry must have convinced them we were important fellows, indeed. As for the rapids, she said, Richie was a good boatman and could probably negotiate them while blindfolded. So, up the river we went.

Ekwok is a small village of about twenty-five houses and ninety-seven residents. Half the houses are modest, prefab, tract houses equipped with central heat, electrical appliances, color television; the other half are tiny, low-ceilinged shacks lighted by a single bare bulb. One family fishes salmon commercially down in Bristol Bay. The others either work at the lodge or eke out a subsistence living by fishing. Hanging throughout the village like so much laundry are slabs of chum salmon, air-drying. The salmon is mostly for the dogs, Richie told us. The dogs are no longer used for transportation (everyone has snowmobiles for that) but for dog sled racing.

John was taken to Luki Akelkok's steam house, where Morry was waiting. Nick and I were ushered to the steam house of Philip Akelkok, Luki's brother and the recent past president of the village corporation.

A steam house is a little, ramshackle wooden shack with two rooms, a small cooling room that is screened against mosquitoes and a larger steam room, where the oil-drum stove is half buried in a pile of cobble-size rocks. Water is ladled from a five-gallon bucket and tossed onto the heated rocks to flash into superheated steam. Each bather is provided with a washcloth, which must be kept wet. The cloth serves two purposes: to breathe through, protecting your lungs from the otherwise searing dry heat of the room, and to wet your hair to keep it from scorching. From time to time, when it gets too hot to bear, you duck out into the cooling room to have a beer.

Whether it's a hallowed tradition or a practical joke, I don't know, but Eskimos always test their white visitors by seeing how much heat they can stand. It's also a form of punishment. The only difference is that when you are being punished, a big native sits before the door, blocking your escape; when it's only amusement, you can always decide to lose face and bolt for the door. I don't know how John and Morry fared (and I suspect they were blocking his door), but Nick and I were sorry representatives of our race. Nick begged off from steaming on account of a heart condition, and I couldn't stand much heat. But we sure held our own with the beer in the cooling room.

While we sat in the cooling room, Philip Akelkok regaled us with stories of the good old days, when the native peoples would gather periodically to trade goods and sing and dance and feast together. I asked Philip if he remembered any of the songs, so he sang two of them. They reminded me of Russian folk songs such as *Ochi Chórnyi*, "Dark Eyes."

After the steaming ended, Nick and I were taken to Luki Akelkok's house, where John and Morry were waiting. (Morry's legs seemed fine.) Luki lives in one of the prefab houses. As we sat there in his kitchen, drinking coffee and beer, and talking about the oil-drilling threat to Bristol Bay and other problems facing Alaska's native peoples, a *Mary Tyler Moore Show* rerun kept yammering away on the color TV hanging from the wall on one of those hinged-arm contraptions they put in hotels.

Finally we left Luki's and headed for the boat. Morry said he'd forgotten something and went back to Luki's house. He was gone nearly an hour. By the time he returned, as usual with only the vaguest of explanations, John had disappeared on the back of a three-wheel ATV driven by Letia Hurley, a pretty, disaffected village girl who worked at the fishing lodge but hankered to move to San Diego or Santa Monica, I can't remember which.

Eventually, we gave up waiting for John and went back down river to the lodge, Morry muttering all the while about John's making trouble for him again and how the Akelkok brothers might decide to neuter John "if he messed with that girl." Nick and I tried to calm Morry down by telling him how honorable a young gentleman we knew John to be—even though we'd all just met on the flight up from Seattle. Richie was sent back up to the village to wait for John, who returned to the lodge as soon as the boat could get up to the village and return. Morry spent most of the night muttering, pacing, and chain-smoking, John said.

Nick and I slept like babies in our room, dreaming of salmon leaping under a starlit sky.

4
TRAVELING TACKLE

As for the rest of your tackle, you can pretty much go with what you've got, as long as it's appropriate to the demands that will be made on it. Just give everything a close inspection and a thorough tune-up before you depart.

Reels

"Smaller and lighter" are watchwords for traveling anglers, except when it comes to reels. When traveling halfway around the world to fish, I want reels that can survive a hard knock or two, and that pretty much rules out the fleaweights. Like most people, I started out buying modestly priced fly reels. (My first ones were an Orvis Madison, a Pfleuger Medalist, and a Cortland LTD—and I still use all of them, especially the LTD.) Since then I've edged up into slightly higher brackets: Loop, Zeus, Hardy, Scientific Anglers System 2, and Valentine planetary-gear reels, for instance. I'm not looking for cachet, but for more sturdiness, smoothness, durability, and dependability. That's the first principle in selecting reels for traveling.

▶ For traveling afar, choose reels for their dependability as well as their appropriateness to the fishing. If you will be fishing light lines for spooky brown trout, you will probably want a small reel.

Just get one that's up to the rigors of traveling, not an el-cheapo lightweight.

The other reel-selection principles are equally simple:

▶ Unless you are experienced at palming a reel on big, fast, or long-running fish, choose reels with good, dependable drags. Even for trout fishing, I prefer reels with good drags, in case I injure my palming hand or can't figure out the dynamics of a fish that's new to me.

▶ Carry backup reels, but not too many of them. Reels are relatively bulky and heavy, but you need a backup in case something happens to your main reel. For this reason, my backup reels are often lightweight jobs, such as Cortland's inexpensive but dependable

Valentine planetary-gear reel and an Arctic char fly, with Siberia's Lake Lubalakh in the background.
(Author's collection)

LTD graphite reels. If I could convince my new wife that we need new reels more than new kitchen cabinets, I might be tempted to get a few STH Cassette reels because the cassettes are lighter, smaller, and less expensive than spare spools. That raises the next point:

▶ Don't use extra reels to carry extra lines. Yes, it's the easiest, handiest way to switch lines, but you just can't afford the extra bulk and weight when you are traveling. If you want to have a number of lines loaded and ready to go, carry them on spare spools rather than reels.

I've seen more reels fail on fishing trips than I've seen rods break. Considering the extreme frailty of a graphite rod's flimsy tip and the way so many people mistreat their rods while fumbling to land or tail a fish, that's amazing.

▶ Be prepared for reel failure: Carry reel lubricant (both oil and grease), some drag disks and washers, screws, and a hobbyist's or jeweler's set of small screwdrivers. If your reel has a suspect part, one that's old and worn or showing a hairline crack, say, replace the part before setting forth on that trip of a lifetime. At the very least, carry a spare part. If the make or model of your reel is known for certain kinds of mechanical fallibility, be prepared with drag springs, pawls, gears, spacers, bearings, whatever.

Fly Lines

Because they take up relatively little room, don't weigh very much, and affect the fishing so much, fly lines, leaders, and flies are almost exempt from the spartan, minimalist approach otherwise strongly urged on traveling fly-fishers. This is one area in which I think it's better to risk taking too much, to be sure you aren't taking too little. That long-belly, intermediate-tip fly line you've never got around to using? If you leave it home, it will almost certainly turn out to be the very line you need to cope with conditions.

To make room for all the fly lines you might need, take appropriate steps.

▶ Leave the packaging home. Cardboard boxes and plastic spools take up a lot of room in your luggage. However, if the boxes and spools are part of a rewinding mechanism, as they are with Cortland LazerLines, you might decide the speed and convenience are worth lugging the extra bulk.

▶ Don't carry all those extra lines on reel spools either, unless you really can't stand the inconvenience of loading and unloading your reels.

▶ Carry your lines in twist-tied loose loops, so you can carry a whole bunch without crowding out that liter of single-malt Scotch or the novel you've been meaning to get around to one of these days. Ziplocked plastic sandwich bags, prominently labeled with permanent markers, are great for carrying lines and leaders too.

▶ Shooting tapers are great for traveling. With one reel spool, you can fish on top, deep, or anywhere in between. I keep a Loop reel loaded with nothing but backing and a thin running line and use it with 5-, 6-, 7-, and 8-weight shooting tapers. The Loop is especially well suited to this use because it can carry a lot of backing and line for its light weight.

☞ TRAVELER'S TIP

From experience I've learned it's a good idea to take along a small number of logically unnecessary things for those one or two days a week when even the local experts have trouble catching fish. That's when you wish you had brought something you decided to leave behind. To avoid such disappointments, after deciding what I really need, I always pack a few extras.

When the logical tackle isn't working, perhaps a high-speed sink tip, or even a full sinking line, or saltwater streamers or a steelhead pattern might save the day. I put these few flies and lines in a small, zip-locked plastic bag that doesn't take up valuable space.

—Sugai Yasuji
president, Chikyu-Maru Co., Ltd.,
publishers of *Outdoor Life Magazine*
Tokyo, Japan

I usually make my own shooting tapers because I find that with my casting style (that's a euphemism for "ineptitude"), a shorter, heavier taper works better. Let's say I'm using a 6-weight rod. Rather than fish with conventional, thirty- to thirty-eight-foot, 6-weight shooting tapers, I'll maybe use twenty-five-foot, 8- or 9-weight tapers. (Shortening a taper by eight to ten feet adds three line sizes to the necessary casting weight.) That way I don't have to pick up and aerialize so much line on the back cast to load the rod.

Floating lines are probably specified most often by lodges, camps, guides, outfitters, or booking agents, with sink-tip lines recommended less often. Some will suggest you bring both. Saltwater outfitters may nominate intermediate lines as the first choice. Whenever someone suggests that I carry full sinking lines, I get the same feeling I used to get on ski runs with names like Slingshot, Suicide, or Grizzly: *I'm going to die.* I can't cast sinking lines well, they wear me out early in the trip, and I have precious little fun fishing them. So, as I used to do on the ski slopes, I head somewhere else or resort to the piscatorial equivalent of snowplowing—sink tips and weighted leaders, about which, more later.

Weight-forward or double taper? WF lines are great for shooting line, DTs for making delicate presentations or aerializing a lot of line. Pay attention to all the advice you read in books and magazines or hear from friends, booking agents, or your fly-shop guru, but pay closer attention to your own gut. The real questions you must answer are: *What do you like to use?* and *What lines can you handle proficiently?* Even if Lefty Kreh, Ted Williams, and Killer Joe down at the Fly Flicker say a long-belly, weight-forward, no-stretch intermediate line with a twenty-foot, Hi-D sinking tip is what you need, you won't have much fun or catch many fish if you can't handle such a line. If you can cast, mend, and control a normal weight-forward sink tip better and more comfortably, that's what you should use. Carry the recommended line as a backup, maybe, but don't commit yourself to relying on it.

In recent years, a lot of salmon and steelhead anglers have taken to using add-on sink tips of various lengths and densities. That certainly provides a lot of flexibility, but it also requires compensatory casting. If your rod loads properly with a given line, adding a few feet of sinking tip overloads it. Good casters can compensate, by aerializing less line and shooting more. But I think Stu Apte has come up with a better idea.

The Multi Tip Fly Lines in the Stu Apte Signature Series, sold through Johnny Morris's Offshore Angler catalog, have a braided loop connector at the end of the front taper, where the level tip section begins on other fly lines. Separate tips are connected to the line by fast, loop-to-loop connections. Because the line doesn't have a built-in tip, switching densities doesn't affect its weight or casting performance as much as adding a second tip to a regular fly line. The lines are weight-forward, low-stretch floaters (available in weights 6 through 13), and they come packaged with floating and medium-density sink tips. For another $15.99, you can buy the other pair of tips: a clear-core intermediate and a fast-sinker. The tips are color coded, and their lengths vary from fifteen to twenty feet, depending on the density. The line (with two tips) sells for $49.99, so for sixty-six bucks you practically have four top-quality fly lines, a real bargain. And you don't need to carry extra reels, spools, or backing, all of which add weight, bulk, and considerable cost. I've just started using them, and I am impressed.

Leaders

Prior to discovering Stu Apte's Multi Tip lines, I had just about retired my sink-tip lines altogether, preferring to use instead Airflo's versatile braided-leader *series*. (In case you can't find them in your shop, contact Angler Sport Group, 6619 Oak Orchard Road, Elba, New York 14058; phone 1-800-332-3937 or 1-716-757-9958; fax 1-716-757-9066.) I emphasize "series," because that's what makes them special. You can buy the leaders separately or in packaged sets—trout, salmon, and lightweight. (The four lightweight trout leaders are for upstream nymphing for trout in fast pocket water or for making stealthy presentations in clear or glassy-calm waters.)

The entire Airflo range includes braided sections that range in length from four to ten feet and in floating, intermediate, antiwake (called antiskate in the salmon set), slow-sink, fast-sink, super-fast-sink, and extra-super-fast-sink densities. Given all the permutations of length, strength, and density, the Airflo series offers thirty-five different leaders. The intermediate leaders are untreated, the floating leaders are treated with a floatant, and all the sinking leaders are impregnated with a tungsten-filled polymer.

Airflo leaders do change the weight and casting characteristics of a line, but a lot less than do accessory sink tips, split shot, or weighted flies. And they fish deeper. Remember, no matter how fast or deep a line or tip sinks, a fly fished on a monofilament leader won't be as deep as the tip of the line. So, the closer the fly is to the part that sinks, the deeper it will fish. You can use tippets of almost any length with the Airflo leaders—from less than two feet in upstream or long-tumble nymphing to twenty feet or more in casting to spooky brown trout in still water.

I can't tell you the number of times the Airflo leaders have made a major difference in both fun and effectiveness. Using them in the North Fork of the Shenandoah for smallmouth bass, I can fish any fly right down on the bottom. Using conventional leaders, I had to stick with split shot or heavily weighted flies, both of which I hate to cast and cause my forearm tendonitis to flare up. One day, briefly, four of us were fishing the Hourglass Pool on Russia's Varzina River, a short, deep, fast pool immediately below a mile or so of really heavy white water. Later in the season, when the water drops, the pool can be fished with whatever flies or leaders strike your fancy. But in higher water, you must fish either a high-density leader or a very short leader on a high-density line, or you must stand on the one rock in the last rapids that allows you to drift your fly into the pool from above. One of those, or go fishless. In the ten minutes I fished Hourglass from below the rapids, using a super-extra-fast-sinking Airflo leader, I connected with (but lost) two salmon, while the others were unable to get their flies down to where the fish were holding.

You've probably heard from famous fly-fishing gurus that braided leaders won't turn over properly or that they spray too much water in casting. All due respect, but most of these guys tried braided-butt leaders when they first came out (and weren't very good), made up and closed their minds, and haven't tried braided leaders since. I can turn them over as well as or better than regular monofilament leaders, and I'm no tournament caster. Only the untreated intermediate braided leaders are guilty of spraying water on the cast (but not much more than do knotted mono leaders). To minimize the spray or its effects, put some oomph into your first back cast, or make your first false cast away from the target, over water you've already fished.

Whether you use braided, knotted, or unknotted leaders, you will need to carry the following:

▶ Several spools of leader and tippet material. Don't scrimp on the X-sizes you think you will most use. If the fishing is great, or if you simply change flies often, you will go through a lot of tippets. And bring enough monofilament to tie up tapered leaders from scratch. Your jet-lagged mind may forget that plastic bag full of pretied leaders back at camp or in some en-route hotel room, or it might fall out of your vest or bag or otherwise disappear. If you've packed a selection of leader wheels, you're immediately back in business. Carry what you like. I like Maxima all the way down to 5X and sometimes 6X. I just wish Maxima's large-diameter wheels would fit in the tiny vest pockets provided for leader and tippet materials. Vest manufacturers, please take note.

▶ Shock tippet material for toothy or rough-skinned quarry, or for fishing around abrasive structure (rocks, piers, reefs, wrecks). You can use wire (solid or stranded), coated wire, or heavy mono. For stranded wire, you'll probably want to carry crimp sleeves and a crimping tool, unless you're really good at figure-8 knots, or fused twists for nylon-coated wire.

A word of warning if you decide to use Climax Duramax or one of the other microfilament tippet materials: Be sure it isn't stronger than your backing line. The stuff is so fine and flexible, you may have to use really strong tippets to get the fly to turn over properly. If the microfilament tippet is stronger than your backing, and you get into a really big fish, you might be saying good-bye to your whole fly line.

Cautious travelers might opt for packing a spare spool of backing. I usually don't, because it's so bulky. But when I do, it's nearly always Cortland Micron, mostly because of its fine diameter, which means I can get more backing on the reel spool. I've dabbled with the new Spectra (spun polyethylene) and Kevlar lines as backing, but it's hard to know in advance how much backing will fit. Usually it's less than you think it will be. Sometimes a lot less.

Flies

No matter where you go or what you are fishing for, some locally favored flies will almost invariably seem to work better than anything else. (Whether they are truly superior is moot. Once the guide insists

☞ **TRAVELER'S TIP**

I contact locals, guides, or outfitters to find out what patterns are cur-
rently working, in what sizes, and what they personally recommend
for their area. Do you need a longer rod because wind is a problem
there? Do you need a heavier line to buck the wind? Do you need to
bring along a light outfit for prime conditions in calm, clear water?

—Ron Spomer
professional photographer
and outdoor writer
Troy, Idaho

that your flies are no good and that you need a Whatso Special, your
confidence will sag a bit, and you won't fish as authoritatively as you
should.) If local flies are recommended, by all means try them. But
you can't count on flies being available locally. So you ought always to
bring a fair number of flies with you. What flies?

▶ Ask the booking agent which flies are hot and which are not, where
you are going, when you are going. In addition, ask the agent for a
telephone or fax number of the lodge, operator, or guide.
▶ If you can, get in touch within a week or two of departure, to find
out what's cooking.
▶ Pore over back issues of fishing magazines and newsletters for
articles and reports on the waters you'll be fishing.
▶ Ask the references you will get from the booking agent or operator—clients who fished the same waters at the same time the year
before.

Armed with all this information, head for the fly shop or the tying
table. After my first salmon trip to Russia's Kola Peninsula, I read
through the camp logs of a couple of rivers, preparing for my next
trip. It was readily apparent that British anglers fishing early in the
season took a lot of fish on a pattern called Ally's Shrimp. All I knew
was that it was a mostly orange, shrimp-imitating fly. I figured I
might do just as well fishing General Practitioners, Lady Carolines,
Polar Shrimp, and a couple of my own orange patterns: Rusty Prawn
and Kola Prawn. But my curiosity got the best of me, so I did some

calling around and finally located two or three tying recipes for Ally's Shrimp. I tied some in a few variations and sizes. The first day I tried one, a day when nothing much was happening, I caught a bright hen salmon on my fourth cast. Although I can't explain why, Ally's Shrimp turned out to be the best of the orange flies. Guess what pattern will henceforth enjoy a prominent place in my Russian salmon assortments?

▶ Because flies are both small and light, I'm convinced it's a good idea to carry a lot of them. (If only fly boxes weren't so bulky!) Just don't do what I usually do, and carry one or two each of umpty-zillion patterns. All too often, one particular pattern works better than anything else in God's creation, and you'd better have at least half a dozen of them.

▶ Some tiers like to travel with a vise and tying kit. I'm not one of them. It's too much bother, and anyway, I never know what materials to bring. Fortunately, more lodges and camps are stocked with

---

✍ TRAVELER'S TIP

Wherever you go, the traveling angler must have money. What I mean is, go to the tackle shops and buy all the stuff you want, even though it isn't appropriate, because at some point or another, at some place in the world, it will come in handy.

Flies that I bought in France turned out to be just the thing in Chile. Down in South America, crane flies are the dominant insects. They have them in all sizes. Even though they've got mayflies, caddises, and all the other things, there are more crane flies than anything else. I found that one of the French caddis patterns, which is tied with a clipped-hackle body and wings extending sort of out to the side, like a crane fly's, worked fantastically well.

So my advice is, always buy more tackle and take more stuff than you "need." And when people say, "Well, God, here comes the tackle store again," don't be ashamed, because it just might come in handy.

—Jack Hemingway
author of *Misadventures
of a Fly Fisherman*
Ketchum, Idaho

vises and materials. At some, one of the guides or someone else in camp will tie and sell you flies. At others, you pay a nominal fee for materials and tie your own. Both systems suit me a lot better than carrying my own tying kit.

▶ No matter what kind of trip you are on, it behooves you to carry a fairly good assortment of flies *you* like and trust, flies *you* know how to fish well, flies that produce for *you*. We all have our favorites. Once I get west of, say, Missouri, I must have some Yellow Humpies in my box or I get flustered. I don't know why. I don't actually spend that much time fishing them, and they certainly haven't taken as many cutthroats and other western trout for me as, say, Elk-hair Caddises. It's just one of those things. I put fishing the West without Yellow Humpies in the same category as watching a movie in a theater without popcorn: It can be done, but what's the point?

Besides your personal favorites, a few patterns are so productive, they almost qualify as universal, go-anywhere, catch-anything patterns. You really shouldn't travel without them. A. J. McClane used to say he could go anywhere in the world and catch trout with nothing but Muddler Minnows and Adamses. I suspect McClane could have gone anywhere in the world and caught trout on anything. The proof of the pudding is that *even I* could probably go anywhere in the world and catch the occasional trout on Muddlers and Adamses. Personally, I wouldn't go anywhere in the world and fish for any of the salmonids without a few Royal Wulffs. I nearly always catch fish on Royal Wulffs. Why they work so well for me is another of angling's happy mysteries.

Nor would I go on a saltwater trip anywhere in the world without a healthy assortment of Lefty's Deceivers. Depending on its size and color, and how fully it's dressed, the Deceiver seems to be able to attract almost anything that swims, from summer flounder (fluke) and snappers to sharks and billfish. (For Arctic char in salt, fresh, or tidal waters, try tying a red-orange-and-yellow Deceiver on a long-shanked hook, with the dressing just beyond the hook bend.) You can fish it fast or slow, on floating lines or high-density shooting heads, in the tropics or in reasonably high latitudes. Thank you, Lefty Kreh.

Before worrying about patterns, let's look at principles. Wherever you are planning to go, and whatever you hope to catch, your fly selection must include large, medium, and small flies, bright ones and dull ones, light flies and dark, flies that fish on the surface, those that plumb the depths, and those than can be fished in midwater. You should have noisy flies as well as quiet ones. Now, a word like "noisy" means a lot of different things. It covers the sonic spectrum from raucous sailfish poppers to comparatively quiet tentwing caddises. But when the trout are fixed on what the Brits call skittering sedges, you'd better have some flies that will boogie in the surface film.

Okay, that said, here are some of my personal favorites, flies I simply can't imagine traveling without.

FOR TROUT

▶ Nymphs: Light, medium, and dark nymphs in small, medium, and large sizes, both weighted and unweighted (Orvis's all-purpose nymph selection is perfect), Pheasant Tail and Gold-ribbed Hare's Ear nymphs, Prince, Zug Bug, scud or freshwater shrimp patterns, assorted stonefly nymphs in fast water, dragonfly or damsel fly nymphs in still water. In Patagonia, filoplume mayfly and damselfly nymphs. Bead-head variations have breathed new life into a lot of old patterns.

Bonefish, tarpon, and sailfish flies. *(David Stocklein/Frontiers)*

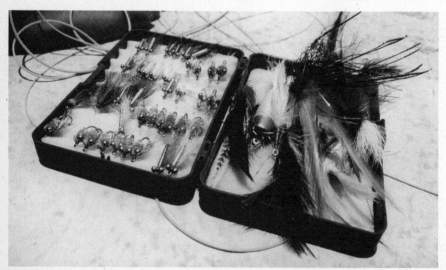

▶ Muddler Minnows, for sure, including some black, yellow, and white Marabou Muddlers. Woolly Buggers too? Of course. And I've had a lot of success almost everywhere with the Miller Woolly Worm, supposedly a pattern specific to Arkansas's White River, which I've never fished.

▶ Streamers and wet flies, such as Mickey Finn, Zonker, Whitlock Sculpin, and soft-hackle patterns.

▶ Emerger patterns: Carry a selection of your choice, because I haven't settled on any favorites.

▶ Dry flies: Troth-style Elk-hair Caddis, Adams, Blue-winged Olive, Pale Morning and Evening Duns, Wulffs (especially the Royal), Griffith Gnat, Tricos (White-Winged Blacks), Improved Sofa Pillow, Humpies and Goofus Bugs, Irresistible, Stimulators in several colors, Renegade or black and brown Bivisibles in riffles, and parachute flies in several sizes and shades. In still waters and back eddies, the tentwing Europa 12 often takes fish even when sedges aren't hatching.

▶ Terrestrials: Joe's Hopper, Letort Hoppers and Crickets, black and cinnamon ants, and, where the fish are large, deer-hair mice. When terrestrials are evident, few other flies will work as well. (I find they often work even when the critters they are supposed to imitate are nowhere to be seen. I caught a lot of trout in the Julian Alps on Montana grasshopper patterns.)

FOR SALMON

▶ Traditional patterns, mostly in hairwing and reduced variations (because I can't tie or afford the fully dressed, married-wing originals): Blue Charm, Hairy Mary, orange prawn patterns in spring and fall, Rusty Rat, Jock Scott, Black Dose, Green Highlander, Black Sheep (particularly effective in Iceland), Doctors in several color variations (especially Silver Doctor).

▶ Waking flies: Muddler Minnows and Marabou Muddlers, Bombers, Buck Bugs, Surface Stonefly, and deer-hair mice. Top producers in Russia.

▶ Dry flies: Wulffs, Macintosh.

▶ Predominantly black flies in all types and patterns, in many sizes and at all times.

▶ Steelhead and Pacific salmon patterns: Skykomish Sunrise, Skunks, Waller Waker, Polar Shrimp, Whit's Electric Leech, Winter's Hope, Popsicle, Purple Flash, Teeny Nymph, Comet, Squamish Poacher.

There used to be a major distinction between flies meant for *Salmo salar* and the West Coast salmonids, but no more. Earlier in this century, the influence went from Atlantic to Pacific, but now steelhead and Alaskan salmon flies are making major inroads in Europe and the Maritimes.

I feel about Glo-Bugs and most other egg patterns the way I do about British tube flies and buoyant strike indicators: They're often miraculously effective, but I'll use them only in a real pinch. I simply don't enjoy fishing with them, and enjoyment is what I'm fishing for, not fish.

FOR FRESHWATER BASS

▶ Topwater flies: Poppers and bass bugs in several sizes, shapes, styles, and colors.
▶ Bottom-bouncing: Clouser Deep Minnow and Crayfish.
▶ Streamers and the like: Zonker, Matuka Sculpin, many leech patterns, Dahlberg Diver, Harry Murray's Lead-eye Hellgrammite, Chuck Tryon's BUB Fly (in both Black and Banana).

FOR SALTWATER SPECIES

Saltwater fly-fishing is growing so rapidly, new patterns constantly are being developed and usurping the places of honor long held by old standbys. I can't keep up with the developments, so my personal favorites are mostly old-hat.

▶ Bonefish and permit flies: Clouser Deep Minnow, Crazy Charlie, epoxy flies of various pedigrees, Bonefish Special, Bendback, Snapping Shrimp, most crab and shrimp imitations.
▶ Tarpon flies: Lefty's Deceiver, Joe Brooks' Blondes, Apte Tarpon Fly, Cockroach, Deepwater Whistler, Bunnies.
▶ Barracuda flies: Long needlefish flies in green, yellow, and sometimes reds and oranges.

▶ Flies for inshore species such as striped bass and bluefish: Poppers, sand eel patterns, Surf Candy, Gibbs Striper, Blondes, Deceivers, menhaden patterns.

▶ Sailfish and offshore flies: Big poppers and streamers, Blanton Whistler, Baja Streaker, big-game tube flies with or without foam popper heads.

▶ Flies for dolphin, small tuna, cobia, and the like: Lefty's Deceiver (especially green-and-yellow for dolphin, pink for albacore), Merkin, Chum Fly, Abel Anchovy.

If you need flies you can't find in the shops or find tying recipes for, get in touch with Robert J. Nichols II at Bud's Bugs, 26183 Chambers Avenue, Sun City, CA 92586; phone 1-909-679-1647. He has a sixty-page catalog that lists some flies I've not seen anywhere else. The prices are good too. Besides the roughly 1,000 patterns in the catalog, Bud ties custom flies from samples, descriptions, or original designs. In fact, most of his tying is done on custom order. "Send me a description of what you need," he says, "and I will tie a sample of it and send it to you for approval or modification. Some of my customers can come up with some pretty unusual patterns, and I get great pleasure in trying to keep up with some of these concoctions." (Bud Nichols also builds truly custom rods, to exact requirements and specifications worked out with customers "to achieve maximum accuracy and the best possible actions.")

Before we leave flies altogether, let me terminally irritate purists by singing the praises of two molded-plastic "flies" that are really fly-rod lures (as are many of the lipped and foam-bodied flies now being fished). I speak of Walt Rogers's incredibly effective Frisky Fly and Bingo Bug. The former looks something like a paper airplane with a curved spine, and the latter has a rounded lip and some chicken feathers molded into the wing. Neither casts worth a damn, both spin and twist leaders when fished on a floating line in fast water, and they probably aren't legit on many fly-only waters. But they will take fish of every persuasion when nothing else will.

I nearly always carry a few Bingo Bugs and Frisky Flies and will resort to them when a skunking seems imminent, so long as their use is permitted. They've failed me only once: on rainbows recently released from a hatchery on private water in the Ozarks of southern

Missouri. Conversely, on Slovenia's Krka River one morning several years back, I took a dozen rainbows in less than half an hour on silver and green Bingo Bugs when nobody else had had a take or even a refusal in two hours. By the time you read this, one of the big chains might have decided to sell these plastic wonders, but in any event you can buy them direct from Chuck Salinas (Walt's nephew) at Frisky Plastics & Company, 1512 S. Oregon Street, Yreka, CA 96097; phone 1-800-433-4744.

Resources

MAIL-ORDER TACKLE CATALOGS FOR TRAVELING FLY-FISHERS

Anglers Image, 5969 Cattlemen Lane, Sarasota, FL 34232; phone 1-800-858-0903, 1-813-371-3200; fax 1-813-371-0782

Angler's Workshop, P.O. Box 1044, Woodland, WA 98674; phone 1-206-225-9445; fax 1-206-225-8641

Dan **Bailey's** Fly Shop, P.O. Box 1019, Livingston, MT 59047; phone 1-800-356-4052, 1-406-222-1673; fax 1-406-222-8450

Bass Pro Shops, 1935 S. Campbell, Springfield, MO 65898; phone 1-800-403-6000, 1-417-887-3567; fax 1-417-887-2531

L. L. **Bean,** Inc., Freeport, ME 04033; phone 1-800-221-4221, 1-800-341-4341, 1-207-865-3111, 1-207-865-3161; fax 1-207-797-8867 (U.S.), 1-207-878-2104 (Canada, International)

Cabela's, Inc., 812-13th Avenue, Sidney, NE 69160; phone 1-800-237-4444, 1-800-237-8888; fax 1-308-254-6745

Classic & Custom Fly Shop, P.O. Box 1072, New Hartford, CT 06057; phone 1-203-738-3597; fax 1-203-738-0824

Cold Spring Anglers, P.O. Box 129, Carlisle, PA 17013; phone 1-800-248-8937, 1-717-245-2646; fax 1-717-245-2081

Cortland Line Company, Inc., P.O. Box 5588, Cortland, NY 13045; phone 1-607-756-2851; fax 1-607-753-8835

Feather-Craft Fly Fishing, P.O. Box 19904, St. Louis, MO 63144; phone 1-800-659-1707, 1-314-963-7876

Fin-Nor Corporation, 2021 S.W. 31st Avenue, Hallandale, FL 33009; phone 1-305-966-5507; fax 1-305-966-5509

Fishing Creek Outfitters, R.D. 1, Box 310-1, Benton, PA 17814; phone 1-800-548-0093, 1-717-925-2225; fax 1-717-925-5644

The **Fly Shop,** 4140 Churn Creek Road, Redding, CA 96002; phone
1-800-669-3464; fax 1-916-222-3572

The **Frugal Flyfishers,** 487 E. Main Street, Suite 287, Mt. Kisco, NY
10549; phone 1-800-241-0125

The **Hook & Hackle** Company, 7 Kaycee Loop Road, Plattsburgh, NY
12901; phone 1-800-552-8342 (U.S.), 1-800-248-8342 (Canada),
1-518-561-5893, 1-518-561-9523; fax 1-518-561-0336

The **Global Flyfisher,** 2849 W. Dundee Road, Suite 132, Northbrook,
IL 60062; phone 1-800-457-7026; fax 1-708-291-3486

Hunter's Angling Supplies, Central Square, Box 300, New Boston, NH
03070; phone 1-800-331-8558, 1-603-487-3388; fax 1-603-487-3939

International Angler, 503 Freeport Road, Pittsburgh, PA 15215;
phone 1-800-782-4222, 1-412-782-2222; fax 1-412-782-1315

Kaufmann's Streamborn, Inc., P.O. Box 23032, Portland, OR 97281;
phone 1-800-442-4359, 1-503-6400; fax 1-503-684-7025

Madison River Fishing Company, P.O. Box 627, Ennis, MT 59729;
phone 1-800-227-7127, 1-406-682-4293; fax 1-406-682-4744

Bob **Marriott's** Flyfishing Store, 2700 W. Orangethorpe Avenue,
Fullerton, CA 92633; phone 1-800-535-6633, 1-714-525-1827; fax
1-714-525-5783

Murray's Fly Shop, P.O. Box 156, Edinburg, VA 22824; phone 1-703-
984-4212; fax 1-800-984-4895, 1-703-984-4895

Offshore Angler, 1935 S. Campbell, Springfield, MO 65898; phone
1-800-633-9131, 1-417-881-3567; fax 1-417-887-2531

Orvis Services, Inc., P.O. Box 798, Manchester, VT 05254; phone
1-800-548-9548, 1-802-362-3622, 1-703-345-4606; fax 1-802-362-
3525, 1-703-343-7053

Pennsylvania Outdoor Warehouse, 1508 Memorial Avenue, Wil-
liamsport, PA 17701; phone 1-800-441-7685, 1-717-322-3589; fax
1-717-322-5281

Urban Angler Ltd., 118 E. 25th Street, 3rd floor, New York, NY 10010;
phone 1-800-255-5488, 1-212-979-7600; fax 1-212-473-4020

Interlude ⟶

THE WRONG STUFF

The routine had become depressingly familiar since our little band of American fishing writers had arrived in what was then Yugoslavia. After being driven to new water, we would meet our new guide, who would invariably speak little or no English. We would exchange nods and handshakes, get a few basics translated through our English-speaking tour guide (who didn't speak fly-fishing), and open our fly boxes so the guide could start us fishing with the proper flies. But always the guide would knit his brow into a frown, shake his head from side to side, and mutter something in Serbo-Croatian or Slovene. No matter where we were or what we were fishing for, we always seemed to have the wrong stuff. Then the guide would shrug and select something from our boxes, always something black. It seemed to make little difference whether it was a big black stonefly nymph or a tiny black midge. Large or small, wet or dry—it hardly mattered, as long as the fly was black.

We'd all carried small selections of old dependables—the flies you can't imagine fishing without—and had planned to purchase the "hot" flies locally. But there weren't many places you could buy flies in Croatia and Slovenia. The few stores that carried them had pitiful selections, crudely tied, and the stores were located in the cities, not near the trout streams we were fishing.

Every time we passed through Zagreb or Ljubljana, the capital cities of Croatia and Slovenia, respectively, we hit as many sporting-goods stores as we could and bought whatever flies we could find. They nearly always turned out to be the wrong ones for the next waters we would fish. The store proprietors tried to be helpful, but their suggestions seldom panned out. The majority of European anglers are what the Brits call "coarse" fishermen—those who fish for carp, barbel, tench, and other cyprinids with ultralong poles or ultra-light spinning tackle. Either Croatian and Slovenian fly-fishermen are very, very few, or they live near the trout streams and tie their own flies. The flies we could find for sale were cheap by our standards, in every sense of the word. Still, a 60-cent fly is awfully expensive when your monthly salary is only $150, especially when the fly is likely to come unraveled after just a few drifts.

But on our last river, the Sava Bohinjka—up in the Julian Alps of Slovenia near the Italian and Austrian frontiers—we thought it would be different. This time we were confident we had the right stuff. Quite by accident, Dave Finkelstein and Evelyn Letfuss had bought a few specimens of a fly called the Romar, the first time we passed through Ljubljana. *Romar* is Slovene for "pilgrim," and pilgrims we surely were. The Romar is nothing more, really, than cinnamon-colored hackle palmered on a hook, a Bivisible without the bivisibility. But on the Sora River, in the alpine foothills around Škofja Loka, the Romar had been pure dynamite on grayling and not a bad choice for brown trout. Fishing other flies, Ed Ricciuti and Jack London had waded through a chest-deep pool without taking a fish; Dave and Evelyn, fishing Romars, waded into the same pool ten minutes later and started raising fish on virtually every cast. It seemed to make no difference whether they placed their casts near either bank, in the middle of the stream, or next to each other's waders.

When we rendezvoused at our minivan as twilight fell over the valley and listened to Dave's and Evelyn's account of their last half hour, the rest of us fell prey to green, piscatorial envy. We had all caught fish, but Dave and Evelyn had really scored big on their Romars. So, on our way to the Sava Bohinjka, we stopped briefly in Ljubljana and rushed to the few sporting-goods stores in town, buying up all the Romars we could find. No one had fewer than half a dozen of the things. We were loaded for bear—well, for trout and grayling, actually.

Jack and Ed had stayed behind an extra day in Ljubljana to do some more research for stories they wanted to write. So the rest of us had the Sava Bohinjka to ourselves the first day. We first fished the river where it came roaring out of Lake Bohinj. It was the fastest water I'd ever fished, and I couldn't seem to get the hang of fishing five-second drifts at what seemed like ten to fifteen knots. We didn't risk our precious Romars, though, because the opposite bank—just twenty feet away—was festooned with low-hanging, fly-eating tree branches. (Anyway, we had been told there were mostly trout here, and we wanted to save the Romars for the grayling we hoped to find later.) Our guide, river warden Jože Borisek, suggested that we use dark dry flies and fish them without floatant on short leaders. Really short leaders: "One meter, no more," he said in English, holding his hands apart, lest there be any doubt as to his meaning. He wanted them *in* the surface film or just under it, he explained through our bilingual tour guide, Danilo Breg. In this fast water, the trout wouldn't be able to see flies floating on top of the surface film; anyway, the fish were used to feeding on drowned insects.

After an hour or so of frustration—during which we managed to take a few small trout, this *we* not including yours truly—we moved downstream to a stretch that offered a variety of waters.

On the drive to the new spot we learned there would be plenty of grayling as well as trout and that a big fishing tournament held here in the Bohinj Bistrica district the previous weekend had been won by several big grayling caught in the part of the river we were about to fish. As soon as the van rolled to a stop, we piled out and put our rods together. Dani told us that Jože wanted to see what flies we had, so he could start us fishing properly. Out came the boxes—and the smiles. This time we had it nailed.

Jože peered into our fly boxes, frowned, muttered something in Slovene, and pointed out two or three black flies. But we wanted to fish for grayling, we protested, for *lipan*. Dani translated; Jože said something else in Slovene and pointed at the same black flies. What about all those Romars lined up in our boxes? we asked. That had been *the* grayling fly on the Sora. Dani passed this on to Jože. We didn't need a translator for his reply: "Sora is Sora, Sava Bohinjka is Sava Bohinjka." We had the wrong stuff again.

We plodded down to the river behind Jože and Dani, not entirely dejected, but not exactly encouraged either. We tried the black flies, with slight success. We tried the Romars, with none. We tried this and that, and caught a few trout—both browns and rainbows—but no grayling. By this time we had been joined by Jože's fellow river war-

den, Vojko (Vojc) Carl, who decided to fish with us. He tied on a black
fly and started wading downstream, casting as he went. He took one
fish down by the road bridge, then fished his way out of sight around
the bend. (When we next saw him, he was bearing three big grayling,
each about sixteen to eighteen inches long.)

After Vojc disappeared around the bend downstream of the bridge,
I decided to follow his example and headed downriver.

Having had such limited success on everything else I had tried—
various dry flies and nymphs, a tent-wing caddis, and a couple of
feather-wing wet flies I had left over from a trip to Scotland the year
before—I decided to try a Royal Wulff. I hadn't the slightest idea
whether this attractor pattern would appeal to these fish. But what
the heck: I like to fish the Royal Wulff, and I couldn't do much worse
than I had done with the recommended black flies.

Here, and upriver by the lake, I had noticed what I thought were
fish fleeing before us as we waded through the rocky shoals toward
what looked like the prime fishing waters. It had been at least fifteen
or twenty minutes since Vojc had waded through, so I tried casting to
the likeliest-looking spots in the very unlikely looking, ankle-deep
water ahead of me. In eight or ten casts, I took five rainbow trout.
Small fish, to be sure—nothing more than ten or eleven inches, and
most of them six to eight—but not bad, considering how skinny the
water was. I had intended to follow Vojc downstream around the
bend, but I got sidetracked experimenting in the waters just below
the bridge.

I tried fishing all sorts of flies and casting to lots of different spots:
Muddler Minnow, Adams, Zug Bug, Light Cahill, Bivisible; to big rocks
submerged in the deep channel, to trees lying alongside the current
on the other side, to eddies and pools and pockets. It all started coming together. There seemed to be fish almost everywhere, mostly rainbows, but a few browns too. Periods of fast fishing would be followed
by interludes of casting practice. Then the fish would turn on again
and I'd be landing or losing fish on every third or fourth cast. Sometimes, briefly, on virtually every cast. I even caught trout on black
flies. But nothing on Romars; Jože had been right about that.

It had been like that earlier and elsewhere. Initially discouraged
by discovering we were not properly armed with the locally
endorsed flies, we would begin fishing without much confidence
(but with plenty of frustration). Naturally, fishing that way we didn't

catch many fish. But once we stopped cursing fate and quit feeling sorry for ourselves, when we fell back on what we knew and on fishing for fun, the burden of helplessness always seemed to slip off our shoulders. Here, a light-colored dry fly would do the trick; there, a dark-green nymph. Behind a little log dam on the Krka after a fishless and strikeless two hours, and in the high, fast, roiled waters of the Sora after a ten-hour downpour, it had been a purist's nightmare: a molded-plastic-and-chicken-feather Bingo Bug. (When I had shown Walt Rogers's strange creation to the guides, in both cases they had rolled their eyes at its suspect worth but nodded assent to its ragged-edge legality.) During our last day on the Sava Bohinjka, my hot fly was Joe's Deer Hopper, even though we hadn't seen any sign of grasshoppers in the stream or in the fields along the banks. Whatever and wherever, it had always been *something*.

What I have finally learned after a lot of these experiences is that when you're fishing at the right time in the right place, even the wrong stuff doesn't much matter. What matters more is keeping your cool, remembering what you know about fish and fishing, and studying the water. Like everyone else, I have been outfished on a lot of outings and skunked on others. But I've had my high-hook days in the sun too. I haven't been keeping a log, but my recollection has me convinced that having the "right" or the "wrong" flies on the end of my tippets hasn't routinely placed me in one category or the other. But whenever I have let my confidence slip, the fishing went with it.

Now that I've largely overcome my fear of fishing the wrong stuff, I get a kick out of turning a slow day around by fishing something no one else has ever seen. Often it's the Miller Woolly Worm, a fly designed for Arkansas's White River, that has caught fish everywhere in the world I've tried it, from Montana's Madison and Maryland's Gunpowder Falls to Siberia's Tirekhtyakh. It's fun, carrying and fishing a lot of different flies, but it isn't really necessary. Still, I can't resist carrying more flies than I could possibly need. You just never know when one of the odd ones will come in handy.

One day up in Lappland (what the Swedes call their portion of Lapland, an area that includes the northern portions of Norway, Sweden, and Finland and the northwesternmost corner of Russia), the hot fly, the one that guaranteed fish, was something that had never before taken a fish for me. Come to think of it, I don't believe I've caught anything on it since. But on that day, on that river, it was the fly you simply had to have. According to the rule books, though, it was definitely the wrong stuff to be carrying.

It was the day following *Midsömmer*, the summer solstice, very early in the season north of the Arctic Circle. Tjuonajåkk (also spelled Tjuonajokk), the fishing lodge where we were staying, wouldn't even open for business until the day of our departure. Fishing was—let's be charitable and call it slow. If you resorted to worms, one Swede instructed by demonstration, big brown trout could be had. But we hadn't traveled thousands of miles to dunk worms. Unfortunately, the trout weren't interested in feather, fur, and floss fakery.

Toward the end of the afternoon, a few hundred yards below where the Kaitum River flows out of the lake called Vuolep Kaitumjaure, we had located a group of mostly submerged rocks that held a few grayling that occasionally would succumb to reddish-brown nymphs.

The next day, after a fruitless all-night trip up to some tarns and streams near the Norwegian border and a morning nap, we struck out in several directions, trying to locate willing trout. By late afternoon the three of us—I was fishing with Lars Georgsson, Sweden's press officer in New York, and Jan Olsson, the fishing writer for the daily newspaper in Göteborg (Gothenburg) and Sweden's representative to the International Game Fish Association—were back hammering the grayling rocks. The action was even slower than it had been the previous day.

Of a sudden, a great dark storm cloud loomed on the horizon, bearing straight for us. Coincidentally, the grayling started feeding on the surface. Not just around the rocks we were fishing, but everywhere. Hundreds, no, thousands, of delicate rise rings pocked the surface of the river as far as one could see. They were taking something off the surface. In the gathering gloom it was hard to make out exactly what was hatching, but it was black and tiny. Midges or Tricos, maybe. About size 28. I had some tiny White-winged Blacks and Griffith's Gnats that would probably work, but I'd have to retie my leader, down to a 7X or even 8X tippet. What with the storm approaching so fast, I didn't think there'd be time.

Then I noticed two small, black deer-hair water beetles in my box. The smaller one was tied on a small hook, maybe 18 or 20, but the body was many times bulkier than the tiny bugs on which the grayling were feeding. At least it might turn over my 5X tippet. So I decided to give it a shot. With one eye on the fast-approaching storm, I cut off the nymph and tied on the smaller of the water beetles, greasing it with a lot of Mucilin paste, so it would float high on the film.

It was like casting poppers to feeding bluefish. The grayling were fighting over the fly, and I was getting a strike on every cast, sometimes two or three strikes. (European grayling are avid strikers but horrendously inaccurate. You have to wonder how they survive on this energy budget.) Lars and Jan weren't having any action, so they waded through the rise rings of a lot of uncooperative grayling and lined up close to me. I kept catching grayling after grayling, and they kept coming up empty. Between the two of them, they had a few strikes and took one fish.

"What the devil are you using?" Lars asked, leaning over and peering through his Coke bottle–bottom spectacles as I unhooked another grayling.

"A deer-hair water beetle," I said nonchalantly, as if it were the most natural thing in the world. "Black. With a lot of Mucilin. They're really effective if you keep them riding high on the film. Pretty good on cutthroats and splake too." Sometimes I can't resist pulling chains.

"Water beetles?" Jan said incredulously. "Do you have an extra?"

"Not one small enough," I said. "A size twenty-eight trico or midge pattern would match this hatch."

Before Jan and Lars had finished retying their leaders, the storm hit, putting the fish down and driving us out of the water.

That night we had a few nice sautéed grayling fillets with our Scotch and crudités, our crackers and cod-roe paste, while our guide fixed a savory reindeer stew.

"Gary, how did you know to carry deer-hair beetles?" Jan asked, pencil poised over notepad, ready to immortalize my answer in Sweden's largest daily.

"Well, you know, Jan," I began pontifically, then paused for effect while I took a sip of eighteen-year-old Macallan single-malt, "sometimes it pays to carry the wrong stuff."

5
KIT AND CABOODLE

If rods, reels, lines, leaders, and flies were all there were to fly-fishing, fishing travel would be a snap. But they aren't and it isn't. Maybe it's because the tackle is so light that fly-fishermen (well, some of us at least) carry so much stuff when we go anywhere: waders, rainwear, clothing, books, booze, sundries, snacks, and all the other gewgaws and gadgets we seem to need whenever and wherever we go fishing. And do we ever have the gadgets and gewgaws! Hanging in a fly shop, a fishing vest isn't a whole lot more substantial than some of the bits of fluff in the Victoria's Secrets catalog. But by the time I've loaded all the pockets for fishing, my vest weighs almost as much as an auto mechanic's tool box and takes up more room than anything else in my kit, and I can't ever find anything when I need it.

Of all the nontackle things about which I could pontificate, I'm going to limit myself to the important ones: waders, other foot gear, hats, sunglasses, clothing, rainwear, and luggage. As for vests-versus-bags and most other trip-packing decisions, let's face it: Personality and style weigh more than wisdom.

Wader Wisdom

Waders—with either integral boot feet or separate wading brogues—will probably be the heaviest, bulkiest thing you carry on your fly-fishing travels. If you'll be fishing offshore or on some subtropical bonefish flat where you don't need waders, count yourself lucky and skip ahead to the next section. But the rest of us need waders—usually, and unfortunately, chest-high waders.

On far-flung fishing trips, you probably will be spending more time in your waders than you do fishing closer to home—ten to twelve hours a day, maybe more if you are fishing early summer in the Land of the Midnight Sun. (Stupidly, I once put in a twenty-three-hour day in Swedish Lappland.) If you find your present waders uncomfortable, you'd better think about getting some more comfortable ones. Even if you think your waders are fine, here are some hints that will make life less miserable.

▶ Wear two pairs of socks, for warmth and to prevent blisters. The inner pair should be thin and supple, a hydrophobic synthetic or warm, slick silk. Outer socks should be thick, bulky wool or high-tech synthetic. I used to wear ragg wool socks, but now I mostly wear Thorlo Trekking socks. I haven't tried Gore-Tex or neoprene wader socks. Be sure your boots are big enough; if your feet are cramped they will be cold and uncomfortable.

▶ When wearing stocking-foot waders, always use wader gaiters or neoprene wading booties, to keep too much silt, sand, and fine gravel from accumulating painfully underfoot. You *must* wear the booties to prevent sand and gravel from damaging lightweight waders.

▶ Don't wear trousers under your chest waders, just long johns and thick polypropylene fleece pants.

▶ To keep pants from riding up when you put waders on, use duct tape, a neoprene reel tender, or a pair of Pant Guards around the ankle.

☞ TRAVELER'S TIP

For cold weather, you've gotta have boot-foot waders. Forget the stocking-foot, they're terrible. With the boot-foot waders, there's that air space around your feet. I haven't had cold feet since I got them.

—Harm Saville
president, Nor'East Miniature Roses, Inc.
Rowley, Massachusetts

▶ Similarly, wrap duct tape around the ankles of lightweight stocking-foot waders, to minimize bunching underfoot, a trick I learned from the Ozark fly-fisher Chuck Tryon.

▶ To keep hip boots from pulling your pants down, support them from your shoulders with Compleat Angler Hip Boot Suspenders.

▶ Wide suspenders are more comfortable than narrow ones. Ditto for suspenders that have an H back rather than an X back.

▶ Elastic wader belts are safer and more comfortable than nonelastic belts. Even if you don't wear a wader belt at home, take one along. You may encounter pretty horrendous wading conditions.

Hip boots or chest waders? Hippers are certainly more comfortable, but chest waders will give you more wading freedom. And if you are accustomed to fishing in chest waders, you'd better take them along, even if the agent or outfitter says hippers are all you'll need. Why? Because habit will take you in over the tops of the hip boots at least once a day. Waist-high waders are billed as the perfect compromise. To me, they don't look much less hot or uncomfortable than chest waders, and they won't let you wade all that much deeper than hip boots. When wading shallow in chest waders, just roll them down to waist level and use a wader belt to keep them up.

Stocking-foot or boot-foot waders? Stocking-foot waders give you a wide choice of wading boots and offer better ankle support. Boot-foot waders are easier to put on and take off, and may be more comfortable in the foot. Stocking-foot waders may be slightly less bulky than boot-foot waders made of the same material. But the real advantage of stocking-foot waders in traveling is that you can carry both chest and hip waders without adding much bulk or weight.

Rubber, canvas, neoprene, coated-nylon . . . ? Old-fashioned rubber and canvas waders are just too heavy and bulky for traveling. I haven't tried the new, form-fitting latex waders, which are said to be comfortable, but my experience with rubber gloves leaves me feeling clammy and skeptical. I guess I feel about Gore-Tex waders the way I feel about twenty-five-year-old Macallan Scotch: On the one hand, I'm intrigued, but on the other, I really can't afford to develop a taste for $275 waders and $130 whiskies. Most traveling fly-fishers opt for neoprene or lightweight nylon waders.

If you are cold-blooded and fishing very early or late in the season, when the water temperature is close to freezing, you may need neoprene waders. I hate to carry the bulky things, even to a local stream, let alone halfway around the world. But they are warm. For me, too warm. Hiking in them is thermal torture. Unless both air and water temperatures are *really* cold, I wind up soaked in sweat and miserably uncomfortable, even if I spend the day mostly just standing around casting. The other thing that bugs me about heavy waders is the extra resistance they offer to moving water when wading. (Admittedly, my cheap, thick neoprenes don't fit like an Armani suit, so yours may not be as likely as mine to carry you downstream.) At 45°F (7.3°C) and up, I'm outa those neoprenes and into my lightweights.

For my first trip abroad, I bought a pair of Red Ball Flyweight coated-nylon, stocking-foot chest waders. Eight years later they developed their first leak, an easily patched pinhole. Except for Flyweight hippers, and in recent years a pair of hot, heavy neoprenes I hardly ever wear, those Flyweights had been my one and only waders. They have scrambled over a lot of sharp rocks, been stretched beyond reason climbing hills and into and out of float planes and helicopters, and subjected to a long, unplanned hike through an alder forest in Swedish Lappland.

I could wear those Flyweights still—and do, around home—but three hundred miles from nowhere is not a good place to suffer a

---

☞ TRAVELER'S TIP

Many view clothing for fly-fishing as an outdoor-clothing fashion statement, but for us clothing is technical equipment. Function is of primary importance, whether you are dressing for the trout stream or salt water. Cold-weather clothing can be summed up in one word: layering. Tropical fishing wear should dry quickly and be well vented and—most important—loose fitting. Polarized glasses help you see into the water to spot fish and structure, but they also protect your eyes. Many are piercing body parts, but it's still not fashionable to pierce one's eyes.

We tend to favor subdued colors for freshwater species and pastels for saltwater; avoid bright colors anywhere. We are not advocating camouflage, but you shouldn't stick out like a sore thumb.

—Steven A. Fisher
partner, Urban Angler Ltd.
New York, New York

foot-long parting of the seams when the waders finally succumb to mistreatment and old age. They've been replaced for traveling by (surprise, surprise!) a new pair of Red Ball Flyweights. Actually, they've been replaced by two pairs of Red Balls.

When I got the new Flyweights, I also decided to try a pair of Red Ball Flyweight Supplex Neoprene Foot chest waders. For all their virtues, lightweight stocking-foot waders can be quite uncomfortable underfoot. The polyurethane-coated nylon fabric used in the regular Flyweights bunches up in wrinkles and folds between your sock and the wading sock that goes between wader and boot. I doubt that Supplex—a soft, thin nylon microfiber that feels almost like cotton—will be as durable as the 200-denier nylon fabric used in the regular Flyweights, but are those neoprene-foot Flyweights ever comfortable! They're easy to get on and off, and you hardly notice you're wearing them while they're on. I first tried them on a six-week trip to Russia, mostly spent north of the Arctic Circle on the Kola Peninsula. Except for the first week, when the Kharlovka was at 37°F and full of ice floes (more or less forcing me to wear neoprenes), the Supplex Flyweights were all I ever wore. With silk or polypropylene long johns and thick, polypro fleece pants underneath, the waders kept me warm and comfortable.

Backup waders? When you are traveling afar, you really ought to consider bringing an extra pair of waders. If you wear boot-foot waders, the extra bulk and weight may be prohibitive. But if you wear stocking-foot waders, a backup set won't add much to your luggage. I've always traveled with both chest and hip waders, and I've recently started carrying a backup set of chest waders, either neoprenes for really cold water or a second set of Flyweights for emergencies. (I know anglers who carry lightweight waders to wear inside their leaky neoprenes! I can't imagine a more uncomfortable solution.)

Wader repair: It has often been observed there are only two kinds of waders: Those that leak a little and those that leak a lot. No matter what other packing decisions you make, carry patches, seam cement, and whatever else your wader manufacturer says you might need to stem the tide.

▶ Aquaseal—repairs large rips, tears, and seam separations in waders, especially neoprenes
▶ Cotol-240—cleans area to be repaired and cuts Aquaseal drying time from twelve to two to three hours

▶ Seam Grip—similar to Aquaseal; use with Seam Cleaner and Seam Excel accelerator

▶ SimmSeal—plugs punctures and small leaks in neoprene waders in three hours.

▶ K-Kote Seam Sealer 3—seals seams in all synthetic materials (also "stitches" holes in Gore-Tex and other fabrics)

▶ Neoprene wader patch kit—neoprene patching material

▶ Wader patch kit—for rubber, coated-nylon, and canvas waders

▶ Lightweight wader patch kit—super sticky tape and gap-filling cyanoacrylate cement

▶ Bicycle inner-tube tire patch kit—repairs latex waders

▶ Angler's Cement—waterproof cement used to attach felt soles, wader patches, and the like

▶ Sportsman's Goop—flexible, waterproof repairs to rubber (including latex and neoprene), vinyl, leather

▶ Shoe Goo or Kiwi Athletic Shoe and Boot Patch—similar to Goop

▶ K-Kote Recoat 3—to recoat leaky, worn areas on urethane-coated nylon waders

▶ Barge Cement—flexible, waterproof cement for attaching felt soles, repairing waders, and the like

▶ Zap-a-Gap cyanoacrylate cement—helps patches and tape stick to waders; many other repair and tackle-rigging uses

▶ Pliobond cement—flexible cement for patching waders (and to coat knots and all leader-to-line connections)

▶ Duct tape—everyone's panacea

Many other kinds of cements, patches, and potions can be used to stem the tide. If there's one thing you really mustn't stint on, it's stuff to patch and repair waders. Take everything anyone's ever recommended to you. If your waders leak—and they will, sooner or later—you will be one wet, cold, and miserable puppy until you can get them patched.

Wading Boots and Boot Soles

Wading boots are available in so many styles, you ought to be able to find exactly what you need. Lightweight canvas boots are easier to carry but may offer less ankle protection around boulders. (I suffered painfully bruised ankle bones wearing unpadded canvas wading shoes in Montana's rocky Gallatin Canyon.) I've noticed more and more traveling fly-fishers wearing Orvis's Lightweight Wading Shoe, a padded, coated Cordura nylon boot that all who wear them swear by.

Unless you will be wading on nothing but mud, sand, or fine gravel, be sure you get felt-soled boots. And if the going gets really rough, with glacial polish, moss, slime, seaweed, snow, or ice on big rocks, consider using waders or boots with studded felt soles. Studded soles are great when you need them but are otherwise a pain. They are noisy, and the damage they can do to floors will not endear you to lodgekeepers. I've tried a compromise I really like: aluminum drive rivets. They are almost as secure as studs, but they aren't as noisy on rocks or as damaging to floors. Use a proper size bit to drill a hole into (but not through!) your wader soles, and pound the rivet in with a hammer. (Put a wooden block of some sort inside the wader, to use as an "anvil.") You need seven rivets for each shoe: two side by side on the heel, a box pattern of four under the ball of the foot, and one in the toe. Some catalogs and fly shops carry them in kit form as Kleet Feet.

Alternatively, you can carry any of the following slip-over accessories to make your felt-soled boots more secure.

▶ Cleated sandals
▶ Studded sandals (e.g., Korkers)
▶ Cleated rubber overshoes (e.g., Stream Cleats)
▶ Spiked golfing rubbers
▶ Wading chains (also sold in shoe stores and cobbler's shops as SnoShuz Polar Model shoe chains)

Of these accessories, wading chains are the lightest and most compact, and can be carried in a vest pocket, but they can be knocked off. Still, they're cheap enough that you can afford to buy a spare set.

Speaking of spares, cautious anglers might want to carry the following backups on a trip:

▶ Boot laces
    (Remember the sorry spectacle of Tonya Harding at the 1994 Winter Olympics?) Because of all the soaking and drying, wading-boot laces won't last very long. And unlike your shoelaces, they

may not show signs of fraying to warn you when they need replacing. You can always use backup boot laces to pinch hit for the wader suspenders you forgot at home.

▶ Felt sole replacement kit, including soles (and sometimes heels), coarse sandpaper, and waterproof cement

Maybe it's just me, but so far I've had precious little luck replacing felt soles on waders or wading boots. They always seem to come loose in no time at all.

▶ Extra pair of lightweight wading shoes or boots (e.g., Orvis Pack-and-Travel Wading Shoe)

I don't carry backup boots, but I am sometimes haunted by the memory of Don Proebstel hunkered down beside a campfire on the banks of a Siberian river, trying to sew the soles back onto his brand-new boots, using a pocketknife and some monofilament leader material.

More A-Foot

If you will be fishing from a boat or wading the flats, other footwear is in order.

Some boat anglers like to fish barefoot. There's a word for it: stupid. Slipping on wet fiberglass and breaking your neck is just the first of the hazards. Getting a 6/0 tarpon hook deeply embedded in your foot will really put a damper on your trip, not to mention traumatic amputation of your toes by a shark, bluefish, or barracuda. Your best bet, when fishing from a boat, are deck shoes. I'm particularly fond of the razor-thin, wave-slit soles such as those on Sperry Top-Siders. The uppers can suit your fancy. If you simply must have that open-air feeling on your feet when you're in the tropics, at least wear deck-soled sandals to prevent falls. But stay away from large, angry fish thrashing on the sole of the cockpit. When boat fishing in cold, nasty weather, knee-high rubber boots with deck soles are in order.

For wet wading, in fresh or salt water, you have several choices available:

▶ Regular or lightweight wading shoes or boots
▶ Wading sandals

▶ Float-tube boots
▶ Reef boots
▶ Locker-room slippers or sandals
▶ Hightop basketball shoes

The nature of the bottom will guide your selection. On mud, sand, or fine gravel, you can wear anything. Cobbles require felt soles. Big rocks require felt soles and ankle protection.

In camp, you will want something comfortable to wear. Try to find out whether the ground is damp or dry. If it's dependably dry, anything will do. If it's wet, go with waterproof boots, either rubber-bottom jobs or ones made with Gore-Tex. Here are some of my favorites:

▶ Slip-on camp boots (e.g., Sorel Fish Hawks, Bean's Lodge Boots) for schlepping to and from the shower
▶ Comfortable hiking boots with secure soles and good ankle support whenever any hiking may be involved
▶ Après-ski and similar boots for lounging around your cabin or the lodge
▶ Moccasins (with soles) or moccasin-style loafers for camps with flat, dry, solid terrain (also good for those urban stayovers at either end of the trip)

And do yourself a favor: Break in new boots before going on the trip. If you don't have time to break them in the old-fashioned way, by wearing them for several days, you can put them on, stand in a tub of water until they are thoroughly soaked, and then wear them until they are fairly dry. That will make the leather conform to your feet. Depending on manufacturer's recommendations, you might want to treat them with saddle soap, mink oil, silicone, or some other leather preservative once they are dry.

Polarized Points of View

You need glasses to protect your eyes from errant fish hooks, sunglasses to protect them from damaging ultraviolet light, and polarized glasses to locate fish and lies underwater. Period. This is not a negotiable item.

As for frame style, plastic vs. glass lenses, color of lenses, or pho-tochromic lenses that darken as it gets brighter, suit yourself. What-ever it takes to make you wear them. You can buy cheap or expensive, dimestore or designer. Just make sure they filter out most of the ultraviolet spectrum, both UV-A and UV-B. Removable leather side shields give extra protection against sidelight and glare. Tinted side panels are less effective but may keep you from feeling claustro-phobic, as some people do when wearing side shields.

If you already wear corrective lenses, consider these alternatives:

▶ Polarized clip-ons
▶ Polarized Solar Shields that fit over your glasses (if you can stand the bulky things)
▶ Prescription Polaroids (if you can afford them)

And wear a Croakie or some other kind of strap to keep the glasses from falling off and breaking or being lost.

Bring something to clean your sunglasses (eyeglasses too, if you wear them). A soft, cotton handkerchief at the very least. Better, lens tissues and cleaning fluid (which you can use on your camera as well). This is especially important when fishing salt water, because merely wiping glasses will smudge them. Before you go, coat your sunglasses and spectacles with Rain-X (which you can find in auto supply stores), and they'll resist spotting for at least two weeks.

Topping Off

Whether you are heading north or south, to polar regions or the trop-ics, you need a good hat to protect you from sunlight, rain or snow, heat or cold. Many anglers like to wear baseball-type caps. I don't, because I have a long French nose (more Yves Montand than Cyrano de Bergerac, thank you). I used to wear swordfisher caps (baseball caps with exceptionally long bills) but seldom do anymore. I like hats that will protect my ears and neck as well as the nose and lips. I gen-erally wear these hats when I go fishing:

▶ Florida Keys up-downer guide hat
▶ Broad-brimmed, washable-cotton Tilley Hat

▶ Knit watch cap—to be worn in cold weather under the Tilley or the hood of a rain jacket

The Tilley and many of my up-downers have cord to keep them from blowing away in a boat or a stiff wind.

Tweedy Irish country hats, Tyroleans, deer stalkers, and tam-o'-shanters look awfully nice on fly-fishers, but they don't offer much protection against the sun. Straw hats are okay in the tropics and under the bright sun anywhere, but they're not much good in a rain.

I've recently acquired a Desert Rhat, a white, high-tech, long-billed cap with a long detachable cape to fully protect the neck and ears. Once I get used to looking like a cross between a French Foreign Legionnaire and a toxic-waste handler, I may like it for fishing the flats under the blazing tropical sun.

In subtropical waters, I like hats with vented panels in the crown, to keep my head from overheating. Eddie Bauer makes hats and caps out of terry-cloth toweling material. Soaked and wrung out, they keep you cool by evaporation. I just wish they came with broader brims or longer bills.

Fishing caps and hats should be dark on the underside of the visor or bill. Otherwise they can reflect glare down over and behind your sunglasses.

Fishing in the Rain

Wherever you go, you'll need rainwear of some sort. Among the choices available:

▶ Old-fashioned oilcloth slickers—pretty much restricted to the sailing set these days
▶ Tightly woven and treated cotton and polyester-cotton poplin—very comfortable but merely water-*repellent*
▶ Waxed cotton (e.g., Barbour)—instant cachet among salmon fishers and trouting traditionalists, but a bit heavy and bulky
▶ Coated nylon—waterproof and cheap, but you'll be soaked in sweat
▶ Gore-Tex and similar microporous materials—waterproof, breathable, and the best all-around choice

---

☞ TRAVELER'S TIP

I've been caught without raingear, when my baggage got lost. And so I used what I refer to as a Belizean Burberry, which is a plastic trash bag with holes poked in it for your head and arms. It's not so much that it keeps you dry, but when you get soaking wet and then run the boat, it keeps you from freezing to death, even if you're wet underneath, because it stops the wind.

—Don Moser
editor, *Smithsonian*
Washington, D.C.

Some guys prefer to take light, cheap, plastic or plastic-coated nylon waterproof jackets to the tropics. If you're *sure* it's the dry season where you're headed, I guess that's okay, but I prefer to carry good Gore-Tex raingear wherever I go. That way, if it blows up unseasonably rainy, I won't be quite so miserable.

The thing to keep in mind about Gore-Tex clothing is this: The Gore-Tex is just the waterproof film hidden between two layers of fabric. The actual characteristics of the rainwear are determined by the fabrics used in the shell and liner, and in any insulation. Two Gore-Tex rain jackets may be equally effective, but one will be heavy and stiff and the other one supple and light. I once had a jacket that drove me nuts because it was so noisy. Every time I moved my arms, the fabric would *zip-zip-zip* loud enough to be distracting.

Rain jackets with hoods will keep you drier than those without. They also will better protect the back and sides of your head from wind-blown flies.

Clothing

A single word to the wise when packing clothes for a fishing trip: layers. Especially in the high latitudes, but even in the tropics. During those high-speed runs early in the morning or late in the afternoon, the tropics will feel surprisingly chilly. Conversely, in the high Arctic it can be so hot in midsummer that you will be tempted to go shirtless.

Pack both long- and short-sleeved shirts, no matter where you are going. The long sleeves are needed in the tropics to protect you from a sun that can be cruelly intense in midafternoon. If you are heading toward the poles, you won't need many short-sleeved shirts, and at the beginning or end of the season you may not need any. I'd take at least one anyway; you can always use it as an extra undershirt.

For fishing in the tropics, carry loose-fitting garments made of light, airy, fast-drying fabrics. With the explosive growth of saltwater fly-fishing in recent years, particularly on tropical bonefish flats, numerous special lines of lightweight clothing have been developed especially for anglers. These often incorporate fast-drying fabrics, ventilation vents, bellows pockets, and extra roominess around the armpits to facilitate fly-casting. Although these lines of clothing were developed for the tropics, I think they're great fishing togs anywhere in midsummer. Look for these brands and lines:

▶ 10-X (Sun & Fun Wear—sounds dumb, but the clothes are great)
▶ AFTCO (yep, the same people who make roller guides and solid aluminum butts for big-game rods)
▶ Columbia Sportswear (Casting Shirts, Whidbey, and Easy Access)
▶ Ex Officio (Baja Plus and Double Haul)
▶ Orvis (Bonefish Scrubs)
▶ Simms (Tarponwear)
▶ Willis & Geiger (Balloon Cloth)
▶ Wrangler (Angler)

A lot of these shirts, shorts, and pants come in bright, gaudy colors that fairly scream "Tropical!" but I'd stick to the tans and blues that won't frighten fish off the flats.

Fishing in higher latitudes under more boreal conditions, you will need a larger variety of materials and weights. Begin with the long johns you will wear under your waders. The brand isn't important, but the material is.

▶ Silk or silk blends for comfort across the greatest range of temperatures
▶ Polypropylene knits and fleeces (Synchilla, Thermax, Polartec, Capilene, Alpen Fleece, whatever) when it gets really cold

Wear cotton underwear only in warm weather. Cotton is bulky, only sort of warm, and takes forever to dry. Wet cotton is cold, clammy, and uncomfortable.

For layering in colder climates, your fishing wardrobe ought to include a lot of these:

▶ The *chlorophylle haute technologie* brand of poly-cotton—tightly woven, relatively lightweight fabric that buffers the wind, dries fast, resists soiling and wrinkling—a good all-around choice in all but tropical climates

▶ Wool shirts and pants—Filson, Pendleton, and Woolrich are almost synonymous with quality, value, and versatility in wool clothing but now have lots of competition

▶ Cotton flannel—marginally okay in moderate climes, but wool is better

▶ Wool sweaters—nothing is warmer when wet, but fleece jackets are more versatile

▶ Polypropylene and polyester fleece—Patagonia's SST jacket, a longtime favorite of steelheaders and salmon fishermen, has stimulated welcome competition from other brands

▶ Thinsulate—good insulation down to around 0°F

▶ Goose down—warmest and most compressible insulation, but it isn't warm when it gets wet or heavily soiled

▶ Polyester fibers: Hollofil, Quallofil, Thermoloft—bulkier than down but warmer when damp or wet

And don't forget a sweater or soft fleece pullover for wearing in the evenings. Don't get it sweaty and smelly by wearing it while fishing. You'll feel almost civilized, sitting down to dinner in something so clean, dry, and warm.

Lotsa Luggage

Veteran travelers have a motto for packing: "When in doubt, leave it out." They say you ought to be able to carry all your luggage half a mile (or a kilometer, for metric types) without aid of a cart! Apparently I'm still learning the ropes, because I simply can't travel that light when I'm going fishing.

Ideally, you should travel with just three (or four) pieces of luggage:

▶ A large duffel (or two smaller ones) as checked baggage
▶ A carry-on bag
▶ A rod case—either checked or carry-on (or both, if you're an equipment freak)

I cheat: So I can bring all the neat stuff that seems absolutely essential, I wear on the airplane one of those photojournalist vests with more than a dozen pockets—fully loaded with notebooks, phrase books, paperback foreign dictionary, passport case, tiny toilet kit, bird book, compact binoculars, sunglasses, microcassette recorder, paperback novel, point-and-shoot camera, some film, candy, antacid tablets, acetaminophen tablets, eye drops, saline

Dave Whitlock stowing about the largest travel duffel that can fit in airline overhead compartments. *(Bass Pro Shops/Offshore Angler)*

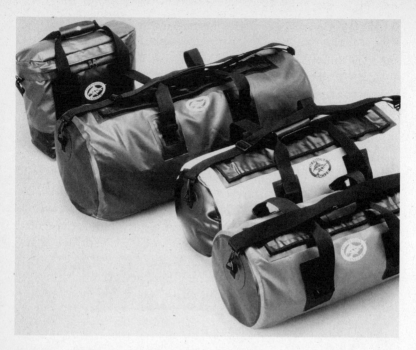

Splash-proof gear bags for fishing in rainy weather or from boats.
(Offshore Angler)

nasal spray, keys for the luggage locks. Whatever won't fit in the
carry-on bag.

Leave your rigid or hard-sided luggage home; it weighs a lot and
takes up too much room. At some point, you will be traveling by jeep,
bush plane, helicopter, or boat with limited cargo space. Good duffels
are easy to come by these days, many of them designed specifically
for traveling fly-fishers. Here's what to look for:

▶ Rugged construction—heavy fabric, reinforced seams, handles and
   D-rings that will take the stress of the loaded bag
▶ Both handles and shoulder strap—preferably padded, in both
   cases
▶ Outside compartments to help you organize the contents
▶ Easy access—main compartment accessible from the top, prefer-
   ably by U-shaped rather than straight zipper

▶ Waterproof materials, if you will be fishing from boats
▶ Square or rectangular cross section—makes access easier and will carry more
▶ Corner wheels—optional, but handy, the bigger the duffel

Prices vary from $50 to more than $300, and the quality varies from mediocre to superb, so shop carefully. Discount luggage shops don't always offer much value for the money.

Inside your duffel, also carry a knapsack you can wear while fishing and an assortment of plastic bags that will find many uses during a week's fishing. I sometimes carry a cheap, ultra-lightweight, zippered duffel. When packing to return from a fishing trip, I rarely can get everything back into the big duffel. So I put all the dirty clothing in the extra duffel and hope for the best. If it gets counted as extra baggage, it's light enough that the penalty isn't unbearable.

Because your luggage may sit on an open baggage cart in a downpour, pack everything in plastic garbage bags if you aren't using a waterproof duffel. I use transparent bags or ones of different colors, so I can identify underwear, shirts, pants, socks, and so on. I put smaller things in zip-locked, clear-plastic freezer bags.

Mark your duffel for easy identification at the airport. Besides the required identification tag, put something gaudy on it. Adhesive tape tends to come off, so I tie on several ribbons of the bright, fluorescent-orange tape used to mark off construction sites and crime scenes.

Never put in your checked baggage anything you really must have. Whatever else you decide you want to have on the plane, your carry-on bag ought to accommodate at least these things:

▶ Money: Cash and traveler's checks
▶ Travel documents: Passport, visas, customs and currency declarations
▶ Prescription medicines and other medication in their original containers
▶ Medical documents: Prescriptions, letter from doctor, and the like
▶ Travel address book with all the names, addresses, and telephone, account, and policy numbers you might need
▶ Photocopies of passport, visas, airline and other tickets, reservation confirmations, and so on

☞ **TRAVELER'S TIP**

To keep misdirected checked luggage from completely ruining a trip, I always carry essentials with me on the airplane, including at least two four-piece fly rods. I carry my reels, loaded with the proper lines, a basic assortment of flies, and necessary accessory items in a shoulder bag that will fit beneath the seat or in an overhead compartment. When packing the shoulder bag, I make certain it does not contain knives or other articles that might create a problem at the security checkpoint.

If fishing is to be done from a boat, I include a wet bag in my luggage to carry cameras, extra jacket, and accessory items that I want to keep dry in the event of rain or for protection from the spray when running in a small boat. If a real wet bag is not available, I pack a couple of folded plastic garbage bags in my gear. Then I place my shoulder bag in the garbage bags to protect it from getting wet.

—Leon Chandler
retired vice president, Cortland Line Co.
Cortland, New York

Being a devout pessimist, I assume my checked baggage will be lost. As the whole point of the trip is fishing, my carry-on bag must accommodate a lot. In addition to the above:

▶ Waders, wader belt and suspenders, wading boots, and two sets of wading socks
▶ One set of long johns and poly fleece pants
▶ Reels, fly lines, leaders
▶ Fly boxes
▶ Vest (fully loaded), fishing hat, and Gore-Tex jacket (although I often wear this aboard)
▶ One or two pairs of camp socks, one complete set of layered clothing sufficient for the coldest day likely, and two changes of underwear
▶ Toilet articles
▶ Backup reading and sunglasses (primaries are on my person)

▶ Camera and film (in a clear-plastic freezer bag or lead-foil bag)
▶ Bird book and compact binoculars
▶ Fishing logs, notebooks, reference and reading materials

Such a bag obviously pushes the carry-on size limits. Many bags have been designed specifically for carrying fly-fishing gear aboard. They're great, but mostly too pricey for my budget. I use a large, compartmented bag designed specifically for carrying wet boots and waders. Only twice, on commuter-size aircraft, has it been disallowed as a carry-on. Once, flying to northern Quebec with far too much stuff, I wore my fully loaded fishing vest on the plane, so it wouldn't count as a carry-on.

Before you check your two-piece (or three-piece, two-handed Spey) rods as baggage, be reasonably certain they will survive the trip. I once traveled with someone who put his rod tubes in a golf bag. Interesting. But when I check rods, I use one of the following:

▶ A rectangular cross-section, heavy-gauge aluminum rod case that is, alas, no longer made
▶ Three aluminum rod tubes, taped together
▶ Heavy, rugged case made of three- or four-inch-diameter Schedule 40 PVC pipe

More often, I carry on board the plane three, sometimes four, travel rods, their short tubes taped together—usually slung over my shoulder with a strap, hoping they won't count as a carry-on. One of these days I must finally buy one of those super rod safes that will hold four multipiece rods and several reels.

☞ **TRAVELER'S TIP**

I always take a field guide to the birds whenever I go on a trip. Heck, half the fun is looking at birds, anyway.

—Jack Samson
saltwater columnist, *Fly Rod & Reel*,
formerly editor of *Field & Stream*
Santa Fe, New Mexico

Minimal Miscellany

You could stuff your vest pockets full of gadgets (and most of us do), but only a few things are truly necessary on a fishing trip. In addition to the lifesaving stuff mentioned in Chapter 7, here are the traveling fly-fisher's essentials:

▶ Hook sharpener—hone, auto ignition points file, ceramic stick, and so on, to make the most of the strikes
▶ Forceps/hemostat—used as a hook disgorger
▶ Flashlight—flex-neck light, "pinch" light, mini lithium flash, one of those lights that fasten onto a cap bill
▶ Stream thermometer
▶ Tape measure
▶ Pliers—Abel Pliers if you can afford them, otherwise Sargent Sport Mates
▶ Needle and thread—small needle and normal thread, plus a larger needle and button-and-carpet thread
▶ Safety pins in several sizes
▶ Pocket knife—a *small* Swiss Army knife is ideal
▶ Line cutter/nippers—at least two; easily broken or lost
▶ Small piece of metal tubing—for tying nail knots
▶ Scissors—small folding ones are safe to carry
▶ Brass beads in several sizes—slipped on the tippet before the fly is tied on, for getting flies down deep (I prefer them to split shot, but carry one or the other.)
▶ Rubber bands—always good to have on hand
▶ Tape—plastic, fabric, duct, adhesive, whatever there's room for; it's all useful
▶ Dental floss or tape—for whipping, repairing, tying, securing things
▶ Permanent-ink felt tip marker—fine or extra-fine point Sanford Sharpie
▶ Towel—wear it as a shawl for warmth, roll it up as a pillow, or dry yourself off away from the shower house
▶ Candy—if you have a sweet tooth (When the fishing gets tough, a hard, sour candy, some M&Ms, or miniature Snickers bar often will fill me with new resolve.)

▶ Booze—if you're an imbiber (When the fishing gets *really tough,* only a belt of dark rum, Russian vodka, or eighteen-year-old Macallan Scotch gives me the will to go on.)

Resources

KIT-AND-CABOODLE CATALOGS

Most of the mail-order tackle catalogs listed in Chapter 4 sell waders, boots, luggage, clothing, and other accessories. The following catalogs do not offer tackle.

Buck's Bags, P.O. Box 7884, Boise, ID 83707; phone 1-800-284-2247 and 1-208-344-4400; fax 1-208-344-6244 (*Travel bags*)

Clear Creek Co., Inc., P.O. Box 182, New Hampton, IA 50659; phone 1-800-894-0483 and 1-515-394-2048; fax 1-515-394-2048 (*Rod tubes and cases, travel bags*)

Clemens Custom Tackle, Inc., 444 Schantz Spring Road, Allentown, PA 18104; phone 1-610-395-5119; fax 1-610-398-2580 (*Rod bags, fly boxes, creels, nets, accessories*)

Compleat Angler, Inc., 1320 Marshall Lane, Helena, MT 59601; phone 1-406-442-1973; fax 1-406-442-9900 (The *wader-accessory catalog: belts, suspenders, felt soles, pack, patch kits*)

D. B. Dun Inc., 10487 Overland Road, Boise, ID 83704; phone 1-800-574-1021; fax 1-208-344-4893 (*Rod and reel cases, wader bags, travel cases*)

Early Winters, P.O. Box 4333, Portland, OR 97208; phone 1-800-458-4438 and 1-800-821-1286; fax 1-503-643-1973 (*Travel clothing and gear*)

Eastern Mountain Sports, Vose Farm Road, Peterborough, NH 03458; phone 1-603-924-9571; fax 1-603-924-9138 (*Outdoor clothing, luggage, accessories*) [EMS no longer produces a catalog, but contact them for the address of their nearest store.]

Fly-Tech, 3313 Park Lake Drive, Fort Worth, TX 76133; phone 1-817-346-8887; fax 1-817-346-1030 (*Waders, rainwear, accessories*)

Fly Tyer's Carry-All, Box 299, Village Station, New York, NY 10014; phone 1-212-242-2856; fax 1-212-989-2989 (*Folstaff wading staff, The Carry-All*)

Giorgio Benecchi's Products, Via Giotto, 279, 41100 Modena, Italy; phone 011-39-59-341-190; fax 011-39-59-342-627 (*Sauvage leather rod and reel cases, accessories*)

Lewis Creek Co., 3 Webster Road, Shelburne, VT 05482; phone 1-800-336-4884, 1-802-985-1099; fax 1-802-985-1097 (*American-made waxed-cotton outerwear*)

Mark Pack Works, 230 Madison Street, Oakland, CA 94607; phone 1-510-452-0243; fax 1-510-452-3022 (*Polarplus clothing, tackle bags, rod and reel cases, luggage*)

Northwest River Supplies, Inc., 2009 S. Main Street, Moscow, ID 83843; phone 1-800-635-5202, 1-208-882-2383; fax 1-208-883-4787 (*Neoprene footwear, dry suits, waterproof boxes and bags*)

Patagonia Mail Order, Inc., P.O. Box 8900, Bozeman, MT 59715; phone 1-800-336-9090, 1-800-638-6464, and 1-406-587-3838 (*Outdoor and travel clothing*)

The J. Peterman Company, 1318 Russell Cave Road, Lexington, KY 40505; phone 1-800-231-7341 and 1-606-268-2006; fax 1-800-346-3081 and 1-606-266-6367 (*Travel clothing and bags, and the Peterman Owner's Manual is the most entertaining catalog extant*)

Precision Flyfishing International, 14109 Dartmouth Court, Fontana, CA 92336; phone 1-909-428-2054; fax 1-909-428-2339 (*Luggage, accessories*)

REI, Recreational Equipment, Inc., 1700 45th Street East, Sumner, WA 98352; phone 1-800-426-4840, 1-800-828-5533, 1-206-891-2500; fax 1-206-891-2523 (*Luggage, outerwear, accessories*)

Sequel Software, Inc., P.O. Box 3185, Durango, CO 81302; phone and fax 1-303-385-4660 (*Outdoor and travel clothing*)

Spirit River Inc., 2405-68 Diamond Lake Boulevard, Roseburg, OR 97470; phone 1-503-440-6916; fax 1-503-672-4309 (*Tackle Satchel, Expedition Carry Alls*)

SwiftSure Incorporated, 1509 Queen Anne Avenue N., #267, Seattle, WA 98109; phone 1-800-337-9438 and 1-206-283-3539; fax 1-206-283-3539 (*Waders, tackle bags, accessories*)

10x Products Group, 2915 LBJ Freeway, Suite 133, Dallas, TX 75234; phone 1-800-433-2225 and 1-214-243-4016; fax 1-214-243-4112 (*Sun & Fun Wear*)

Tilley Endurables, 300 Langner Road, West Seneca, NY 14224; phone 1-800-363-8737 and 1-716-822-3952; fax 1-800-845-5394 [900 Don

Mills Road, Don Mills, Ontario M3C 1V6, Canada; phone 1-800-363-8737 and 1-416-444-4465; fax 1-800-845-5394 and 1-416-444-6977] (*Great, but pricey, travel clothing, shoes, bags*)

A. A. Williams Co., P.O. Box 177, Rancocas, NJ 08073; phone and fax 1-609-267-5506 (*The Sportsbag*)

YOLKY PALKY!

Doragiye Amerikanskiye druz'ya . . ."

Omigod, Kim Sanch was at it again. Cautious hands flew to cover glasses, but it was too late: The vodka bottle had already made the rounds.

Kim Sanch is Kim Aleksandrovich Koryakin, chairman of the Yakut Society of Hunters and Fishermen and the local host of our fishing visit to Siberia. The other is Russian for "Dear American friends," the usual opening of Kim's toasts. Whether under banquet conditions in Yakutsk, or at the rustic table of our base camp on the cobbled banks of the Kyundyudey River, Kim kept us well toasted. In the noisy helicopter, his toasts were usually silent ones, just a lift of the cup and a nod.

Now, Kim Koryakin is a man of some consequence in Yakutia (then the Yakut Autonomous Soviet Socialist Republic), and when he toasts, you toast. It isn't that Kim likes to drink so much (I watched him sometimes surreptitiously refill his glass with soda water or fruit juice), but he does like to lift a glass in long, florid toasts to peace, friendship, brotherhood, cooperation, wildlife, nature, the environment, the end of the Cold War. Like most of the other Russians and Yakuts we met, Kim seemed genuinely to like Americans. Everywhere we went, we were fairly besieged with toasts, smiles, handshakes, hugs, and kisses. Once I got past my Cold War preconceptions (I grew up in the Middle West during the McCarthy era), it felt a lot more brotherly in the Soviet Union than it usually does back home in, say, New York City.

We had come to Siberia to fish for (a) fun and (b) science. The first part is easy to understand, but the second may need some explaining. Taxonomists in the United States and Russia disagreed on whether the lenok is a single species or two. Tests that had been done up to that point—mostly morphometrics and electrophoresis—were inconclusive, and so the idea was to get a few American fly-fishermen together with some American and Soviet scientists and collect tissue samples for DNA analysis back in the States. Participating in the venture were Trout Unlimited, the Soviet (now Russian) Academy of Sciences, the Russian Society of Hunters and Fishermen (of which the Yakut Society is a branch), Soviet Sports Connections (an American expedition outfitter, now defunct), and *Fly Rod & Reel* magazine (represented by yours truly).

Key to the economic feasibility of the Siberian Scientific Expedition for Salmonid Fish Species Identification 1991 was the participation of paying customers: anglers who would serve as specimen collectors. We had six. From the Headhunters Club of Columbus, Ohio, came Jack Klages, Tom Fitzpatrick, Vernon Crawford, and Jack Edwards, a brave bunch of can-do men in their late sixties and early seventies; from California, the father-and-son team of Ken and Mike Holland, who took to the Siberian wilderness as if they'd grown up there. We had three scientists. Sergey Alexeev, a young biologist with the Soviet Academy of Sciences in Moscow, had studied lenok for a decade or so and had already visited many of the streams we would fish. (Sergey had packed all his scientific, camping, and fishing gear—including an inflatable raft—on his back. We had a chartered Mi-8 helicopter, a typically Russian machine, big, dirty, ugly, and built like a tank.) From Colorado State University came Dr. Robert Behnke, America's foremost salmonid taxonomist (and TU's representative), and Don Proebstel, a Ph.D. candidate who would be doing the mitochondrial DNA analysis. Our leader was Bill Davies, then president of Soviet Sports Connections (and now of Kola Salmon, Inc.), a Russophile and Russian history buff who lives in Russia half the year.

And we had a large supporting cast. Soviet Sports Connections furnished Aleksandr' Berkan, its general manager in the USSR and a real bilingual go-getter, and Gennady Dubovitsky, field manager, fish-savvy guide, and excellent streamside cook. Kim Koryakin's Yakut Society of Hunters and Fishermen supplied the guides, boatmen, and camp hands we needed. Confusingly, but typically, we had two or three each of the most common Russian names: Sasha, Sergey, Volodya, Valery. (At the three Kola Peninsula salmon camps I would fish in 1994, ten of the fifteen guides would be named Sasha, although one was usually called Big Alex.)

Our guides were a most interesting and hard-working lot. They weren't professional guides as we understand the term. These were amateur sportsmen who guided for the chance to meet and talk to American sportsmen and to visit remote places that were otherwise beyond their means. Among their number were an ophthalmologist, a professional forester, two or three mining and civil engineers, a sculptor.

> *Pachimu?* (Why?)
> *Patamushta* (Because.)
> > —conversational gambit
> > evolved over seven decades of
> > Soviet Communist rule

Much of the time we split into two or three groups for fishing, so we could cover a lot of different waters. The Ohioans usually fished together as a group. The Hollands fished together too, sometimes joining the scientists or me in our explorations. Over a seven-day period we collectively fished a lot of water: the Kyundyudey, Iundyulung, Muna, Dyanishka, Buntatay, Tirekhtyakh, Begilzhan, Upper Yana, and Sobolakh-Moyan rivers (as well as some streams whose names I never knew or have since forgot) and a lake called Lubalakh. (The last we fished to investigate a rumor of landlocked salmon; they were big Arctic char.) Some of the rivers fished well, others didn't. Overall, the Tirekhtyakh was the best water we found: fishably small and floatably deep, with good rock and gravel bottoms and plenty of fish: both forms of lenok, and taimen as well.

The *Brachymystax* species, locally called lenok and limba, are charlike salmonids that perhaps most closely resemble our bull trout, itself a largely unknown fish. These were the fish the scientists were most interested in catching. But the anglers were all hoping for a shot at *Hucho hucho taimen*, the largest of all salmonids. The taimen, or Siberian salmon, looks sort of like a skinny Atlantic salmon, to which it is in fact related.

These are funny rivers: not nearly so rich in insect and "minnow" life as North American trout streams, yet the fish are generally large (two- to four-pound lenok were reasonably common, and we caught a few to seven and eight pounds and lost some even bigger; the taimen reach weights well in excess of one hundred pounds). These fish must be slow-growing and old, therefore easy to fish out. I wish I could report that the Russian and Yakut sportsmen had our conservation ethic, but they are still in the find-'em, catch-'em, kill-'em, and eat-'em phase. From the helicopters we saw a few solitary taimen that looked to be four or five feet long, but we just couldn't get them to rise to a fly or even to take a metal spoon. We took a few taimen, but in the five- to ten-pound range.

We checked the stomachs of all the fish we killed in the name of science. A few were empty. One was stuffed with snails. Quite a few were full of caddis cases. We saw numerous hatches of small mayflies, but not much evidence to indicate the fish were feeding on them. Nor did we find evidence they were feeding on forage fish, of which the rivers had precious few. Several fish had mice, voles, and shrews in their stomachs. How they find so many mammals to eat, I don't know.

As almost everyone had predicted, huge deer-hair mice were the lures of choice, although smaller hair mice and Muddler Minnows and Dahlberg Divers and even Humpies took fish. Besides standard American deer-hair mice, I had a couple of enormous, almost-impossible-to-cast Lemming Meringue Flies I had received from the Cornell ichthyologist Ed Brothers, who'd invented the pattern while on a taimen trip to Outer Mongolia the year before. The Hollands had a lot of success with huge, black streamers that John Bailey had tied for them, based on a lenok and taimen trip he'd made earlier to Mongolia. But the mice were what really turned them on. Lenok have large jawbones and tough mouths, and it isn't always easy to hook them securely. They will, however, come back to a fly that is cast right back to the same spot.

As for the rest of the tackle: floating lines of whatever size would carry the fly, and the rods to cast them. Vernon Crawford used a 6-weight rod the whole trip and had a ball, but I can't cast well enough to launch big, air-resistant flies on so small a rod. Most of us used 8- or 9-weight rods. You don't really need to balance the rod to the fish, unless you happen to hook into a big taimen. Even though both lenoks are big and strong, they aren't really very good fighters. They splash on the surface but don't jump. Even the one small taimen I caught fought more like a char than like a salmon or grilse. But those who have caught large taimen say they jump well and fight hard, like salmon. We heard one unverified story that, when asked how many times big taimen jump when hooked, a local fishermen said, "Just once, unless you miss with the rifle." These guys haven't yet fully embraced catch-and-release fishing.

There are Arctic grayling here and there in the rivers and tributaries (and also in Lubalakh), and they are a lot of fun on light tackle. But as I was almost always loaded for lenok or taimen I didn't really try for any.

Microchips? Why, we make the biggest ones in the world!

—typical Russian joke

Toward the end of our Siberian stay, we split up into three groups for a two-day, two-night float trip. Behnke, Proebstel, Alexeev, and I were dropped with two guides on the Tirekhtyakh, between the Lena River and the Verkhoyansk Mountains. The two Californians and two guides had earlier been dropped on the Dyanishka, some 160 miles to the south. The four Ohioans and their guides would be dropped on a river about midway between us and the Californians; because of map-reading confusion, it still isn't clear which river it was.

The two days we floated the Tirekhtyakh, we experienced all sorts of fishing. Shortly after the chopper dropped us off, Don Proebstel, using spinning gear, took a small taimen and a lenok in a riffle just upstream of the deep, swift pool Bob Behnke and I were casting flies to without any success. (During the whole trip the rest of us chided Don for fishing spoons, spinners, and huge Magnum Rapala plugs, and we made sure to stay ahead of his raft during the float trip, lest he fish out every hole before we got there. He kept reminding us that he was on the trip for science, not fun, and that he had to collect a certain number of specimens before he could afford the luxury of fly-fishing. He was The Meat Fisherman, nevertheless.) Bob and I made him trade places with us after he'd taken his lenok and taimen, but we went fishless in the riffle too. I guess they wanted hardware.

The guides were still inflating rafts and readying gear when it started raining. Hard. We hunkered down under the rafts and under the tent that had been thrown, tarplike, over the pile of camping gear. After a while Kolya and Sergey (the guide, not the biologist) decided it would be prudent to move downstream in the rain. The rocky bar we were on was too low to risk camping on if the river rose suddenly. That was when I discovered that my Gore-Tex rainsuit had died; I might as well have been wearing terry cloth. (Fortunately, it rained only that first day and night. The next day we were back to blazing sun and sweltering heat—just the thing for spending twelve hours in neoprene chest waders. Davies's packing list had been explicit on neoprenes, so I had left my lightweight waders behind—never again.) We had three rafts: one for the camp gear (which Sergey and Kolya took turns rowing), one for the young scientists, Alexeev and Proebstel; and one for the old-timers, Behnke and Soucie.

We fished rather fitfully in the rain, to no effect. We put ashore a couple of miles downstream on another rocky bar that looked no better to me than the one we'd just left, but I deferred to the guides' experience. They were right. The big Mikoyan chopper returned briefly, to drop off Bill Davies, whose gear had inadvertently been off-loaded with ours. We huddled together under the rafts as we watched the Mi-8—which was heading back to Yakutsk, some 400 miles distant, for a crew change—lift off and quickly disappear in the zero-visibility, zero-ceiling mist, fog, and driving rain. Our wilderness vulnerability suddenly dawned on me. We were at least 160 miles from the nearest human habitation. If the chopper went down in this weather before it got high enough to radio our positions over the mountains, no one would even know where to begin searching.

The next day shaped up very nicely, clearing just after breakfast. Off we went, Behnke and Soucie, with Davies rowing, in the lead. We all had excellent fishing that day. Bill and I both had slashing attacks from a fish that surely would have gone ten pounds, but neither of us could hook up well and truly. The big lenok was lurking in a deep pool where a small tributary entered the main stream. It would blast up out of the depths after the floating mouse. Momentarily I had the fish on twice and Bill, once. Then it gave up on us. Out in the sunnier part of the pool, we could see dozens of smaller lenok—to maybe four pounds. While Bill rowed us around in circles, Bob and I caught and released most of them. Finally they got wise to us and stopped rushing at our flies.

In case you are wondering why Bob and I weren't keeping the fish for science: Because of the intense sunlight and heat, the scientists decided it was too risky to keep fish in both rafts. To ensure good results from the DNA analysis, the tissue must be taken from a live or really fresh dead fish. Don Proebstel had the stringers and cooler in the other raft. Anyway, he also had the spinning tackle, so he would surely outfish the rest of us. Even scientists and journalists get to fish for fun sometimes.

For the next two days, we caught lenok (both forms) in pools, riffles, and runs; in head waters and tail waters and in eddies and pocket water; while wading and while floating. We fished wide stretches with clean gravel bottoms; narrow, swift channels of intimate beauty that were flanked by heavy forest; braided channels and back waters. We fished in shadow and in full sunlight. Sometimes we caught fish, sometimes we didn't. It was hard to discern a pattern. Overall, we caught a lot of fish.

At the end of the first day, Bob Behnke was terribly fatigued and had a moderate case of *panos*, Russian for traveler's trot. He skipped dinner. Kolya found a plant with a name that sounded like *kurikopter*, boiled its roots, and gave Bob the infusion to drink. Whatever it was, Bob felt fine the next morning.

Ne vieshai lapshu na ushiy. (Don't hang a noodle on my ear.)

—Russian way of saying
"Stop pulling my leg."

Meanwhile, the young biologists, Don and Sergey, were doing their scientific thing, measuring fish (they had more than thirty of them) and cutting, chopping, preserving, and labeling tissue specimens— heart, liver, kidney, muscle, and fin. I watched them for a while, but the mosquitoes finally drove me to the tent. They were at it until after midnight, and the next morning Don's face was all lumpy and swollen from the bites. Field biology sounds glamorous, but it sure has its down sides.

The next day the fishing was slower, and the sunshine gave way occasionally to light, sporadic showers, but it was a pleasant float nonetheless. I managed to take a couple of blunt-nosed lenok and several of the sharp-nosed limba, and Bob did somewhat better. We had developed a tag-team approach. I would cast a deer-hair mouse and if I missed the strike or failed to keep the hooked fish on, Bob would mop up with his Muddler Minnow. Sometimes we had double-headers that would dart every which way under the raft.

Bill got quite a chuckle out of my fishing because almost every time I'd look away from my mouse—scouting for submerged snags or rod-threatening limbs, or just watching Bob play a fish—I'd get a strike. And miss it. I set what Bill said was surely a Siberian and per-haps a world record: While floating down through a long riffle, I had the same fish on *seven* times (Bill remembers six) before finally land-ing it. On the seventh strike it took the whole, virtually life-size mouse inside its mouth. It wasn't about to let me pull its prey away again.

We saw a little wildlife, but not much, which was typical of the whole time we spent in the Soviet Union. On this particular float we saw one moose, some waterfowl, lots of terns and wagtails, one small flight of swans. We saw sign of fox and bear and elk, some of it fresh, but no animals. From rafts and helicopters over a seven-day period, we saw fewer than a dozen moose, four reindeer, not really very many numbers or species of birds. One day, on a helicopter flight I wasn't on, some of the others saw four snow sheep. A strange place, Siberia.

Before heading downstream the second day, Bill and Kolya had agreed that our lead raft would stop around two or two-thirty, on a beach or bar wide enough for the helicopter to land. The chopper was to pick us up at four o'clock. We found a good spot: an island that had plenty of driftwood for a cook fire, surrounded by some very fishable-looking water.

After we had deflated our raft and gathered a huge pile of fire-wood, I decided to fish the river right in front of the campsite while waiting for the other rafts. Almost immediately I had several fast, short, missed strikes from what I took to be a grayling, so I switched to a yellow Humpy. It turned out to be a small limba. Then I caught one of about three and a half pounds. I went back to a deer-hair mouse and caught a small taimen of maybe five or six pounds, my first and only Siberian salmon. A Siberian grand slam.

The other rafts arrived. Don had two more stringers full of fish, but not the eight-pound lenok he'd managed to lose while stringing up another fish. Bob took Don's spinning rod over to a nice backwater slough right next to a fast riffle on the other side of the island. He returned just in time for lunch, bearing a nice, seven-pound lenok and an account of having caught and released a thirty-inch taimen.

After lunch the young biologists went back to their butchering, and the guides deflated the other two rafts and packed up all the gear. I climbed out of the waders and put away my fishing tackle, so we'd be ready to go when the chopper arrived. Don, who doesn't mind living in his neoprene waders, explored the waters around the island with his spinning rod but didn't have a lot of luck.

Four o'clock came and went. After nearly two weeks in the Soviet Union, we were prepared for a wait. (Coping with frustration and disappointment is a way of life in modern-day Russia as well as the old Soviet Union. Dealing with it is something Americans have to get used to. If you react the way you would in America, it both shames and irritates your hosts. But if you say nothing, it sends the wrong message and only makes you sullen. Bill taught me the appropriate Russian response to screw-ups: You throw your hands in the air, roll your eyes, and say, *Yolky palky!* It means "A stick for a Christmas tree," and it works like a charm, always producing grins and redoubled efforts rather than frowns.) The hours rolled on. At nine o'clock or so, we gave up. The guides started pitching camp and we started another cook fire.

The guides had two chickens they wanted to boil for dinner. We were tired of boiled fish and chicken, so we gathered forked sticks and split some fish for roasting. We decided to make it a taste test and cooked one each lenok, limba, and taimen. (My taimen hadn't survived the rigors of photography.) The guides boiled the chickens anyway. Boiling is important in Russian camp cuisine, to provide broth for soup or stew the next day.

For breakfast the next day we had the boiled chicken, which we made Kolya brown in the last of the butter. After breakfast, the guides packed up the cooking gear but left the tents up—just in case. Don finally unlimbered his fly rod and went exploring around the island and caught a few lenok and limba. I'd have joined him except the ribs I had busted a few days earlier (the result of too much vodka, mind-numbing heat in a sauna tent, and tripping while tiptoeing over a cobblestone riverbank) were hurting so much from all the twisting and turning and casting in the raft, I decided not to fish. Mostly we just lazed around the campsite, talking, dozing, whatever. Kolya, a professional sculptor and carver, whittled a traditional Yakut toy, a stylized bull, and gave it to me. Sergey Alexeev snuggled up with a book inside his homemade net tent. For lunch we had the chicken broth with everything else we had tossed in. We also fork-roasted a couple more lenok.

After lunch, Bob Behnke smoked his last bowl of pipe tobacco. We wondered how long a wait we might have. Bill was noncommittal. Sergey said he'd waited for helicopters many times in his field research in the Siberian wilderness. I asked him what was the longest he'd had to wait. "Fifteen days." *Yolky palky!* indeed. We had plenty of fish to eat and river water to drink, but nothing else. So we started talking about organizing Russian-American teams to search the woods for mushrooms and other edible plants, and something that Bob could smoke in his pipe. Before we got started, we heard the *pocka-pocka-pocka* of the helicopter. It was 2:45 PM. We were so grateful to see the chopper, we didn't even wonder about the lame excuse offered for the twenty-three-hour delay.

> *Ni pukha ni pera.* (Neither down nor feathers.)
>> —Russian way of wishing good luck on departure
>> (perhaps equivalent to our "Break a leg.")

We spent one more night at the Tirekhtyakh River base camp, then left the next morning for Yakutsk. We had absolutely foul weather during the flight, heavy rain, dense clouds. When we stopped to refuel at Sangar, which was closed to fixed-wing aircraft because of the slipperiness of the wet clay runways, we picked up two locals who had connections to make in Moscow. The excitement of the flight out from Yakutsk was noticeably missing. The Ohioans had had poor fishing on their float trip. The rest of us were just sobered by the closing of a most interesting and exciting chapter in our lives. We were really looking forward to a hot shower, though. After seven days in the wilderness, mostly under a hot sun in neoprene waders, we were a dirty, funky lot.

Back in Yakutsk late that morning we had another unpleasant surprise. There was no hot water for baths or showers. Nor was there any cold water. The city's main water line was being repaired or replaced, and there wouldn't be any running water until 6 PM. *Yolky palky!* again. Thirst drove Bob Behnke and me to a free-market truck that was parked in a lot next to the hotel, selling melons. We bought one small watermelon and a large Persian melon for about $2.75—a steal for us but highway robbery for the Yakuts.

Another banquet. More dancing. More toasting. This time Kim offered a short one: *Za khrabrost'!* "To courage!" Even the teetotalers drank to that one. It was a big party, because we were joined by the next group of American anglers, all from Pennsylvania, who were heading out the next morning for a six-day float trip. Based on our group's experience, it was decided they would float the Tirektyakh. (The abortive Communist Party coup—which we missed by a couple of days—happened while the Pennsylvanians were floating the Tirekhtyakh, but it would all be over by the time they got back in touch with civilization.)

Early the next morning it was farewell to Siberia. The flight back to Moscow would be even longer this time, because a big storm center to the west was forcing us to take a much more southerly route. It would take two stops and nearly twelve hours. (Because fuel was so inexpensive in the Soviet Union—we were paying about 5 cents a gal-

Russia's first airliner, the *Antonov 2*, still widely in use. *(R. Valentine Atkinson/Frontiers)*

lon for jet fuel—their engines and motors are outrageously inefficient in fuel consumption. I'm told they don't have a single civilian airplane that can fly nonstop from Moscow to New York.) After refueling in Chita, we flew over Lake Baikal on our way to Omsk. Until a year or so before, the industrial center of Omsk had been one of the Soviet Union's closed cities; no foreigners or tourists allowed, not even for refueling. Another surprise was waiting for us there. Because of the length of the flight, the pilots would not be allowed to continue on to Moscow unless they had eight hours of rest. Nor could we leave the airport to visit the city, because we didn't have Omsk on our visas. The thought of an eight-hour stay in the airplane or the Deputies' Lounge was unbearable. It was suggested that the flight dispatcher might be encouraged to waive the rules. Most of us were willing to chip in fifty to one hundred bucks apiece. The pilot went to see the dispatcher. It took 1,000 rubles ($32 at the 1991 exchange rate), and Bill Davies suspected the pilot pocketed half of it.

Another night at the Intourist Hotel in Moscow, with a nice dinner and a little dancing at a fancy restaurant. Most of the crew went to bed, but Mike Holland and I decided to visit Red Square for some late-night photography and to watch the midnight changing of the guard at Lenin's Tomb. I had a pleasant conversation with a beautiful Muscovite named Mari, whose father, an American Communist, had emigrated to the Soviet Union during the McCarthy years. Only extreme fatigue and abject cowardice caused me to decline her kind and affectionate offer. But she insisted on a kiss (no charge), and I was happy to oblige. (I told you Russians are fond of Americans. On the charter flight out from Moscow to Yakutsk, we had to refuel at Norilsk, a dreary mining town in the icy middle of nowhere north of the Arctic Circle. The price for our being allowed to stretch our legs and walk into the terminal was an American kiss good-bye for the female official in charge.)

The next morning the Ohioans headed out to Sheremetyevo and the States. Bob and Don were meeting with Sergey and his colleagues at the Soviet Academy. The Hollands and I went sightseeing with our guides, Lidia Berkan and Lilia Azarova. On the way out to the airport that afternoon, Mike Holland and I were saying how much we'd like to spend another couple of days exploring Moscow. But duty called. (When we got together for a night of jazz in New York the next Monday, the day of the coup, we both were bummed out that we hadn't been able to stay and see the former Soviet Union through the first step of its long, harrowing road to democracy and free enterprise.)

There were no tearful good-byes at the airport, because we had to struggle through long, sluggish lines. The baggage check-in was so disorderly and mismanaged it reminded me of the DMV offices back in New York, only worse. I doubt we'd have managed it in time but for the efforts of Tanya Davies, Bill's wife at the time, a truly take-charge woman. ("Tanya the terrible" Bill calls her, now that he is married to another Russian, "Nina the wonderful.")

Looking out the window as we took off, I was struck by how different it felt from the landing. Then everything had seemed so strange and foreboding—thanks to all those Cold War spy movies and novels, let alone U.S. government propaganda. Now it was bittersweet, like leaving a good friend's or close relative's after a particularly pleasant stay. Despite the patented Soviet screwups and the occasionally slow fishing, the trip and the whole experience had been terrific. It had even been, as some Russians say (but never in mixed or polite company), *Zayebis'!* And it doesn't get much better than that.

A taxonomic coda: Don Proebstel's DNA studies have proved pretty conclusively that there are two species of *Brachymystax*. To this angler's eyes, the differences were obvious: One has a sharply pointed nose, an underslung mouth, and large rosy blotches along the sides. This is the *Brachymystax lenok* described in the scientific literature but usually called "limba" by the locals. The other, wrongly called just plain lenok by most, and leopard lenok by Bill Davies, has a blunt nose and a troutlike terminal mouth, and its gray to brown flanks are spattered with raggedy-edged black spots. It has, as yet anyway, no scientific name other than *Brachymystax* sp. (although some have suggested *Brachymystax tumensis*).

Whatever the scientific names turn out to be, let me put in an oar for their common English names, lest the scientists settle on the noneuphonious descriptive names they were using on the trip: sharp-snouted and blunt-snouted lenok. Sharp-nosed and blunt-nosed, maybe. Better yet, how about lenok and leopard lenok, or maybe even fireball lenok and leopard lenok?

6
PAPER TRAILS

American bureaucracy takes a back seat to no one's governmental or organizational nonsense, but if you've never traveled abroad, you ain't seen nothin' yet. Something about the crossing of borders seems to bring out the worst bureaucratic urges in the species. No amount of logic, good will, or common sense can prepare you for the documentitis that rages through the ranks of those charged with policing borders and gates. Dot those *i*'s and cross those *t*'s and try to keep a smile on your face. Actually, some of the nonsense is pretty humorous, if you will just let yourself see beyond the impatience and frustration.

If you book through a competent booking agent, you will be told what documents are necessary. If you don't happen to be an American citizen traveling on a U.S. passport, you'd better mention the fact, in case the agent doesn't ask.

Passports and Visas

If you don't hold a currently valid passport, mark your place, put this book down, and go get one. Don't wait until you need it. It can take a lot longer than you think, especially during and just prior to peak traveling seasons. And if you need to get a visa for the country you'll be fishing, you may need to send a photocopy of your valid passport with your visa application. You also may have to send photos with your visa application, so get enough extra copies when you have your passport photos made. If you wait until the last minute to get or renew a passport (as I did the last time), you'll run up a lot of telephone and Fed Ex bills. You'll also deplete the supplies in your liquor cabinet, nursing yourself through the anxieties.

You may be able to apply for a passport by mail if you meet *all* the following conditions:

▶ You have a passport that was issued within the past twelve years.
▶ You can find and submit your most recent passport with your application.
▶ You had attained your sixteenth birthday by the time that passport was issued.
▶ You still use the same name (unless it was changed by marriage or court order).

If you qualify for a mail-in application, you must send all of the following things to one of the thirteen passport agencies listed elsewhere in this chapter.

▶ A completed, signed, and dated Form DSP-82, Application for Passport by Mail (available at passport agencies, one of the courts or post offices that accept passport applications, or your travel agent)—include your date of departure for speedy processing; otherwise it will take several weeks
▶ Your previous passport
▶ Two identical 2-by-2 passport photos
▶ A check, money order, or bank draft for $55
▶ If your name has changed, the original or a certified copy of the court order or marriage certificate that shows the change of name

If you can't meet all four of the tests just mentioned, you will have to apply in person at a passport agency or one of the thousand or so post offices, federal, state, or probate courts authorized to accept passport applications. Show up with the following.

▶ A completed Form DSP-11, Passport Application, which *must not be signed* until you are asked to do so
▶ Two identical passport photos

▶ $65 (but *not* in cash at *some* post offices and clerks of court)
▶ Documentary proof of U.S. citizenship

If you were born in the U.S., one of the following will do:

✔ Previous passport
✔ Certified copy of your birth certificate
✔ Note from a state registrar stating that no birth record exists, *plus* the best available secondary evidence:
  • Baptismal certificate
  • Hospital birth record
  • Early census
  • School records
  • Affidavit of someone who has direct personal knowledge of your birth
  • Et cetera (It's a good idea to call the passport agency and talk this one over first.)

If you were born abroad, you can use one of the following:

✔ Certificate of Naturalization
✔ Certificate of Citizenship
✔ Form FS-240, Report of Birth Abroad of a Citizen of the United States of America
✔ Form FS-545 or DS-1350, Certification of Birth

As for visas, let's hope your booking agent is on the ball and sends you the visa application form in plenty of time. When in doubt, contact the embassy or consulate of the country you plan to visit. Again, this is a process that can drag on a lot longer than you think. In some cases, six to eight weeks or more.

Hey, nobody said planning for a foreign fishing trip was simply an expensive version of "I hear they're biting. Want to go fishing?"

Correct Currency

Check *The Wall Street Journal* or call your banker for current exchange rates. Get used to doing the mental arithmetic when costs and prices are quoted in the foreign currency. You don't want to get home and discover you've paid $2,000 for a souvenir trinket.

If you can, change a little money into the foreign currency before you leave home. At the very least, do it en route, at the currency-exchange agents in international airports. Don't change much, because you will be charged a fairly stiff fee, which is usually a percentage of the money changing hands. You usually can get a better deal at your destination. But you may need a little of the local currency when you arrive, to pay for things like renting airport baggage carts. Also, local laws may forbid citizens from accepting foreign currency, in which case you'll need some local currency to tip baggage handlers and bellhops upon arrival.

While abroad, pay for as much as you can with credit cards. You will get better rates and won't have to pay exchange fees. Also, if you are in a country that has a high rate of inflation, your credit card company may not make the conversion until your bill is mailed, guaranteeing a better exchange rate.

Carry as little cash as you can, but carry as much as you need. Don't forget that many foreign countries charge steep airport departure taxes. Some charge as much as $50, and sometimes you must pay for them in cash. If you have too little cash remaining, you may not be able to board your flight.

In many countries you will be importuned by locals to change money on the black market. Abroad, U.S. currency may be hard to come by and is often the vehicle of choice for hedging against inflation. You will often be offered a very attractive rate of exchange. Don't do it. Some of these are scams to unload counterfeit money (and do you really think you could spot a phony 100 balboa note?) or screenings by bandits and pickpockets simply to find out whether you are carrying a lot of money or where you carry it. Or the offer may come from an undercover cop. Some countries take currency-exchange violations quite seriously.

Plan to make all your tips in U.S. currency (if local laws permit). Dollars don't inflate as fast as most currencies, and will be much appreciated by guides, mates, cooks, and others who exert themselves to make your fishing trip a good one. And don't just carry hundreds, fifties, and twenties. Tens, fives, and singles will come in handy for casual tips, buying small souvenirs, paying for laundry, settling bar bills, and the like. Carry twenty to thirty one-dollar bills, maybe five to ten fives, and five tens. On the larger denominations, suit yourself.

If you are going to Russia: Russians have a thing about new money. If a bill is badly wrinkled, dirty, faded, even slightly torn, or stamped or written on, you may not be able to use it. Even Russian banks may refuse such bills. I've had decent-looking bills turned down because they were "old." In other words, they were from a series printed earlier than 1990! Don't bother arguing, you will always lose. Ask your bank to give you new bills.

Another Russian currency joke: Upon arrival at Moscow's Sheremetyevo Airport, you will need to be carrying at least $3 to $5 worth of rubles. Why? Because periodically some uniformed twit decides the baggage carts in the customs area (one of which you will probably need) can be rented only with rubles. Naturally, there is no place to change money, and no one else can legally change money for you. Sometimes you can use dollars, sometimes packs of Marlboro cigarettes. Be prepared.

Security Blankets

Before leaving home:

▶ Make photocopies of the photo and signature pages of your passport, visas, airline and other transportation tickets, reservation confirmation forms, traveler's check serial numbers, and anything else of real or informational value. A photocopy of your birth certificate can considerably speed up the replacement of a lost or stolen passport. So can two extra passport photos. Put all these things in a zip-locked plastic bag that gets packed in a money belt or your most secure piece of luggage.
▶ Put a photocopy of your passport, visa, and transportation tickets in every piece of luggage you take, including rod cases and carry-ons. First put them in zip-locked plastic sandwich bags.
▶ Leave another copy of everything with a family member, neighbor, or friend who will be sticking close to home while you are away.

Should anything go astray, these photocopies may ease the otherwise tortuous ordeal of replacing them.

▶ Carry with you, in at least two places, the following information: telephone numbers (fax numbers too) for your home, neighbor, office, bank (including account numbers), insurance agent (also policy numbers), physician, dentist, police department, travel or booking agent (whoever sold you the trip and travel tickets); insurance carriers and policy numbers; addresses and telephone numbers of the nearest U.S. embassy or consulate, American Express office, your bank's correspondent bank (your banker can furnish this info), airline ticket or sales office, any relatives, friends, friends of friends, or other contacts you may have that might come in handy in an emergency; your travel itinerary and schedule; prescriptions for corrective lenses and medicines (using generic chemical, not brand, names).

▶ If you are traveling with medicines that may be considered "controlled substances" (read *narcotics*) here or abroad, or if you have syringes and hypodermic needles with you, leave the medicines in their original containers and carry a copy of the prescription or a letter from your doctor, so you won't be mistaken for a junkie or a dealer. Even that won't suffice for certain drugs in certain countries. Check with their embassy or consulate to be safe.

If you will be carrying foreign-made cameras, tape recorders, radios, binoculars, watches, or other equipment that isn't obviously used, be prepared to prove to U.S. customs upon your return that you didn't buy them abroad. If you can't, you may be shelling out import duties or, worse, having your stuff confiscated if you have more than one article of a type bearing a registered trademark. (I've never heard of anyone being taxed or hassled over foreign-made rods and reels, but anything could happen when you're dealing with petty bureaucrats.)

▶ Carry (with your passport) receipts, bills of sale, or an insurance policy listing the equipment by description and serial number.
▶ If you don't happen to possess all these documents (and who does?), take the gear (which must bear serial numbers) to the customs office at the departure airport and get a certificate of registration.
▶ Alternatively, you can try listing all your suspect equipment by brand, model, and serial number and
(a) have the list notarized before you leave the States or
(b) put the list in a sealed envelope and stamp and address it to

yourself on the *back* of the envelope. Mail it to yourself at the post office, asking the clerk to cancel the stamps so the dated cancellation runs across the edge of the sealed flap.

Because these alternative procedures probably aren't listed in the customs manual, you may have to argue their impeccable logic if customs gives you a thorough going-over. (They seldom do these days.)

Car Cares

If you plan to rent a car while you are abroad, you need to find out whether the country in which you will be driving recognizes your U.S. driver's license. Many don't. If your travel or booking agent isn't absolutely sure, call the embassy or consulate. (While you're at it, find out whether they use road permits. Instead of toll roads, some countries have permits that allow you to use divided highways. It's sort of like paying the tolls in advance. If you drive without one, you can be busted.)

If your U.S. driver's license is not good where you will be going, get an international driver's license. Automobile clubs like the AAA can issue one. Bring with you:

▶ $10
▶ Two more passport-size photos

Car insurance is another potential problem area. Your auto policy is invalid in most countries, and the required coverage that comes with the rental car in many countries is minimal.

▶ Buy additional coverage when you rent the car. Carry as much insurance as you would back home.

If you plan to drive your own car into or through Canada or Mexico to go fishing, your driver's license is okay, but your insurance might not be. Check with your insurance agent or carrier to see if it's valid in our neighboring countries. Even if it is, it may not be enough.

▶ Most provinces in Canada require that you carry at least $200,000 in liability coverage.

▶ Mexico requires that you have theft, third-party liability, *and* comprehensive insurance; otherwise, you'll be required to post a multimegabuck bond.

North or south, you usually can buy auto insurance on either side of the border.

Customs and Currency Declarations

Most countries (including the U.S., upon your return) require you to fill out a customs declaration form when you arrive. Sometimes the airline cabin crew hands the forms out, sometimes you pick them up at the destination airport.

▶ Take two copies—just in case you mess one up.

Some countries will allow you to bring a fair amount of stuff in, so long as you label them "gifts." In other countries, "humanitarian aid" are the magic words. Nobody ever got arrested for carrying "gifts and humanitarian aid"—unless, of course, they were smuggling.

Speaking of magic words, "duty free" is misunderstood by most travelers. When applied to the goods purchased in duty-free shops, the term means the goods and articles are free of duty and taxes only in the country in which they are sold and from which they must be exported. Those same "duty-free" goods may be subject to import duties at the other end of the flight. (These days, the prices charged by airport duty-free shops are rarely as low as those charged in major cities, where discounts are readily available.)

Certain countries—Russia and Zimbabwe, for example—require currency declarations as well.

▶ Be sure to get two of these forms upon or prior to arrival. You will need another copy to fill out upon departure, and you may have a hard time finding an English-language form at the airport.

When you depart, you will turn in both forms: the one you filled out on arrival and the departure form. Don't lose the declaration you filled out on arrival. Keep it with your passport and visa during your stay.

Reservations and Reconfirmations

Most airlines, including U.S. carriers, require that you reconfirm reservations at least seventy-two hours prior to international flights, or risk having your seat sold to someone else. You won't be able to reconfirm from many fishing camps and lodges. Unless the lodge or camp operator or his booking agent tells you in writing they will do it for you, take care of it yourself. Upon arrival, go to the airline's ticket counter, explain the situation, and ask for immediate reconfirmation. If possible, get it in writing. If the counter is closed and you must do it over the phone, record the date, time, and the name of the person you are talking to.

Duties, Restrictions, and Prohibitions

When it's time to return from your trip, you probably will be carrying souvenirs—perhaps even a fish or two. Relatively free and unrestricted as international travel is today, there are veritable thickets governing what you may and may not carry across national borders.

Legalistically, fish are no problem—fresh, frozen, or smoked. Logistically, they are a major pain. By the time you get home, your "fresh" fish will be anything but—unless you are returning from Alaska. The airlines and airports up there and in Seattle, where you probably will be changing flights, have special stickers, cold-storage lockers, and other facilities to make carrying fish as painless as possible. Elsewhere, it's a nightmare of thawing, dripping, smelly excess baggage. I don't bother anymore, not even with salmon. But it's your choice.

As for other souvenirs, keepsakes, mementoes, and plunder, you are facing a veritable jungle of laws and regulations. For openers, keep all your sales receipts. You may need them to establish what retail price you paid and that you obtained an article legally.

EXPORT RESTRICTIONS

Many nations around the world have become quite protective of their cultural treasures and resources, and have imposed bans or restrictions on what can be taken out of the country. These are some of the things that can get you in trouble, unless you have filled out all the forms, obtained export licenses, and paid stiff export duties: pre-Columbian artifacts from Mexico and other Latin American nations, masks and textiles and other "archaeological and ethnographical materials" from some Latin American and African nations, antiques (including religious icons and samovars) from Russia, works of art from many places, almost anything purchased on the black market.

Some countries also restrict or prohibit the export of their currency.

IMPORT DUTIES

Except for gifts (limited to a value of $200 per day per person), anything you ship back home is subject to U.S. import duties. When you carry things with you, some of your returning souvenirs are exempt. Returning from most countries, your exemption is $400, based on the fair retail value of the goods. Returning from American Samoa, Guam, or the U.S. Virgin Islands, your duty-free exemption is $1,300. And your exemption is $600 when returning from from certain favored nations, including these fishing spots: the Bahamas, Belize, Costa Rica, Guatemala, Honduras, Jamaica, the Netherlands Antilles, Nicaragua, Panama, and the British Virgin Islands.

Booze and tobacco are treated differently. You may bring back, duty free, one hundred cigars and two hundred cigarettes. If you are twenty-one years of age or older, you also may bring back one liter of alcoholic beverages without being socked with import duties.

If you do get hit with import duties, the rate could range anywhere from 2.1 percent to 34.6 percent, according to a schedule so arcane I doubt anyone can explain it. (Usually they just levy a flat 10 percent tax on your overage.) Duties are payable on the spot, in cash or by check, although at some ports you can charge it to your Discover, MasterCard, or VISA.

It's a good idea to declare everything you are bringing back and to pack it all together in one bag. Anything you've failed to declare can be confiscated, and you can be fined.

PROHIBITED OR RESTRICTED IMPORTS

Certain articles are considered so "injurious or detrimental to the general welfare of the United States" you may not bring them into the country: absinthe, liquor-filled candy (where prohibited by state law), lottery tickets, narcotics and other dangerous drugs, obscene articles and publications, seditious and treasonable materials, hazardous articles (including toxic substances, fireworks, certain toys), and switchblade knives (unless you are a one-armed person).

You also may not import pirated copies of copyrighted books, records, cassettes, and computer programs; drug paraphernalia; plants, cuttings, seeds, unprocessed plant products, most fruits and vegetables, meats, and many other food items.

Beware of articles made of hides, fur, hair, or feathers; if the creature is on foreign, international, or U.S. endangered species lists, or if it is banned from trade by CITES (the Convention on International Trade in Endangered Species), you could be facing a fine and confiscation of the verboten items. In general, avoid anything made from wild birds, spotted cats, sea turtles, crocodiles and caimans, coral (especially black coral), lizards, and snakes. And that's just the tip of the iceberg.

The situation is so complicated, you'd best get copies of the Customs Service, USDA, and Fish and Wildlife Service publications listed elsewhere in this chapter.

Finally, Fishing Licenses

On my various fishing trips, I've had licenses or permits issued by national governments, state and local bodies, even private organizations. On some private waters, no license was necessary. In the former Yugoslavia, you needed permits on "private" waters but not on public. Go figure. When you book your trip, find out what the deal is.

▶ Who is taking care of the permit or license? "No problem" is not a sufficient answer. Know precisely who is taking care of this important matter.
▶ Is the cost of the license or permit included in the trip cost? (I've had it both ways.)
▶ If not, how much is it, and must you pay in cash?
▶ U.S. or local currency?
▶ Are all species covered? (You might want to be flexible.)

Resources

PASSPORT AGENCIES

You can apply for passports or passport renewals at some post offices, federal or state courts, or any of the thirteen passport agencies.

Boston Passport Agency, 247 Thomas P. O'Neill Federal Building, 10 Causeway Street, Boston, MA 02222; phone 1-617-565-6698 (24-hour *R*ecording) and 565-6990 (*P*ublic *I*nquiries)

Chicago Passport Agency, 380 Kluczynski Federal Building, 230 S. Dearborn Street, Chicago, IL 60604; phone 1-312-353-5426 *(R)* and 353-7155 or 353-7163 *(PI)*

Honolulu Passport Agency, C-106 New Federal Building, 300 Ala Moana Boulevard, Honolulu, HI 96850; phone 1-808-541-1919 *(R)* and 541-1918 *(PI)*

Houston Passport Agency, 1100 Mickey Leland Federal Building, 1919 Smith Street, Houston, TX 77002; phone 1-713-653-3159 *(R)* and 653-3153 *(PI)*

Los Angeles Passport Agency, Room 13100, 11000 Wilshire Boulevard, Los Angeles, CA 90024; phone 1-310-575-7070 *(R)* and 575-7075 *(PI)*

Miami Passport Agency, 3rd floor, Federal Office Building, 51 S.W. First Avenue, Miami, FL 33130; phone 1-305-536-5395 *(R)*, 536-4448 *(R*, Spanish), and 536-4681 *(PI)*

New Orleans Passport Agency, T-12005 Postal Services Building, 701 Loyola Avenue, New Orleans, LA 70013; phone 1-504-589-6725 and 589-6161 *(PI)*

New York Passport Agency, 270 Rockefeller Center, 630 Fifth Avenue, New York, NY 10111; phone 1-212-541-7700 *(R)* and 541-7710 *(PI)*

Philadelphia Passport Agency, 4426 Federal Building, 600 Arch Street, Philadelphia, PA 19106; phone 1-215-597-7482 *(R)* and 597-7480 *(PI)*

San Francisco Passport Agency, 200 Tishman Speyer Building, 525 Market Street, San Francisco, CA 94105; phone 1-415-744-4444 *(R)* and 744-4010 *(PI)*

Seattle Passport Agency, 992 Federal Office Building, 815 Second Avenue, Seattle, WA 98174; phone 1-206-553-7941 *(R)* and 553-7945 *(PI)*

Stamford Passport Agency, One Landmark Square, Broad and Atlantic Streets, Stamford, CT 06901; phone 1-203-325-4401 *(R)* and 325-3538 or 325-3530 *(PI)*

Washington Passport Agency, 1425 K Street, N.W., Washington, DC 20524; phone 1-202-647-0518 *(R)* and 326-6020 *(PI)*

Recordings include general passport information, location of the passport agency, hours of operation, and information regarding emergency passport services during nonworking hours.

PASSPORT, VISA, AND OTHER REQUIREMENTS

Here are the basic paperwork requirements of some of the places you might conceivably want to fish. If you plan to try your luck in such places as Afghanistan, Laos, Estonia, Pitcairn Island, Burkina Faso, or the Apostolic Nunciature of the Holy See, you're too adventurous to need help. Do your own research.

Most of the countries that admit U.S. citizens without a passport require a photo I.D. and proof of U.S. citizenship. Whatever documentation the foreign country you are traveling to requires (passport, visa, tourist card, nothing), Uncle Sam requires proof that you are a citizen or a legal resident before he'll let you back in the country. Carrying a passport is easier than any of the other acceptable documentary proofs. You're less likely to lose or misplace a passport while traveling abroad.

When combining business with pleasure on a fishing trip, a passport, visa, or other paperwork may be required for business travelers, no matter what is or isn't required of tourists.

A few countries require that your passport be valid at least six months beyond the planned end of your visit. If it is due to expire within that six-month period, you will have to renew your passport before you depart. Your travel or booking agent should advise you if this is the case, but it's always worth asking.

The time limitations noted in the following list ordinarily apply to visitors traveling without a visa or, where visas are required, on a tourist visa. If you plan to stay longer, you will need to check with the country's consulate or embassy to make special arrangements.

The documentary requirements that follow were in effect at the time this was written, but nations change their rules all the time, so be sure to check.

Antigua and Barbuda (No passport or visa required; onward/return ticket or proof of sufficient funds required; 6 months)

Argentina (Passport required; 3 months)

Australia (Passport, visa, and onward/return ticket required; 3 months)

Austria (Passport required; 3 months)

Azores [Portugal] (Passport required; 3 months, extendable)

Bahamas (No passport or visa required; onward/return ticket required; 8 months)

Barbados (No passport or visa required; onward/return ticket required; 3 months)

Belgium (Passport required; 90 days)

Belize (Passport, onward/return ticket, and proof of sufficient funds required; yellow fever vaccination may be required; 30 days, extendable)

Bermuda (No passport or visa required; onward/return ticket required; 21 days)

Bhutan (Passport and visa required; apply for visa 2 months before departure, visa issued at entry checkpoints; yellow fever vaccination may be required)

Botswana (Passport required; 90 days)

Brazil (Passport and visa required; yellow fever vaccination may be required; 90 days, extendable)

British Virgin Islands [Virgin Gorda, Tortola, Jost van Dyke, Anegarda] (No passport or visa required; onward/return ticket and proof of sufficient funds required; 3 months)

British West Indies [Anguilla, Montserrat, Cayman Islands, Turks and Caicos] (No passport or visa required; onward/return ticket required; 3 months)

Canada (No passport or visa required if you have no criminal record, including DWI; 180 days)

Canton Island (see Kiribati)

Cape Verde Islands (see Portugal; yellow fever vaccination may be required)

Chile (Passport required; 3 months, extendable)

China, People's Republic of (Passport, visa, and letter of invitation or hotel reservation *and* letter of confirmation from China International Travel Service required)

Christmas Island (see Kiribati)

Colombia (Passport and onward/return ticket required; entry permit issued at port of entry; 6 months)

Costa Rica (Passport and tourist card required; 90 days, extendable or with exit visa)

Côte d'Ivoire [Ivory Coast] (Passport required; 90 days)

Croatia (Passport and visa required; visa issued at port of entry)

Cuba (Passport, visa, and Treasury Department license required; many restrictions apply to U.S. citizens)

Denmark (Passport required; 3 months)*

Dominica (No passport or visa required; onward/return ticket required; 6 months)

Dominican Republic (No passport or visa required; tourist card from consulate or airline required; 2 months)

Ecuador (Passport and onward/return ticket required; 3 months)

England (see United Kingdom)

Finland (Passport required; 3 months)*

France (Passport required; 3 months)†

French Polynesia [Tahiti, Society Islands, Tuamotu, New Caledonia, French Southern and Antarctic Islands, Gambier, French Austral, Wallis, Kerguelen, Crozet, and Furtuna islands] (Passport required; HIV/AIDS test required for stay of more than 3 months; 1 month)†

French West Indies [Guadeloupe, Isles des Saintes, La Désirade, Marie Galante, Saint Barthelmy, St. Martin, Martinique] (No passport or visa required; 21 days)

Galápagos Islands (see Ecuador)

Germany (Passport required; 3 months)

Greenland [Denmark] (Passport required; 3 months)* [Special rules apply when entering U.S.-operated defense area.]

Guatemala (Passport and visa or tourist card required; 30 days)

Honduras (Passport and onward/return ticket required; 3 months)

Iceland (Passport required; 3 months)*

India (Passport and visa required; yellow fever vaccination may be required; 1-, 6-, and 12-month visas available)

Indonesia (Passport and onward/return ticket required; 2 months, *non*extendable)

Ireland (Passport required; onward/return ticket may be required; 90 days)

Ivory Coast [see Côte d'Ivoire]

Jamaica (Passport or U.S. birth certificate, onward/return ticket, and proof of sufficient funds required; tourist card issued on arrival, must be turned in on departure; 90 days)

Japan (Passport and onward/return ticket required; 6 months)

Kanton Island (see Kiribati)

Kenya (Passport and visa required; yellow fever vaccination and malaria suppressants strongly recommended; 6 months)

Kiribati (Passport and visa required)

Line Islands (see Kiribati)

Los Roques (see Venezuela)

Madeira (see Portugal)

Mexico (No passport or visa required; proof of sufficient funds required; 180 days with tourist card from consulate, tourism office, or airline, 90 days without)

Micronesia, Federated States of (No passport required; onward/return ticket and proof of sufficient funds required; typhoid and tetanus immunizations recommended; 6 months, extendable to 12 months; health certificate may be required.)

Mongolia (Passport, visa, and confirmation from Zhuulchin, the Mongolian Travel Agency, required; 90 days)

Nepal (Passport and visa required; 30 days, extendable to 3 months)

Netherlands Antilles [Aruba, Bonaire, Curaçao, Saba, Statia, St. Maarten] (No passport or visa required; onward/return ticket and proof of sufficient funds required; 14 days, extendable to 90 days)

New Zealand (Passport, onward/return ticket, and proof of sufficient funds required; if not returning to the States, visa for next destination required; 3 months)

Northern Ireland (see United Kingdom)

Norway (Passport required; 3 months)*

Palau (No passport or visa required; onward/return ticket required; 30 days, extendable)

Panama (Passport, tourist card issued by airline, and onward/return ticket required; 90 days on visa, 30 days on airline tourist card)

Papua New Guinea (Passport, onward/return ticket, and proof of sufficient funds required; 30 days)

Paraguay (Passport required; 90 days, extendable)

Peru (Passport and onward/return ticket required; 90 days, extendable)

Portugal (Passport required; 60 days, extendable)

Russia (Passport, visa, and currency declaration required)

Scotland (see United Kingdom)

Sierra Leone (Passport, visa, currency declaration, exchange of at least $100 at port of entry, and proof of sufficient funds required; cholera and yellow fever immunizations are required, malaria suppressants recommended; 3 months)

Slovenia (Passport required; 90 days)

South Africa (Passport required; 90 days)

Spain (Passport required; 6 months)

Suriname (Passport and visa required; purchase of 500 Suriname guilders—about $275 to $300—at port of entry may be required)

Sweden (Passport required; 3 months)*

Switzerland (Passport required; 3 months)

United Kingdom [England, Scotland, Wales, Northern Ireland, etc.] (Passport required; 6 months)

Uruguay (Passport required; 3 months)

Venezuela (Passport, tourist card issued by airline, and proof of sufficient funds required; 60 days, *non*extendable; a 1-year, multiple-entry visa requires proof of sufficient funds, onward/return ticket, and certification of employment)

Wales (see United Kingdom)

Western Samoa (Passport and onward/return ticket required; 30 days)

Zambia (Passport and visa required; yellow fever and cholera immunizations strongly recommended; 6 months)

Zimbabwe (Passport, firm itinerary, return ticket to U.S., currency declaration, and proof of sufficient funds required)

NOTE: A growing number of countries require an HIV/AIDS test for stays of three months or longer, or for students.

*Time limitation on stay begins when entering Scandinavian area: Greenland, Iceland, Norway, Sweden, Denmark, Finland.

†Journalists on assignment, students, ship or plane crew members, and diplomats or other officials must obtain a visa.

Resources

GOVERNMENT TRAVEL PUBLICATIONS*

Uncle Sam publishes a veritable library of booklets that are very useful for planning trips abroad. Some of these are available free at the passport agencies, or they can be obtained (unless otherwise noted) for about a buck apiece from the U.S. Government Printing Office, Washington, DC 20402 (phone 1-202-783-3238) or the Consumer Information Center, Pueblo, CO 81009 (fax 1-719-948-9724). Call ahead for availability, current prices, and ordering information.

Your Trip Abroad $1.25
Foreign Consular Offices in the United States (GPO only) $4.75
Foreign Entry Requirements [for countries that require visas, tourist
    cards, or other documents; updated annually]   50 cents
Tips for Travelers to . . .
    the Caribbean
    Mexico
    Central and South America
    Eastern Europe
    Russia (and the Former Soviet Union)
    the Middle East and North Africa $1.25
    Sub-Saharan Africa
    The People's Republic of China
    South Asia
Background Notes on [170-some different countries]
Passports & Customs [general info]   50 cents from CIC
Customs Tips for Travelers   50 cents
Know Before You Go, Customs Hints for Returning Residents (Free
    from any local customs office or from U.S. Customs Service,
    P.O. Box 7407, Washington, DC 20044)
*Travelers Tips on Bringing Food, Plant, and Animal Products Into
    the United States* (Free from Public Affairs Office, Animal and
    Plant Health Inspection Service, U.S. Department of Agriculture, 4700 River Road, 4th floor, Riverdale MD 20737)
Buyer Beware! (Free guidelines governing restrictions on imports of
    wildlife and wildlife products—including flies!—from Publica-

tions Unit, U.S. Fish and Wildlife Service, Department of the Interior, Washington, DC 20240. *Additional information on importing wildlife products is available from TRAFFIC USA, World Wildlife Fund, 1250 24th Street, N.W., Washington, DC 20037; phone 1-202-293-4800.*)

*Many of these publications are stocked by U.S. Government Bookstores in Atlanta, Birmingham, Boston, Chicago, Cleveland, Columbus (OH), Dallas, Denver, Detroit, Houston, Jacksonville, Kansas City (MO), Laurel (MD), Los Angeles, Milwaukee, New York, Philadelphia, Pittsburgh, Portland (OR), Pueblo (CO), San Francisco, Seattle, and Washington, D.C. Check your phone directory or call directory assistance for the number.

A VIEW FROM
THE BRIDGE

Do you want to try another spot like this?" Erik asked. "Or would you rather try a spot where the fishing will be more difficult, but there will be a lot of salmon to see?"

"Let's go look at salmon," I said. I was tired of blind casting, however promising the water looked.

Erik Erlandsson, a schoolteacher from nearby Bräkne-Hoby, was my guide-for-a-day on the Mörrum, Sweden's best-known salmon river, renowned for the size of its salmon. We had been fishing Beat 32 at Rosendala ("Valley of the Roses"), the uppermost beat on the *Mörrumso Kronolaxfiske-vatten*, the public salmon water on the river. We hadn't risen a salmon, but we'd seen one. I had been wading deep—almost to the top of my chest waders—in the pool right at the top of the beat. A salmon the size of a potentially dangerous shark had porpoised nearby, sending a rush of adrenaline through my veins and my back cast into a tree. I was chagrined at having blown such a good chance. Erik tried to console me by saying it didn't make much difference, salmon on the move seldom take. What a nice lie, I thought.

The Mörrum is a tough river to fish, Erik explained as we walked back toward the footbridge. There are a lot of fish, including some really big ones, but mortality at sea is high, thanks mainly to commercial fishing. Statistics show that only 1 percent of the smolts released from the Mörrum's hatchery return to spawn. (The return rate is much better for sea trout: about 20 percent.) And the river gets beaten pretty hard by anglers—spin-fishermen as well as fly-casters. In June you have a decent shot at big fresh salmon (twenty-four to fifty-five pounds), but they don't take flies as well as the much more numerous, smaller salmon that enter from mid-June through September. Besides, I had only this one morning to fish. I had a noon appointment with Gunnar Eklund, the hatchery manager and head of *Mörrums Fiskeriförvaltning*, the Mörrum fishery administration.

Erik decided we should fish Beat 4, a few clicks downstream of the hatchery. On the drive, he told me a bit about this river that he fishes about 150 days a year.

Salmon begin entering the Mörrum in mid-May, but the fastest fishing is provided by eager grilse which begin arriving in mid-July. May–June salmon average twenty-two to twenty-five pounds, June–July fish are mostly around twelve pounds, and the grilse (July through September) average five. The larger salmon are very difficult to take in the summer. Fishing throughout the day is good in May, but early mornings and late evenings are better in June and July.

Floating lines and relatively small flies (sizes 4 to 10) are favored by summertime Mörrum fly-fishers. You mustn't mend the line on the water, Erik said, or you will put the fish down. To attract a salmon's attention, you must use a variety of casts and placements and work the fly with the line. A nine-foot, 8-weight rod is good for grilse, but if you tie into one of the big fish, Erik said with a grin, you'll wish you were fishing a big 9- or 10-weight rod.

Because of its deceptively strong flow, the Mörrum can be a tough river to wade. As I had already discovered, it takes a lot of concentration to keep from being swept off your feet. Stout wading staffs (not the light, flimsy sticks favored by Americans, Erik pointed out) are recommended even in August when the wading is easiest.

A lot of Swedes like to fish the river in April for big (eight- to sixteen-pound) sea trout. A few fresh trout enter that early, but most of the fishing is for holdovers. The main run of sea trout begins in mid-July, and fishing is fastest in September.

Sea-run brown trout begin entering the river in early spring, but the run really picks up steam in August and September. August fish will average about ten to eleven pounds, with the largest fish running to twenty-four to twenty-seven pounds. Sea trout are so much spookier than salmon that most of the fishing is done in the "evening," beginning no earlier than 10 PM. "If you can see the trout, you are too early," Erik said. "Sit down, away from the stream, and wait until it is dark. Trout begin moving when darkness sets in, and that is when they are most likely to take a fly. Cast to feeding lies and moving fish, and make each cast count because you won't get many. This isn't salmon fishing, so don't thrash a pool with repeated casts."

Beat 4 was entirely different in character from the narrow, forested stream at Rosendala: open and sunny, the river wide and sinuous in its course. And crowded. Whereas we had Beat 32 all to ourselves, we were sharing this beat with maybe six or eight other anglers. Erik pointed at some rocks that weren't being fished. "There are several good lies," he said. "Go ahead and fish them."

"Why don't you show me how?" I countered, still mindful of having screwed up earlier.

"You cast and I'll tell you what to do."

Let me confess that I had little faith in the proceedings, either in my skills or in the willingness of the Mörrum to give up fish in late June, under these conditions. But Erik was a good and patient teacher, retrieving without comment the back casts I dropped on the high embankment, telling me where to cast the fly and how to swim it past the lie. After several good swims produced nothing, Erik suggested I change flies.

"Anything different," he suggested. "Try a different size, color, or shape. Sometimes you have to cast a lot of different things at them before they wake up."

So I went from a Silver Doctor to a basically yellow fly I'd picked up at a local shop. Still nothing, even though the lies looked really fishy and, as Erik had promised, there was plenty of evidence of salmon in the beat. From time to time a salmon would show itself out where the river widened in a slow bend. Sometimes they porpoised, sometimes they free-jumped. Although smaller than the fish that had spooked me earlier that morning, these were nice fish. Fifteen, twenty pounds, maybe more.

"We'd better go," Erik said, pointing out that we were due at Gunnar Eklund's office in fifteen minutes. "But first I want to show you something," he said.

Erik led the way downstream and up the embankment to the railroad bridge that crossed the Mörrum at the bottom of the beat.

"Look," he said, pointing at the three rocks I'd been fishing without event. Each rock held three big salmon. Two of them sheltered one or two smaller salmon as well, probably early-arriving grilse. In each case, the largest salmon lay upstream of the rock, finning slowly, almost imperceptibly, in the brown-stained water. The smallest fish were always downstream of the rocks, in their lee.

"Well, that pretty much proves it," I said. "I'm no salmon fisherman."

"No one else is catching anything either," Erik said, without going so far as to contradict my statement. "I think they just aren't in a taking mood today."

On the short drive to the hatchery office, I asked Erik if it would make sense to have two or three anglers casting shoulder to shoulder and swinging different flies, one after the other, past a fish. "It's not a bad idea," he said. "It's hard to tell what it takes to wake up a resting salmon."

Later that day, after lunch in the *Domänverket* (Swedish Forest Service) cafeteria and a tour of the hatchery, an alfresco afternoon tea on the Eklunds' patio overlooking the river, we watched a young Swedish angler weigh in a fish: a bright, 6.8-kilogram (fourteen-pound) hen, taken on a Toby spoon at the rocks just upstream of the railroad bridge at Beat 4. Less than half an hour after we'd quit fishing those same lies, I pointed out. "She probably wouldn't have taken a fly anyway," Erik said, sensing my self-doubt and disappointment.

For most of us anyway, Atlantic salmon fishing involves a lot of blind casting to likely looking lies and blind faith that the next cast will be the one that does the trick. Whenever I find my back beginning to ache, my toes and fingers numbing in the cold, my faith beginning to ebb, I think of that view from the bridge over the Mörrum, with fish holding on every rock, oblivious to the flies being cast their way and to all the rest of the world's vain strivings. I fish then with renewed vigor and hope, imagining the slow, almost imperceptible tail movements of the fish I'm casting to, now and then a pectoral fin trimming its hydrostatic equilibrium. If I concentrate hard enough, I can almost see the sluggish side-to-side movement of its head, a sign that it has become aware of my fly, signaling that it will take the next good cast. Or perhaps the one after that. No matter. I'm ready.

7

SAFETY FIRST

Fly-fishing trips far afield are fraught with potential for trouble: foreigners traveling in a strange land without command of the language; bush planes, helicopters, and high-speed boats; fast currents and slippery rocks; high hills and deep water; sharp, barbed hooks flying back and forth through the air; fish with spines and sharp teeth; extremes of heat and cold; blazing sun and raging storms; strange food and too much drink; importunities and temptations around every corner.

Still, while minor injuries and maladies are commonplace on fishing trips, I've never been on a trip where someone was seriously injured.

Fishing five or more long, long days in a remote environment can be extremely strenuous, so have a thorough medical checkup about six weeks in advance of your departure. Visit your dentist too. If you need any dental work or conditioning exercises, start on them right away. Have the doctor prescribe the medications you might need on the trip. Ask for a second set of prescriptions using the chemical names of the drugs, in case you have to fill them abroad. The U.S. trade names may be unknown or, worse, misleading. Also, ask your doctor for a To-whom-it-may-concern letter describing your medical condition, any treatments you are receiving, and the medications you are taking—including the just-in-case medicines you are carrying.

If vaccines or inoculations are required or recommended, get them. There's a difference between the two. Required vaccines (usually yellow fever, sometimes cholera) are mandated to protect the host country. The booking or travel agent will know about the inoculation requirements. Recommended vaccines are suggested by the Centers for Disease Control and Prevention to protect the traveler. You may have to discover these on your own by calling the CDC Hot Line at 1-404-639-2572.

The better shape you are in, the less likely you are to suffer either injury or illness while traveling. If you're ordinarily as sedentary and slothful as I am, get your doctor's advice before you embark on a strenuous exercise program to make up in weeks for years of cardiovascular and myogenic neglect.

Shots in the Arm

Few immunizations are required for world travelers these days, but many are recommended. After calling the CDC's Traveler's Hotline to check on current health problems in the area you'll be visiting, consult with your doctor on the advisability of getting the recommended shots.

Let's say you plan to fish in Mexico. Unless you will be arriving from a part of the world known to be infected with yellow fever, no vaccinations are required by the Mexican government for entrance to their country. However, U.S. health authorities *recommend* immunization against diphtheria, tetanus, polio, typhoid, and hepatitis A. (You'll find these immunizations are recommended throughout much of the world.) You probably have the first three. *Important:* No matter where you will be traveling, be sure your tetanus booster is current. Puncture wounds are common in fishing.

Also, malarial outbreaks are common in rural Mexico, particularly on the southwestern coast. Mosquito repellent is all you need to protect yourself against malaria in big cities and the major resort areas on both coasts. But in remote fishing camps? Discuss with your doctor the advisability of taking chloroquine, which you should begin two weeks before you arrive in Mexico and continue for four weeks after you depart.

In other areas of Latin America, except Chile and Uruguay, chloroquine is *strongly recommended*, though nowhere required. And to this list of recommended immunizations add rabies and yellow fever.

When traveling to other parts of the world, immunization against Japanese B encephalitis, meningitis, typhus, and perhaps some other diseases may be recommended. Only you and your doctor can decide what is best for you.

Travel Insurance

Before leaving the country, check with your insurance carrier to see whether you are covered outside the country, and to what extent. Even if you are covered, your policy may not pay for air evacuation if you are seriously injured or fall critically ill in a place where medical standards aren't very high.

If you aren't covered, consider buying a travel insurance policy (not the common-carrier, death-and-dismemberment policy offered by credit card companies). Most travel and booking agents can sell you a trip insurance policy, but you might save some money or get more favorable terms by shopping around. Typically, the policies cost a couple of hundred bucks and last two to three weeks. Find out whether the policy covers preexisting conditions; many don't. Also, find out whether it covers air evacuation; not all do.

Air evacuation sounds like some sort of dramatic M*A*S*H operation, but it's simply being transported by air to a place where you can receive the medical care you need. Even if a country or region has hospitals and clinics, you might not want to use them except in a life-or-death emergency. Even in countries as relatively advanced as Russia, where the medical staffs are generally well trained, the facilities can be dreadful. And I don't mean just big, expensive things like magnetic resonance imaging machinery; I mean things like new, unused hypodermic needles.

▶ If you book a salmon trip to Russia's Kola Peninsula, be sure the insurance you buy will pay for air evac to Finland. Some won't, because of hospital availability in Murmansk.

Major medical and hospitalization insurance isn't all you need be concerned with.

▶ If you are driving into Canada or Mexico, find out whether your auto coverage goes with you and whether the terms of the policy remain unchanged. (See the discussion in Chapter 6.)
▶ Some credit cards automatically provide accidental-death-and-dismemberment coverage (on airlines and other common carriers) or auto insurance (on rentals). Check it out with your credit card company. If you are traveling with a family member, you might have to charge the tickets separately to get accident insurance for each of you.

Insect Repellents

When fishing in the tropics, you need bug dope to protect you from malaria, yellow fever, and God only knows what else. Around salt

---

☞ TRAVELER'S TIP

Bring plenty of mosquito repellent—ideally, something with maximum DEET content. Muskol in the small, light-green bottle has a very high DEET content and is quite popular up here. However, a word of caution: DEET dissolves many types of plastic and mylars. I had a bottle break open in my lens bag and eat away a Swiss Army knife handle, two filter covers, and part of a lens housing, then eat through the camera bag and take the finish off my antique dining table. A disaster! Make sure your hands are completely cleaned of the stuff if you have to touch videotape or any plastic materials like filters, fly lines, leaders, etc. Last summer I spent about 100 days shooting throughout the Alaska bush, and I only put on repellent twice. The rest of the time I kept a cheap cigar burning in my hat band or on the ground near my feet. It works great on insects but also seems to be an effective wife repellent.

—David Hill
senior producer, Alaska Video Post Cards
Anchorage, Alaska

water, you need it to fend off bottle flies and *Aedes* salt marsh mosquitoes, both of which have very painful bites that are easily infected and to which a lot of people are allergic. In the Far North, you need the stuff to preserve your mental health, the mosquitoes, black flies, and no-see-ums are so thick in summertime.

▶ DEET is the most effective insect repellent available, but it's stinky and greasy (not exactly attractive to fish when you handle your flies); destructive of fly-line coatings, leaders, and other plastics; and potentially harmful to your health. Health authorities recommend that you stick to repellents that contain only about 15 percent DEET. Guides are more likely to recommend 100 percent DEET. It's your decision to make.

▶ Some people swear by Avon Skin-So-Soft Bath Oil as a mosquito repellent, but it doesn't work on everyone. I'm one of the unfortunates on whom it doesn't. It's actually beneficial to the skin, but it will damage clear styrene plastics, so don't get it on your leader-material spools, just in case.

▶ Citronella is an old standby, which won't harm fly lines or leaders and apparently doesn't repel fish either. But I think it's only marginally effective at best.

▶ If the bugs are really thick, consider wearing a head net. They bother me so much when I'm fishing I will resort to one only in desperation, but I always carry one in my vest. Some people carry larger nets to protect their faces while they sleep. Not a bad idea. Otherwise you have to resort to burning mosquito coils—very effective, but smelly and noxious.

▶ The Shoo-Bug jacket is a soft, open-weave jacket impregnated with a DEET-based repellent. It's really quite effective. It keeps the DEET off your skin, but you still have to be careful you don't get it on your fly line, leader, or fly.

Sun Screen

Don't go anywhere without it. In summer, the sun is almost as intense at high latitudes as it is in the tropics. At high altitudes, the atmosphere is so thin you can get a tropical-grade suntan even in the mid latitudes where most trout fishing is done. You're not trying to get a tan, so wear SPF 15 or higher. In the tropics, I'll go as high in the SPFs as I can find. I've read in numerous authoritative places that SPF numbers higher than 15 don't really afford more protection, but I feel better when I'm out on the flats wearing SPF 39 sun screen.

▶ Always wear a waterproof sunscreen; they last longer. Every so often, give yourself another coat. And don't forget your ears, the back of your neck, your calves and ankles, and your feet (if you're wearing sandals).
▶ Many sunscreens use PABA—amazingly effective stuff, but it does tend to stain clothing, and some people can't tolerate the stuff on the skin. If you are one of the latter, ask your doctor or pharmacist to recommend an alternative.
▶ Some sunscreens need to be applied at least thirty minutes prior to solar exposure. Others, such as PreSun, are used only to prep the skin to use most efficiently the sunscreen that is later applied.
▶ Just in case you miss a patch of skin and get burned, carry aloe gel or lotion. It really helps heal sun-damaged skin. It also helps cuts and other wounds to heal.

The Traveling Fly-Fisher's First-Aid Kit

Augmented, of course, by the prescription medicines and other supplies you ordinarily require, consider building a little first-aid kit from the following items.

▶ Toilet paper—a hygienic rather than a first-aid item; flattened, partially used roll carried in a zip-locked plastic sandwich bag
▶ Adhesive bandages in several sizes—for minor cuts (preferably waterproof)
▶ Larger gauze pads (2 by 2 or 4 by 4), with or without adhesive—for larger wounds
▶ Adhesive tape (preferably waterproof)
▶ Elastic bandage for strains and sprains
▶ Antiseptic for cuts: tincture of iodine, povidone-iodine ointment, or an antibiotic ointment

▶ Neocortisone or other antipruritic (anti-itch) ointment
▶ Ear plugs—to protect your ears against airplane, helicopter, out-board-motor, and other potentially damaging loud noises
▶ Eye drops
▶ Saline nasal spray
▶ Topical anesthetic for toothaches
▶ Cement, caps, or temporary fillings to patch chipped or broken teeth
▶ Antacid tablets
▶ Tables, capsules, transderm patch, or pressure band for motion-sickness (if needed) [25 mg antihistamine motion-sickness medication (e.g., Dramamine, Marezine, Bonine) plus 60 mg pseudoephedrine (e.g., Sudafed) is an especially effective nonprescription dosage]
▶ Water-purification tablets
▶ Lomotil or similar medication for diarrhea
▶ Antibacterial and antifungal ointment for skin
▶ Diphenhydramine HCL or similar capsules, or a topical antihistamine ointment or lotion (for bug bites, plant allergies, etc.)
▶ Throat lozenges or cough drops
▶ Nasal decongestant capsules, spray, or drops
▶ Analgesic tablets, caplets, or capsules (aspirin, acetaminophen, ibuprofen, or naproxen sodium)
▶ Ointment for aching muscles and joints
▶ Moisturizing lotion for skin
▶ Zinc oxide (in tropics, especially) to protect nose and ears from sunburn
▶ Aloe gel or lotion for sunburned skin
▶ Talc
▶ Antifungal powder or lotion
▶ Tweezers
▶ Braces/bands for back, elbow, knee, or ankle
▶ Foot-care supplies for corns, bunions, blisters, and the like

Pack them in as small a container as will hold them. A plastic tackle box about the size of a large fly box will hold a lot; a large Band-Aid tin will suffice for the spartans in the crowd.

You surely won't need *all* the items listed, particularly not if the camp or lodge where you will be fishing has an adequate, facility-size medical or first-aid kit. Better to be thought of as a hypochondriac than buried as a reckless adventurer.

Be sure you aren't allergic to any of the medications listed, and that your doctor approves.

Lifesavers

A few things that ought to be in your fly-fishing kit have nothing to do with catching fish but a lot to do with keeping you healthy and safe. Felt soles, sunglasses, and a hat to protect yourself from the sun are first and foremost among them. (Okay, okay, all three can also help in the catching of fish by enabling you to spot them underwater and wade to within casting range.) Among the lifesaving things you might wish to consider carrying in your vest or somewhere else on your person:

▶ Wading staff—for wading deep or in fast water (whether aluminum folding staffs are too weak and flimsy is a subject of some debate)
▶ PFD—in really treacherous water, an inflatable or buoyant vest or inflatable SOSpenders
▶ Wader belt—to keep water from filling your waders if you get in deep (elastic belts with quick-release buckles are best)
▶ Compass
▶ Map (unfortunately, not all camps and lodges have maps for clients)
▶ Matches—embedded in wax to keep them dry
▶ Signaling mirror
▶ Pocket or other knife
▶ Side-cutting pliers—for cutting through hooks
▶ Space Blanket—emergency warmth and shelter for cold climates
▶ Drinking water

"Water, Water, Everywhere, Nor Any Drop to Drink"

Not all the water that sustains fish is fit for human consumption. Giardiasis is the scourge of wilderness travel these days. Some call it "beaver fever," but it's human wastes, not beaver droppings, that cause the problem.

☞ **TRAVELER'S TIP**

Several years ago I was fishing offshore of Costa Rica when the boat went dead. It happened around noon and we were adrift until we were picked up around eight o'clock the next morning. Naturally, the boat had no running lights, and we were in an area that was being worked by big Korean trawlers. All night long I kept tearing pages out of my bird book and burning them, so the trawlers might see us.

Now I always carry a little, battery-powered strobe light with me when I go on fishing trips. It's powered by flashlight batteries and isn't any bigger than a small flashlight, so it packs easily in my fishing baggage.

—Don Moser
editor, *Smithsonian Magazine*
Washington, D.C.

Most camps and lodges have filtration equipment or use tested well or spring water, but if you are a worrier or a member of a high-risk group (with chronic, systemic, or immune-system ailments or simply prone to gastric and intestinal upset), don't drink the local water. And that includes ice cubes. In areas known to have contaminated water, it also means avoiding salads and raw vegetables that might have been washed in the water. Buy bottled water, stick to juices and sodas, or use water-purification tablets.

Outdoor equipment catalogs list a lot of filters that supposedly protect the wilderness traveler from *Giardia* and other pathogens, but few of them are worth carrying. The ones that are reliable (e.g., the Katadyn PF) are relatively large and expensive, and the smaller, cheaper others are about as effective as the filters on cigarettes.

▶ Another note for fishermen traveling to Russia: Except in St. Petersburg, industrially polluted areas, and certain areas in southern Siberia, so far the water has proven to be about as good as you might find it anywhere these days. If you are stopping over in St. Petersburg, don't drink the *Giardia*-contaminated water. Don't even use it to brush your teeth. If you run out of bottled water, use vodka.

Almost anywhere, a change in diet and drinking water can cause diarrhea. You can try to control the condition with over-the-counter medications, but be aware that their value and effectiveness are the subject of some debate in the medical community. In any event, the greatest danger from diarrhea is from dehydration. You must rehydrate your body and restore the balance of your electrolytes or you'll be susceptible to other ailments as well as weakened. Drink *a lot* of fluids: GatorAde, canned or bottled fruit juices, sweetened tea made from water that has been boiled at least ten minutes, or this restorative potion:

▶ A 50–50 mixture of fruit juice and tea or boiled water, with as much salt as it will dissolve or you can stand

Should you cut yourself while fishing, let the wound bleed awhile, to carry off any bacteria that might have entered when the skin was broken. Stopping the bleeding too soon promotes infection. Before bandaging it, treat the skin around the wound with antiseptic; if you don't have your first-aid kit handy, at least wash the surface. If you have reason to suspect the water, don't stick an open wound in it. Nor should you put the cut in your mouth. Mouths harbor an enormous variety of bacteria and microbes and are the source of many an infected wound. Unless you have a bladder or urinary-tract infection, in a pinch you can use your own urine as a handy sterile rinsing agent.

Finally, whenever you are fishing away from the camp or lodge, carry drinking water in a canteen, flask, or plastic bottle. Drinking enough fluids will help your strength and stamina, guard against dehydration and heat stroke, and make you feel more comfortable. Around salt water it's even more important to carry plenty of fresh water to drink, especially if you will be fishing from a boat. Boats break down, and rescue isn't always immediately at hand. Don't go out on the ocean in a boat that isn't carrying plenty of drinkable fresh water. Some fools I know think that beer will see them through a crisis. Digesting the nutrients in beer takes more water than the beer contains, so drinking beer actually will hasten your dehydration.

Crime

From time to time you hear of some traveling angler being robbed, mugged, or otherwise being victimized by criminals abroad. Well, it certainly happens, but in so many of the cases I know about, it's almost as if the angler volunteered for the role, his behavior was so reckless. Big cities all over the world are riddled with crime, and criminal predators look for easy prey. It's difficult to imagine easier prey than a traveler who doesn't know the city, the language, the culture, the street savvy. Airports, hotels, and tourist traps are like coral reefs in a tropical sea, where both prey and predators congregate.

It's really pretty easy to stay out of trouble while traveling. Whether you are passing through New York, Miami, Moscow, or Caracas, the rules are the same.

- ▶ Don't flash a lot of money around. Prefer credit cards and traveler's checks to cash, and be careful with them. Countersign traveler's checks only in front of the person who's cashing them.
- ▶ Leave the Rolex home. Travel with a good, dependable, cheap watch. Flashy jewelry, expensive clothing, and ostentatious displays of wealth are criminal magnets.
- ▶ Don't behave like a fish out of water: wearing clothing that brands you as a tourist, gawking while you walk, calling attention to yourself. Dress sensibly, speak quietly, and walk as if you had a purpose. Even when you are lost, act as if you know what you are doing, and ask directions only of cops and others in authority.
- ▶ Luggage tags, labels, decals, clothing, behavior, or anything else that identifies you as an American may mark you as an attractive target.
- ▶ Drink moderately. Heavy drinking impairs your judgment and draws criminals the way blood in the water draws sharks.
- ▶ Never go anywhere with a stranger, no matter how friendly he or she seems, or how wonderful the offer. Never discuss your travel plans with a stranger or newfound bosom pal.
- ▶ Whenever you are jostled, asked for directions or time or a light, told that something is spilled on your clothing, or surrounded by a group of vagrant children, think *pickpocket* and make sure your money is secure.
- ▶ Know how to use a pay phone, and have the proper coins or tokens on hand.
- ▶ Don't use "unofficial" taxis. Use the licensed, clearly marked cabs, even if they are hard to find in some cities.

▶ Don't take shortcuts, narrow alleys, or dark streets. Stick to open, well-lighted places.

▶ Don't get in an elevator alone with someone who looks even vaguely suspicious.

▶ Don't leave cash, traveler's checks, credit cards, jewelry, or other valuables in your hotel room. Use the hotel safe.

▶ Use common sense. A cowboy bar in one of our Western ranching or mining towns could be a dangerous place for an effete city slicker who wore funny clothes and spoke only a few heavily accented words of English. At home, you know better than to wander into a bar that has a whole bunch of Harley hogs parked outside. Use the same sort of discretion overseas. Know the difference between exotic local color and a local hangout for hometown hoods.

▶ Hide a $20 bill in one sock and the same amount in local currency in the other. At least you'll be able to get back to the hotel if you are robbed.

Airports, bus terminals, and railway stations are especially attractive to pickpockets and thieves. In recent years, all over the world, these scenes have become all too commonplace:

▶ You are standing in line, waiting to board a plane or pass through security. A row or some other commotion nearby attracts your attention. The disturbance settles down, the carry-on bag you had placed on the floor has disappeared. *Moral:* Never look away from a piece of luggage that has been placed on the floor. If it's really too heavy to hold, keep your hand on or a leg through the shoulder strap.

▶ You ask another departing passenger—perhaps even a well-dressed one, or a woman with a small child—to watch your carry-on luggage for a moment while you get a drink of water or whatever. You return to your seat in the waiting area to find luggage and "passenger" gone. *Moral:* Never place anything you don't want to lose in the custody of a stranger.

Some people wear money belts, but thieves look for them on tourists. It's better to wear a neck or "shoulder-holster" money pouch, either of which may be overlooked by a holdup man. Eastern Mountain Sports suggests sewing a steel guitar string into the neck strap of the money pouch; "it will foil the plans of any thief who tries to cut the strap." I don't know. I'm not sure I want to frustrate someone who's wielding a knife in the vicinity of my throat.

Except for occasional instances of petty theft, crime is almost unknown in fishing camps and lodges. Usually when theft does occur, it's because anglers have left money or other valuables lying about. Hide your stash, and check it daily. If anything turns up missing, report it immediately to the camp manager. But search high and low for it first. Make sure it's really missing. Much more often than theft, things disappear because their owners have misplaced them.

Resources

CATALOGS

In addition to the catalogs listed in Chapters 4 and 5, many of which carry first-aid kits and other health-maintenance products, the following mail-order suppliers carry products and services to help keep traveling fishermen healthy and safe.

Northwest River Supplies, Inc., 2009 S. Main Street, Moscow, ID 83843; phone 1-800-635-5202, 1-208-882-2383; fax 1-208-883-4787 (*Water purifiers*)

REI, Recreational Equipment, Inc., 1700 45th Street East, Sumner, WA 98352; phone 1-800-426-4840, 1-800-828-5533, 1-206-891-2500; fax 1-206-891-2523 (*Water purifiers and filters, compasses, first-aid kits, etc.*)

Travel Medicine, Inc., 351 Pleasant Street, Suite 312, Northampton, MA 01060, tel. 1-800-872-8633, fax 1-413-584-6656. Mail-order service of Stuart R. Rose, M.D. (*First-aid and dental emergency kits, water filters and purifiers, repellents, bug nets and screens, short-wave radios, books, newsletters, travel insurance*)

GOVERNMENT PUBLICATIONS

Unless otherwise indicated, the following publications are available from the Government Printing Office, Washington, DC 20402-9328, phone 1-202-783-3238, for $1.00:

A Safe Trip Abroad
Travel Tips for Older Americans
Travel Warning on Drugs Abroad
Health Information for International Travel [immunization require-
 ments and recommendations, health precautions, risks in par-
 ticular countries] $6

TRAVEL WARNINGS AND CONSULAR INFORMATION SHEETS

The U.S. Department of State publishes Consular Information Sheets
on every country in the world. The sheets describe unusual entry or
currency regulations, health conditions worth noting, the situation
vis-à-vis crime and security, political unrest and areas of instability,
and drug penalties. They also list addresses and emergency telephone
numbers for U.S. embassies and consulates. From the conditions
described, travelers can make up their own minds. If a situation is
considered truly dangerous, a Travel Warning will accompany the
Consular Information Sheet. In these cases, travelers are advised to
defer travel to a country.

The Consular Information Sheets and Travel Warnings are available free at, by, or through:

▶ All thirteen regional passport agencies (addresses in Chapter 6)
▶ U.S. embassies and consulates abroad
▶ Airline reservations systems (when the reservation is made)
▶ Mail: Self-addressed, stamped envelope to Overseas Citizens Ser-
 vices, Room 4811, Department of State, Washington, DC 20520-
 4818
▶ 24-hour recordings: Dial 1-202-647-5225 on a touchtone telephone
▶ Fax: Dial 1-202-647-3000 from a fax machine's telephone handset
 and follow the prompts you will hear through the receiver
▶ Modem (settings N-8-1): Consular Affairs Bulletin Board (CABB),
 1-202-647-9225
▶ Internet: telnet fedworld.gov (path: D, GateWay system on main
 menu; D, Connect to Gov't sys/database on GateWay menu; 82,
 CABB)
▶ World Wide Web: www.fedworld.gov (same path as for Internet)

HEALTH INFORMATION FOR TRAVELERS

Diabetes Travel Services, Inc., 39 E. 52nd Street, New York, NY 10022, worldwide information on diabetic treatments and physicians

The **International Association for Medical Assistance to Travelers,** 736 Center Street, Lewiston, NY 14092; phone 1-716-754-4883, free medical directory, clinical record, and malaria risk chart from a voluntary organization of hospitals, health centers, and more than 3,000 English-speaking, Western-trained doctors in more than 140 countries

International Travelers Hotline, Centers for Disease Control and Prevention, phone 1-404-332-4559

International Travel Health Guide by Stuart R. Rose, M.D. Annually updated guide to health risks, diseases, other medical problems, services, gadgets, etc., 450 pp., $17.95 + $5.95 S/H from Travel Medicine, Inc., 351 Pleasant Street, Suite 312, Northampton, MA 01060, phone 1-800-872-8633, fax 1-413-584-6656

The Safe Travel Book by Peter Savage, 192 pp. $14.95, in bookstores

Travel Health Clinics, a list of more than 100 clinics staffed by specialists in travel medicine, is available by sending a self-addressed, 8½-by-11 envelope stamped with $1.01 postage to Leonard Marcus, M.D., Traveler's Health and Immunization Services, 148 Highland Avenue, Newton, MA 02165

Traveling Healthy & Comfortably, bimonthly newsletter edited by Karl Neumann, M.D., $29.95 a year [Available from Travel Medicine, Inc.]

Trip Reports, custom-prepared from information updated daily by the World Health Organization and the Centers for Disease Control and Prevention, $10 for the first country, $5 each for additional countries, Immunization Alert, 93 Timber Drive, Storrs, CT 06268, phone 1-800-584-1999

TRAVEL INSURANCE COMPANIES LISTED ON THE CONSULAR AFFAIRS BULLETIN BOARD

Access America, Inc., P.O. Box 90310, Richmond, VA 23230; phone 1-800-284-8300

Air-Evac International, 8665 Gibbs Drive, Suite 202, San Diego, CA 92123; phone 1-800-854-2569

Gateway, Seabury & Smith, 1255 23rd Street N.W., Washington, DC 20037; phone 1-800-282-4495 and 1-202-457-7707

Healthcare Abroad, 243 Church Street N.W., Vienna, VA 22180; phone 1-800-237-6615 and 1-703-281-9500

International SOS Assistance, 1 Neshaminy Interplex, Suite 310, Trevose, PA 19047; phone 1-800-523-8930 and 1-215-244-1500

Near, Inc., 450 Prairie Avenue, Suite 101, Calumet City, IL 60409; phone 1-800-654-6700

Travel Assistance International, 1133 15th Street N.W., Suite 400, Washington, DC 20005; phone 1-800-821-2828 and 1-202-331-1609

Travmed, P.O. Box 10623, Baltimore, MD 21285; phone 1-800-732-5309

World Care Travel Service, 1150 S. Olive Street, Suite T-2233, Los Angeles, CA 90015; phone 1-800-253-1877

Interlude

JUNIOR, CHARLIE, AND THE WHALE

Because of some confusion back in Kuujjuaq (Fort Chimo, if you prefer the English name), we got to Punnik Camp later than usual that Saturday afternoon in August. Still, after offloading and stowing our gear in the cabins and having a midafternoon snack in the dining cabin, there was time for a couple hours of fishing before dinner. So Dick Burdick (Punnik's comanager then, along with the almost legendary Inuit bush pilot Johnny May) sent me downstream with two other clients, a father-and-son team from upstate New York who were in Northern Quebec to hunt caribou. But they'd bought salmon-fishing and bird-shooting licenses as well.

No sooner had our guide—an Inuit of maybe eighteen or nineteen, whose face kept phasing between stoic impassivity and scowling surliness—pointed at some rocks I should fish than he, the two caribou hunters, and the landing net disappeared downstream a quarter of a mile or so. Suddenly and quite unexpectedly, I found myself attached to an eleven- or twelve-pound salmon by a 7-weight rod and a 4-pound tippet (a choice that had caused Burdick's eyebrows to arch considerably). The fish rolled up in the leader and was using the current to try to pull me around the outside of a couple of big rocks sticking up out of the racing water. The guide seemed oblivious to or intent upon ignoring my shouts of "Net! Net, Thomas, net!" and frantic signals when I could free my reel hand. He got the picture finally, and came loping over the loose boulders that line the Whale and got the net under the fish in time. (I will not comment upon his net technique except to note that it is apparently standard Inuit drill to chase fish from behind with the net or to swipe at them as if dipping in a herring run.) Without asking me, Thomas decided to kill the dusky-looking fish. *Oh, no, not again*, I thought, remembering last year.

I had fished the Whale the year before, but nearly two months earlier in the season at a different camp some seventy miles upstream. Punnik Camp is located just six or seven miles upstream of Ungava Bay, and I had hoped to find better guides and fresher fish. Last year all the regular guides were off at a government-sponsored caribou guiding school the week eight of us were trying to fish at the Whale River Salmon Camp. The stand-in guides, unemployed young men from Kuujuaq, had scared the devil out of us by running the motorized cargo canoes at full tilt through the rapids, tempted some clients to break the law by encouraging trolling when the fishing was slow, and ticked us off by running downstream ahead of us, throwing rocks at mink and beavers swimming through the very pools we were supposed to fish. (Now I wasn't so sure we'd have fared better had the regular guides been in camp.) And Quebec promoters and certain famous fishing writers to the contrary, we'd ascertained that the Whale has no early salmon run, that bright fish aren't in the river in late June and early July. This fish, like the salmon I had caught upstream the previous year, was too dark to be a fish fresh in from the sea.

At dinner that night, I cornered Michel Laplante, the research technician who was directing a salmon-tagging operation that was being operated out of Punnik Camp by the provincial government. He told me that in southern rivers, most salmon enter, spawn, and leave according to the book. But in salmon rivers that flow north into Ungava Bay—the Whale, the George, and the Koksoak—the majority of returning salmon do not spawn the year they enter, but winter over and spawn the next year. A few spawn, winter over, and spawn again the next year. Some of the second-year spawners look bright and fresh, if a bit slender; others look dark and spent. You can't tell for sure just by looking; you have to kill the fish and check its gonads. Many local residents call these overwintering fish "resident" salmon. To further confuse things, all three rivers have ouananiche (salmon that never leave fresh water) as well as an estuarine form that spends most of its time in the brackish reaches of the rivers. Laplante told me that nearly a third of all the salmon in the Koksoak are of the estuarine variety; the proportions are considerably smaller in the Whale and the George.

The next day, Sunday, Dick sent me out with Charlie Okkuatsiak, a nearly toothless, weathered old Inuit who was a man of few words, even in his own tongue. Worse, his English was almost as bad as my nonexistent Inuktitut. Grunting and pointing were Charlie's fortes. After an hour or so, I began to detect a subtle difference between the grunts that accompanied Charlie's pointing at where I was to stand versus where I was to cast. Judging by some of the lies Charlie pointed out, it seemed he thought I could cast like Ted Williams. I can't. In fact, my casting would qualify me as the Bob Uecker or Rodney Dangerfield of fly-fishing, if only my jokes were funnier.

In midafternoon, Charlie put me on a big rocky point and pointed at the pool on the other side of a long, wide, shallow shelf. I spent nearly three hours trying to figure out how to get a proper swing through the pool while the currents sweeping around the point and over the ledge were playing tricks with my line. I'd have given up sooner, except that Johnny had flown overhead, circled back, dipped his wings, and pointed at the river. Apparently he could see fish I couldn't in the glare of bright sunlight on rushing water. To make a long story short, I got skunked.

At dinner that evening, Johnny told me that when he had flown over he could see I was casting over and beyond fish, a dozen or more of which were holding in the shallow water right on top of the ledge. "I'd never have looked for fish there," he said, "except that when I looked down to see how you were doing, I saw them."

Monday I discovered the solution to the guide problem. Dick sent Johnny May's fifteen-year-old son, Junior, out with Charlie and me. Junior May was a bundle of enthusiasm, curiosity, and accommodating energy. Most important, he was bilingual. Through Junior I was able to "converse" a little with Charlie and discovered that he knew a great deal about salmon and salmon fishing. I was beginning to feel better. But the wind was blowing so steadily upcurrent from the north (perfect for catching salmon, according to both Charlie and Johnny, but impossible to cast into, according to yours truly), I was completely pooped by noon. I suggested that we head back to camp.

During lunch, I told Dick Burdick that I wouldn't need to tie up Charlie in the afternoon, that Junior was going to take me directly across the river to try a smaller stream for brook trout. Dick asked whether he could send Junior over with a fly rod, and if I would mind giving him a few pointers. Mind? I was flattered. Imagine me giving anyone fly-casting pointers! My fly-fishing is based on general angling know-how, not on casting or other forms of motor-skill finesse.

The wind was still pretty bad down in the relatively deep and narrow tributary canyon, howling through the scrubby forest-tundra vegetation that grew alongside the stream. Still, we managed to fish a bit. Junior was using an old fiberglass rod and a balky automatic reel. Like all first-timers, Junior was bringing the rod down to about 2:45 on the back cast, but he was able to get some line out. He found fish too, including a particularly aggressive one that kept going after his fly. Junior had trouble striking back at it. My oral instruction wasn't working, so I had to show him how by hooking and landing the brookie on a Royal Wulff. Junior was so pleased, we decided to keep the trout—a thirteen-incher with a bright-yellow chin. Other than a bunch of tiny trout we released, that was it for the day.

I was frustrated by the wind both early and late the next day and in midday by fish I could see but couldn't interest. They were holding in the flat, fast water right on top of the large granite shelf we had inadvertently discovered on Sunday. Today the light allowed me to see them, but that was about it. I had one salmon on briefly, but the Buck Bug's hook bent sideways on the strike and wouldn't hold. I kept drifting flies past the others, but the only one that would take, I couldn't hook. Meanwhile, Junior and Charlie used spinning tackle to catch a bunch of sea-run brook trout that Charlie turned into the finest shore lunch I've ever had.

Late in the afternoon we went upriver from the camp, but the wind direction and eddies made it almost impossible to fish the rapids properly. So I tried the flatter, wadeable water at station 12. But I couldn't stand the mosquitoes and gave up after a cursory working over of the area. As I sloshed back to the boat, Charlie saw a big salmon jump right behind me, where I had just been fishing. It was one of those days.

At breakfast the next morning, Johnny May told me Charlie said the salmon would be biting today. Dick asked if it would be all right with me to let Junior take his Orvis boron-and-graphite rod and disc-drag Martin reel. It was fine with me, so long as Dick wouldn't hold me responsible for breakage. Charlie even took along the mismatched fiberglass automatic outfit. We started upriver in the big rapids at 13 and 14, but I couldn't do anything there. So we went downriver to an unmarked spot Charlie knew about.

We picked three likely-looking lies and started fishing. At first I kept trying to correct Junior's back cast, but he wasn't hitting the rocks and he was getting sufficient line out, so I left him alone. It was a good coaching decision. Shortly after I stopped nagging at him, Junior was into a small fish, but lost it. Then I took a four-pound male grilse on a yellow Marabou Muddler. About twenty minutes later, and thirty yards downstream from me, Junior landed a virtually identical fish—his first salmon on a fly. He caught it on a simple squirrel-tail streamer with green dubbing, a fly he would not change after that.

Dick Burdick, who treats Junior like a son, was beside himself with joy that night. (At season's end he gave Junior the boron outfit.) Over a celebratory glass or two that evening, Dick even asked me to come back the next summer to train the guides. It was heady stuff, and under the influence of some good rum I started feeling like Lee Wulff. But I was still sober enough to say no thanks.

After being skunked the next morning on a trip upriver after pike and lake trout, we had a quick lunch in camp and then headed down to what had already become known as Junior's Rock. I didn't like the looks of my leader, and by the time I had tied a new one on, Junior was into a fish. It was a five-pound male that bore one of Michel Laplante's spaghetti tags. (Autopsy later revealed the fish to be a two-sea-year salmon, not a grilse.) I fished to no avail that afternoon except for one nice, acrobatic brookie that jumped three times and had me thinking it was a small grilse. Junior hooked but lost another salmon. After a long rest during a hot, sunny midafternoon, we resumed our casting. Junior had wandered downstream, so another client, Charlie, and I took turns fishing Junior's Rock but came up empty-handed. When Junior got back, he resumed casting at his favorite spot with his favorite fly and took a grilse on his fifth or sixth cast. The kid was a natural.

Saturday was flying-out day, but Charlie and I sneaked down to Junior's Rock for one last shot. Except for a few overeager parr, we got nothing. We did accomplish our main mission, though. Punnik has literally hundreds of salmon lies within a few miles of the main camp, but they had marked and numbered only fourteen of them. So Charlie and I planted a sign that Dick had made up: JUNIOR 15. I wish I could have been there to see Junior's face when he first saw it.

Flying out to Kuujjuaq that afternoon, I marveled again at this great northern country. Besides the big salmon rivers I've mentioned, there are hundreds and perhaps thousands of miles of unfished waters in this vast wilderness. Most of them are trout streams, but a few char wander up them too. In a few you can see salmon holding in the pools below the waterfalls. But the country is so rugged, and the streams so small, you can't land a fixed-wing plane. Oh, for the money to hire a helicopter and a guide like Johnny May!

8
WHEN IN ROME...

Having invested several thousand dollars in a trip, and being steeped in the American notion that the customer is always right, we sometimes forget that we are guests in someone else's land. We also forget that our hosts are steeped in an entirely different tradition and culture, and that it may be as difficult for them to accommodate our ways as it is for us to adjust to theirs. It's as unreasonable for us to expect our angling hosts to understand and embrace our ways completely as it would be for them to expect their foreign guests to become locals overnight. The best either of us can expect is to meet comfortably and amicably about halfway in between.

This meeting of the minds is essential to having a good fishing trip.

Fortunately, it's really not that difficult. Unfortunately, it too seldom happens. Except for checking with people who've fished someplace before and ruling out the operations that made others unhappy or uncomfortable, there really isn't much you can do about the host's half of the bargain. But you are completely in control of your half. It's like any other deal: The more you invest, the more you are likely to profit.

"*Parlez-vous* Fishing?"

When he was managing Manaka Jungle Lodge down in Venezuela and coping with a lot of logistical and other problems every day, Dennis

Welcome to Abaco Island, Bahamas. *(R. Valentine Atkinson/Frontiers)*

Bitton says his patience was most sorely tried by American anglers who would arrive without a word of Spanish and start criticizing the Indian guides for having so little English. "What did these guys expect?" he fairly splutters. "It's their country. They wouldn't expect us to know their language if they came up here for a visit. Anyway, at least the guides went halfway and learned Spanish. These fat-cat Texans, who wouldn't know a word of Spanish, let alone the Indian language, would worry about going out in a boat with a guide who only had a few words of English. So I'd say, 'Look, he knows the boat, he knows the river, he knows how to fish, and he knows where the peacock bass are. How much English does he need to show you where to cast?'"

If you are going abroad, or to Mexico or the French-speaking part of Canada, you will get a great deal more out of the trip if you can speak a bit of the local language. You needn't be a linguist. All you need are some of the polite words and expressions:

▶ "Hello" and "Good-bye"
▶ "I'm pleased to meet you."
▶ "Good morning," "Good afternoon," and "Good night."
▶ "Please," "Thank you," and "You're welcome."

A few local fish names and fly-fishing words and expressions also would be nice to have. These you can't find in pocket dictionaries or

---

☞ TRAVELER'S TIP

Don't try to impose your lifestyle at home on that of a foreign destination. It can be quite different. And you sort of need to accept, if you're doing the best of the best, what's the Russian best or the Argentine best or the Mexican best, or whatever. It may not be as good as the best in your hometown. I guess I'm amazed at how many people measure success by how close the amenities are to their own lifestyle at home. That's somehow missing the point of foreign travel.

—W. M. "Mike" Fitzgerald
president, Frontiers
Wexford, Pennsylvania

phrase books. Ask your booking agent or the camp operator if such a glossary is available.

If you make the slightest effort to speak their language, your guide, the camp manager, and the cook will all work harder in your behalf to show their appreciation. By itself, that can make the difference between a so-so trip and a good one. Sometimes, between a bust and a fine experience.

▶ At the very least, pick up a Berlitz traveler's phrase book and read through it on the flight.

▶ If you really want to score heavily with the camp staff, learn a few colloquial phrases and a bit about the local history and geography. It won't take much to impress them, they're so used to monolingual, monocultural American visitors. And you may be surprised to learn how much more than fishing you have in common with your fly-fishing hosts.

☞ TRAVELER'S TIP

I suppose that what some of us do who travel to fish or fish to travel is to conceive of the trip as a whole, a complete picture. However, what we are likelier to be touched by is a particular moment afield when some critical portion of the whole is revealed and perceived. There's something unforgettable to me in Haig-Brown's coda to The Fisherman's Winter, *when the course of many weeks of traveling and fishing in Chile is reduced, or perhaps magnified, to a riverside conversation of love and family with his guide.*

I believe it can serve us, as traveling anglers and sojourners in life, to say yea to the moment, to be receptive to the passing moments and fleeting images that make up our day afield. As Victor Jara put it in a song, "In five minutes, an eternity," En cinco minutos la vida es eternal. *Certainly, some better part of contentment, at home or abroad, depends on our ability to seize the essential and to recognize the transcendent. Let it happen. Enjoy.*

—John Jenkins
proprietor, Heart of Patagonia Lodge
Coyhaique, Chile

I fondly recall animated streamside discussions of an up-and-coming, unknown young tennis player named Monica Seles, the novels and sporting sketches of Ivan Turgenev, the paintings of Bruno Liljefors and the Group of Seven, the recordings of Charlie Parker, the comparative driving skills of Ayrton Senna and Nigel Mansel, the relative political prospects of Mikhail Gorbachev and Boris Yeltsin, the best way to cook reindeer liver or frost a chocolate cake, the pharmacological efficacy of various tundra plants. I recall some of those conversations much more vividly than I do the fishing particulars of the days in which they occurred.

Not that I was fluent in any of the languages, mind you, nor that the conversations were carried on the the local vernacular. I had but a few words and phrases, and the conversations were in English. But because of my often-hilarious attempts to wrap my tongue around a difficult word or phrase, my hosts warmed up to me and struggled with my language so we could have a real conversation about things we both cared about.

"*Sprechen Sie* Metric?"

Unless you're heading for Merrie Olde England or one of its neighbors in the British Isles, leave your notions of inches, pounds, miles, and Fahrenheit temperatures home. You've got to think metric. It's a lot easier to think metrically than it is to make conversions. In other words, don't try to figure out how many centimeters long a sixteen-inch fish would be, or how many kilograms a seven-pound fish might weigh, just visualize those 40.6 cm and think three, three and a half kilos when you're hefting that fish before releasing it. Celsius temperatures are probably going to be the slowest things to enter your usable metric consciousness.

(To help you think Celsius, normal body temperature is 37°C and a seriously high fever is 40°C. Water freezes at 0°C and you'll want to wear a sweater if the lodge gets below 20°C. A 30°C day is a hot one in trout and salmon country, but still pleasantly warm on the bonefish flats. Even in the tropics, it's hot at 35°C and 38°C is scorching. Trout and salmon begin feeding at around 4°C to 7°C, although 10°C to 18°C would be better, and salmonids start getting very sluggish above 20°C

☞ METRIC CONVERSION FORMULAS

It's easier to think metrically than it is to make conversions. But if you can't get your mind in a metric mood, or if you happen to be one of those math freaks who delights in calculation, here are the necessary formulas.

Temperature Conversion Formulas: Celsius/Fahrenheit

(°F −32) x 0.56 [or 5/9] = °C
(°C x 1.8 [or 9/5]) + 32 = °F

Weight Conversion Formulas: pounds/kilograms

lb x 0.45359237 = kg
kg x 2.204623 = lb

Length Conversion Formulas: inches/centimeters

in x 2.54 = cm
cm x 0.3937008 = in

Length & Distance Conversion Formulas: feet/meters

ft x 0.3048 = m
m x 3.28084 = ft

Distance Conversion Formulas: yards/meters

yd x 0.9144 = m
m x 1.093613 = yd

Distance Conversion Formulas: miles/kilometers
(Speed Conversion Formulas: MPH/KPH)

mi (or MPH) x 1.6093 = km (or KPH)
km (or KPH) x 0.62137 = mi (or MPH)

Distance Conversion Formulas: nautical miles/kilometers
(Speed Conversion Formulas: Knots/KPH)

NM (or Kt) x 1.852 = km (or KPH)
km (or KPH) x 0.54 = NM (or Kt)

to 21°C. For good bonefishing, the water temperature ought to be in the 24°C to 28°C range, and if it's below 19°C or above 32°C, you might as well stay in the lodge and tie flies or read a good book.)

If you're one of those people who can't seem to get the hang of thinking metrically, see the accompanying conversion tables.

Getting Along with Your Guide or Gillie

It's hard to imagine anything much worse than being saddled for a week with a guide you don't get along with, unless it's a week of cold, driving rain while you are saddled with a guide you don't get along with. Bad weather or not, the fishing is likely to be lousy. You won't pay attention to the guide's advice, he won't try very hard to earn the tip he suspects won't be forthcoming, and you will be stewing in your own bile instead of paying complete attention to your fishing.

A few things you can do to minimize the chances of your being saddled with the wrong guide:

▶ If you are particular about the kind of guide you like to fish with, say so up front—before you book the trip. Let the booking agent or camp operator know that you have certain expectations, particular likes and dislikes. He'll do his best to see that you get the kind of guide you want (or tell you flat out you can't be accommodated). Remember, he wants you to have a good trip, so you'll be telling everyone who'll listen what a great experience you had.

▶ When hiring your own flats guide or direct-booking a charter, talk these things over on the telephone. And don't pinch pennies on the phone call; talk long enough that you get some sense of the guy's personality and the sort of chemistry the two of you might have. If you and a guide or charter captain don't hit it off over the phone, chances are better than good you won't hit it off in a crowded boat cockpit either.

▶ Make sure the camp manager and guide understand the way you like to fish. Are you looking for an easy, relaxing day on the water, or are you eager to hike several miles and scramble down a steep canyon to get to where the fishing is really good? The guide may be loath to depart from the usual plan if the manager hasn't told him it's okay.

▶ If guide problems crop up early, nip them in the bud. Don't zip your lips and seethe in silence until you explode. Speak up. Point out to the guide himself what he's doing or not doing that bugs you. If the problem persists, mention it to the camp operator. Don't be belligerently confrontational in either case, but don't be evasive either. A simple, unheated conversation is what's wanted. The guide, the captain, the camp manager needs to understand what the problem is and that you consider it a serious matter. You don't want to give the impression that you are a cranky, demanding person who's impossible to please. Unless, of course, that's what you are.

▶ Getting along with the manager is almost as important as getting along with the guide. If the manager thinks you're a pretty good Joe or Jane, one who's likely to talk up the place in the right circles, he might tell the guide to take you to that special, sure-thing spot or ask the guide to stay out a little late so you can catch that twilight bite. A sure way to get on the manager's *wrong* side is to regale your fellow clients with tales of great fishing at another camp or lodge.

☞ TRAVELER'S TIP

Guides or lodge owners will ask me, "Well, how do you like your room?" and I'll say, "Oh, it's fine." Then they'll look at me and I can see they're having trouble with my answer. So I'll say, "Really, it's fine." Eventually, after dinner one night, the guy will say to me "Americans always say Oh, it's fine, and then they go home and try to stop their check or something."

It's an American propensity, apparently, to respond to a question—"How do you like the food?" "How do you like the bed?" "How do you like the fishing?" "How do you like the plane?" "How do you like your guide?"—by gritting our teeth like the Marlboro man and saying "Oh, fine, fine, no problem." But when we get home we bitch and moan and complain and write letters and stuff like that, instead of trying to correct the problem right on the spot. I've heard that complaint about Americans in more parts of the world.

—Silvio Calabi
editor in chief and associate publisher,
Fly Rod & Reel and *Fly Tackle Dealer*
Rockport, Maine

☞ TRAVELER'S TIP

Always, for starters, use the flies suggested by the guide and fish them as you are instructed. If his approach fails, that is the time to experiment. He'll welcome it. But don't be a smart-ass and go your own way from the beginning. The exception to this would be if you are a Lee Wulff, but most of us don't qualify.

—Nelson Bryant
formerly "Wood, Field, and Stream"
columnist, *The New York Times*
West Tisbury, Massachusetts

▶ Remember that putting you on fish is the guide's responsibility, but catching them is yours. Writing in *Fly Rod & Reel*, John Gierach quotes a Canadian guide who lays it on the line: "Look, I can take you to where the fish are and I can tell you what they're biting, but if you don't catch 'em, that's tough shit, ey?"

It isn't necessary, or even particularly desirable, that you and your guide become bosom buddies. But you should have a good working relationship based on mutual respect and a common understanding of your relationship. Guides are offended when you ignore their advice or tell them you don't want them to net your fish. Some will let you know, others will clam up. Either way, you've probably screwed up the relationship and won't get all the effort and help that otherwise would have been forthcoming. When I'm fishing new water, I always ask for suggestions on patterns and presentations. Even if the advice seems cockeyed, I'll follow it for a while. Later, if I decide to go my own way, I'll explain to the guide what I'm doing and why.

As Randall Kaufmann put it in *Bonefishing with a Fly*: "Your guide is there to make your day more productive and enjoyable. Help him do that. Be kind, courteous, and gracious. *Pay attention.* Show your appreciation when he does well. If a good relationship develops between angler and guide, both of you will look forward to the next day on the water."

Guide-angler relationships can be pretty complicated, considering the different cultures, educations, and other nonpiscatorial things each brings to the party. *Sports Illustrated* ran a short item several

years ago about the ongoing confusion in angling circles between Ted
Williams the fishing and conservation writer and Ted Williams the
fishing baseball great. Usually it's writer Ted who's splashing cold
water in the starry eyes of those who were expecting to fish with a
Hall of Famer. But one day, while bonefishing in the Bahamas, the
Splendid Splinter's guide told him how much he enjoyed Ted's articles
in the fishing magazines. The last of the .400 hitters told the guide that
he wasn't the writer, he was the baseball player. The guide then said,
in cool disappointment, "I don't follow bazebol, mon."

The relationship between a fisherman and his guide isn't that of
lord and master or even employer and employee. Nor is it, as a few
big-name guides seem to think, lowly pilgrim and high priest. It's
client and—well, think of the guide as the carpenter who was sent out
by the contractor you called.

Keep in mind, when assessing your guide's skills, that he's the carpenter, not the architect or engineer or contractor. He isn't responsible for the design, the structural integrity, or the big picture. He's just
the carpenter. But he damn sure ought to know hammers and nails.
Sometimes the knowledge is pretty rudimentary.

Your guide expectations ought to be reasonable for the part of the
world you are fishing. Fishing Scotland, Montana, or the Florida Keys,
you can reasonably have pretty high expectations. But when you are
fishing in some far-flung corner of the Third World, don't expect you'll
be fishing with an expert fly-fisherman. Not unless you are fishing one
of those top-dollar, high-roller places that charge so much they can
afford to import guides from Scotland, Montana, or Florida.

Camp operators in the boonies have a devil of a time finding, train-
ing, and keeping good guides. I've had quite a motley assortment of
guides, from guys who really knew the waters and the fish, and
enough about fly-fishing to put me on opportunities I could handle, to
guys who simply pulled the starter rope and carried the gear. Whatever else he may do or not do, a really good guide will make you a better fisherman than you would be without him. (Or her, I should add,
because there are now quite a few female guides around the world,
and they tend to be good ones.) Out in the Third World, pretty good is
usually as good as they get. This seems to be a particular problem in
the Far North. Even in Alaska.

A few years ago, *The Alaska Angler* published the reports of an
investigative survey that categorized 70 percent of guides at fishing

lodges in Alaska as incompetent. "The guides were predominantly resident and non-resident teenagers who needed a summer job," the editor wrote. "They had neither the fishing nor 'people' skills to handle clients who had invested several thousand dollars." Things are apparently much better now, but they weren't when I last fished Alaska.

One of the Alaskan guides I had—who knew a good bit about the waters and was able to put us on fish fairly consistently—kept pulling us off pretty water because of bears and putting us on muddy banks that were better suited to casting gobs of roe on treble hooks. And every time you'd ask him about the wisdom of using a particular fly, he'd respond, "That's a real killer! Every cast!"

When you are fishing in the Third World (and that includes the back of beyond in Alaska and Canada), you simply must be a bit more patient with guides than you might be elsewhere. These guys are mostly doing the best they can, trying to learn a difficult trade on the job. It's not their fault they've been pushed in over their heads. If a guide isn't trying, or if he's lazy or insolent, your beef is legitimately with him. But if the guide is trying hard but just isn't up to speed, your beef is with management; don't take it out on the guide. Let the camp manager know you think the guide is giving you his best, but his best isn't yet good enough. Perhaps you will be given a more experienced guide. If you aren't, take it up with whoever sold you the trip when you get home.

☞ TRAVELER'S TIP

The most valuable thing I learned from the Indians down at Manaka [Jungle Lodge] was the ability to do nothing. And I mean nothing, absolutely nothing. You don't read. You don't even think. It was really hard at first, then I began to see the wisdom of doing nothing in that hot, sticky climate. When it's too hot to fish, you just lie there in a hammock, doing nothing. The clients who caught on had much more enjoyable trips and probably returned from their fishing vacations with their batteries fully recharged.

—Dennis G. Bitton
freelance writer and formerly
editor of *The Flyfisher* and of
Flyfishing News, Views, & Reviews
Idaho Falls, Idaho

"Most bonefish guides (especially outside the U.S.) live a simple, relaxed life," Randall Kaufmann reminds us. "They are happy when you hook bonefish but do not get unhappy when you do not. Your trip is much more enjoyable if you have the same attitude. Your guide might tell you, 'There will be another bone, mon. Don't worry; plenty of fish. You see.' Relax; you are on island time."

The same thing is fundamentally true about salmon, trout, and other guides. Only the accents and details differ. Relax. Fishing is fun, a recreation. It really isn't a matter of life or death.

Tradition and S.O.P.

Most fishing operations have a standard schedule covering meal and fishing times; some are flexible and will let you fish early or late, others are pretty rigid. Sometimes it's a function of size: Camps with small staffs and a handful of clients at any given time can afford to play it loose. Sometimes it's more a matter of personality: Some managers like to run a tight ship; others, a party boat. Managers of fishing lodges and camps aren't any more homogenized than the managers of corporations, baseball teams, or jazz bands. And sometimes it's a

---

☞ **TRAVELER'S TIP**

Ask whether it's okay to smoke.

I was taken aside by the owner of a lodge I was at and told I was offending everyone by my smoking, even though I wasn't smoking in the lodge. I went around to the other fishermen and apologized, and they said, "What are you talking about? As long as you don't smoke while we're eating, we don't mind."

So I went back to talk to the owner—who is a real health freak and, you know, serves vegetable hamburgers and all kinds of stuff that's good for your heart—and he said, "Well, you reek. Every room you walk into stinks from now on."

And I said, "Okay, call a chopper."

—Harm Saville
president, Nor'East Miniature Roses, Inc.
Rowley, Massachusetts

product of geography, culture, or tradition. Even by fairly relaxed American standards, things can be maddeningly "flexible" in Russia and parts of Latin America. Conversely, they can be terribly tradition-bound on some British waters. Before booking, you'd better find out whether the operation you're considering is compatible with your style. If it isn't, you might be happier elsewhere.

▶ If you book into a camp where schedule is important, you can't reasonably complain that they can't completely accommodate your need to fish early or late, or if they resist holding the kitchen open for you. On the other hand, only a fool expects everything to happen on schedule in *Mañana*land. And if you decide to go salmon fishing in Russia (possibly excepting the Ponoy), you'd better know that all schedules, plans, promises, and decisions should be treated as rumors and that "*yakoby*" (supposedly) is considered an appropriately skeptical response to almost any sort of announcement.

▶ Be prepared to accept local rules and traditions that might seem unreasonable. Trout fishing in the Orkney Islands several years ago, I discovered that one doesn't stand up in a drift boat to cast. Why? Because it simply isn't done, chappie. Seems odd to anyone who's used to stalking bonefish from a flats skiff, but it's the way things are done in Scotland. On some English chalk-stream waters, only dry flies may be used, and they must always be cast upstream and fished dead drift.

▶ If a camp or lodge asks you to pinch down the barbs or to refrain from using double or treble hooks for salmon, comply without complaining, even if it isn't required by law. An operator's long-term interest in resource conservation must always prevail over an individual angler's short-term interest in a week's fast fishing or secure hooking. The operator's conservation concern may be why the fishing's still good enough that you wanted to make the investment in the trip.

▶ Almost everywhere in the angling world, it's considered very bad form to leave your leftover liquor with your guide. Think how upset you'd have been if you'd been given a guide who was seriously hung over the first couple or three days of your trip.

▶ Virtually every camp or lodge has regulations concerning guide drinking. Some don't want you ever to give your guide a drink. Others say a beer at lunch or on the way back from a good day's fishing is all right. At some camps in the Far North, all your drinking is to be confined to your room. In Scotland it's traditional to invite your gillie to have a draft or a wee dram back at the hotel at day's end. If these drinking regulations aren't spelled out, ask.

▶ On some salmon streams, the operator or the guide may want you to kill the trout you catch. If you don't want to, discuss it with the camp manager. On private waters, you may have to kill them because the proprietor won't permit returning egg-eating trout to salmon water. Don't put up a big fuss. If that's offensive to you, find out before you book the trip, and book elsewhere. If it isn't a regulation but simply tradition—as killing your catch is in many saltwater destinations—tell your guide it's against your religion to kill fish or to allow anyone else to kill fish in your presence. That usually works when reason doesn't.

Superstitions

Superstition may be just so much nonsense to you, but in some fishing corners of the world it's almost as important as religion. Arguing about the one makes as little sense as arguing about the other.

▶ If a guide insists on spitting on your fly before you cast it the first time, don't object. It won't harm anything. In fact, research shows that at least some species of fish are attracted to human saliva.

▶ When you show up at the boat wearing a green shirt and your islander guide says green will bring bad weather, don't argue. Apologize for having inadvertently worn the wrong thing. If you have shirts of another color, wear them for the rest of the trip. If you brought nothing but green shirts, explain the situation to the guide. He'll likely find some way of appeasing the affronted gods of wind and weather.

▶ If guide superstition doesn't actually get in the way of the fishing, play along with it. If it does affect the fishing, you don't have to put up with it. Ask the lodge or camp manager to give you another guide.

Sensitivities

In some cultures, American humor and banter are considered offensive, abusive, and insulting.

▶ All in what we consider good humor, we call each other abusive names and punch each other in the shoulder. Others may not enjoy being called S.O.B.s and consider even a light punch an assault or invasion of privacy. In extreme cases, the very behavior by which you mean to let a guide or someone else in camp know you like him can be interpreted as a signal that you dislike the person.
▶ Similarly, profanity, obscenity, or public urination may offend even your rough-and-tough guide.
▶ Keep your antennae working and tune in to local norms and mores. Key your behavior to that of the locals and of the camp manager.
▶ Be especially considerate of the sensibilities of women, who in many other cultures are not considered peers with different plumbing.

Fishing, Believe It or Not, Isn't Everything

Take advantage of whatever else a country, a region, a transit city has to offer. Don't schedule tight connections, which you may miss because of the vagaries of traveling from remote fishing camps and lodges. Most countries have museums and other cultural temples well worth visiting: the Hermitage in St. Petersburg and the Kremlin in Moscow, the Louvre in Paris, the Prado in Madrid, various druid rock formations in Scotland and Ireland, castles and cathedrals all over Europe, pre-Columbian sites in Latin America, the list goes on and on. Some few of them are even fishing related, such as the Sportfiskeforum (Sport Fishing Museum) in Älvekarleby, a small city on the Dalalven, a short, productive salmon river in Sweden. And there are tackle factories to visit: Partridge in Redditch and Hardy in Alnwick, both England; Airflo (Fly Fishing Technology, Ltd.) in Brecon, Wales; VMC in Morvillars, France; Mustad in Gjøvik, Norway; Abu in Svångsta, Sweden—just be sure to work out a visit in advance.

And there are myriad other attractions to whet your other special interests: woolen mills in Scotland, lace factories in France and Switzerland, glass factories in southern Sweden, wineries in France and Austria, breweries in Belgium and Germany, tulip gardens in the Netherlands. If you have the time and interest, combine fishing with other outdoor pastimes: trekking and mountaineering, exploring national parks, kayaking or barging canals, birdwatching. You couldn't get me to go to the trouble of traveling for any of these things, but I love to combine them with fishing—for which I'd travel to the ends of the world.

Before visiting a country or a region that is new to me, I try to learn as much about it as I can without making a graduate research project out of it. I want to know a bit about its ethnology, folklore, religion, literature, art and music, cultural history generally, geography and geology, birds and wildlife, weather and climate. That way I will know what opportunities are available to me, and it will help me to better understand the people I'll be living and working with and how to avoid embarrassing gaffes and blunders.

The most directly useful thing for a visiting fisherman to know, and one of the most frustratingly difficult things to find out, is information on the aquatic life of the region. No, not the sport fishes you'll be targeting, but the forage fish, the aquatic insects, the crustaceans and other creatures that support the aquatic food chain. For example, thanks to Jay Rowland and Joe Kambeitz (British Columbia steelheaders), I now know that the important shrimp species in the Barents Sea is dark red, which explains the success of all those burnt-orange prawn patterns the British like to use. I thought they were bright attractors, not food imitators, because the only orange shrimp I'd ever seen were cooked. And fishing with a fly that imitated a boiled cocktail shrimp made no sense to me. So, to all those unknown salmon-fishing Brits I'd thought merely eccentric or tradition-bound, my profoundest apologies.

LORD OF THE WINDS

Humbly do I beseech thee, O mighty King Aeolus, Lord of the Winds, that thou wouldst command Zephyr to sigh gently in the west, or Notus in the south, that I might find and catch a fish upon the flats, be it bonefish, permit, or tarpon. I shall not kill the fish I seek, nor pollute the waters upon which I navigate, so why dost thou ever send chilly-fingered Boreas out of the north against me, or Eurus howling across the long fetches of the east? What wrong have I done thee, what transgression have I committed, that thou wouldst punish me so? Forgive me, O son of the great Hippotas and husband to the fair Cyane, for I know not what sin has been marked against me in the log book of the gods, and I long to make a fair cast on the flats to a fish I can see. *Tantaene animis coestibus irae?* I join the estimable Virgil in asking: In heavenly winds can such resentment dwell?

—Piscatorial prayer

Too far," the guide said in exasperation as I let another pod of bonefish get away. I stripped furiously, preparing for another cast. "Forget it," said the guide, who shall go nameless, to preserve his well-deserved reputation as a nice guy to fish with. "They're gone."

It was not the first time that day I had failed to see the bonefish in the roiled water and spooked them with a blind cast that was off the mark. "Look," the guide said, with as much patience as he could muster, "you're going to have to see them sooner and cast faster. Especially under these conditions."

Remember Joe Bfstplk, that hapless character in the Li'l Abner comics who always had a rain cloud over his head? That's me on the flats. It doesn't necessarily rain, but it always blows. And I mean always. Not balmy subtropical zephyrs, mind you. I'm talking about real wind: twenty knots or better, small-craft warnings, whole gales, that sort of thing. It never fails to blow when I'm on the flats. You could get rich betting on it.

When it comes to flats fishing, I'm downright cursed. I still haven't caught my first bonefish. Not even on spinning tackle and live shrimp. It's that bad. I've caught tarpon and permit and sharks, but never on the flats. Yes, I've caught barracuda on the flats, but who hasn't?

My failure to learn flats fishing hasn't been for want of proper teachers. Hey, I've been chased off the Lakes by squalls while fishing with Bob Trosset and Marshall Cutchin, and if there are better guides, there aren't many of them.

Like too many flats wanna-bes, I foolishly started without a guide. It was up on the flats behind Tavernier Key, and we did everything wrong: We were four (two too many) in a light, expanded-foam boat, without a push pole, in a brisk wind. We had the tide right, though. We were letting the wind drive us across the flat as the rising waters covered it. But we couldn't see the fish before they saw us. We kept spooking schools of bones. I finally got a decent shot at a lone fish. Luckily, I made a perfect cast with a pink Wiggle Jig. (It was back before I'd taken up the fly rod.) The fish kept picking up the jig by the bucktail, without ever taking the hook in its mouth. It would drop the jig and start to turn away. I'd wiggle the jig and bounce it forward a few hops. The fish would turn and pick it up again. We kept this up until the bone was within two yards of the boat and we were all crouched down below the gunwales. Finally the fish had had enough of this nonsense and skedaddled. It was the closest I've ever come to catching a bonefish.

Even without the wind, my first forays on the flats with a fly rod were spectacularly unsuccessful. As you know, you must be able to cast quickly, accurately, delicately, and far on the flats. All on one cast. In my fly-casting experience, those are almost mutually exclusive propositions. On a good day, I could maybe put two of them together, but never all four. On a bad day, I couldn't put one of them together. And I was (and still am) as prone to bad-casting days as some women are to bad-hair days.

Frantically false-casting in a vain attempt at distance, I'd spook whole flats. When I could get the distance, I'd be wide of the mark or splash the line down right on top of the fish. I'd wrap the line around the rod butt or a cleat, or stand on the so-called shooting coils. I'd hook myself in the back or send the guide diving off the poling platform with an errant cast. It was awful. As my friend Jack London would observe disgustedly, "What an idiot."

Now that I've been on the flats a time or ten, I'm better at spotting fish and muds, and I'm probably no longer the worst caster between Key Largo and the Dry Tortugas. Still one of the worst, maybe, but not the very worst. On a really good day, I can even put three of those casting imperatives together—if the wind would just lie down. But it never does.

The last time I was out on the flats, fishing with another nameless guide, I let boredom blow my best shot. It was a windy day, of course: fifteen to twenty knots, with higher gusts. So we headed for some small flats in the lee of some small keys. After a couple of hours of fruitless poling on flat after flat (the guide spotting fish in the choppy, colored water, and me making feckless blind casts), the guide decided to stake out one flat and chum it. Twenty minutes passed; thirty, an hour. For want of anything else to do, I cast to a little bonnethead shark that was grazing in our chum. You guessed it: As soon as my fly landed, four bonefish came up over the edge of the flat, headed straight for us. As I lifted the line in a rather splashy approximation of a back cast, the fish spooked and ran. The guide had had enough.

"Maybe the wind will settle down tomorrow," he said as he started the engine. If it did, we might even try tarpon out in the channels between the flats.

Next day, we were blown out by small-craft warnings. "I've seen snakebit fishermen in my day," the guide said, "but . . ." He let his voice trail off into the howling wind.

Don't bother contacting the publisher for my phone number. You can't find out my flats-fishing schedule so you can make plans to fish the flats on another day. I've stopped making long-range plans and reservations. Spur of the moment, that's my new approach. I figure that maybe I can catch spiteful old Aeolus when he's occupied elsewhere with his bag of winds. If not, I guess I'll just keep flailing away in the tempests until the Law of Averages catches up with me. It always does, doesn't it?

Appendix A

A FLY-FISHER'S GAZETTEER

The list and descriptions that follow barely skim the cream off the world's fly-fishing possibilities. Worse, the discussions are so brief they are necessarily superficial. You have to look a lot more closely before you can pick a fishing destination that will suit you to the proverbial T. It isn't enough to know the name of a river, say, and the three- or four-month period in which the best fishing *usually* occurs. But you have to start somewhere, and this little gazetteer is intended merely to whet your appetite, to open your eyes to the world of fly-fishing opportunities out there. Maybe, after skimming this gazetteer, you'll turn back to the list of booking agents and outfitters in Chapter 2 and start requesting information. Don't wait until cabin fever makes you stir crazy. The best times and places fill up early, so beginning your research a full year ahead is already cutting it kind of close.

Here's hoping you will find that fishing trip of a lifetime. No, make that merely your *next* trip of a lifetime.

North America

Of the several available definitions of North America, I'm using this one: Canada, Mexico, and the first forty-nine of the United States. (Hawaii is discussed under "Pacific Ocean," Bermuda and Greenland under "Atlantic Ocean," and the Bahamas and the Caribbean islands under "Caribbean and Bahamas.")

North America leads the world parade of continents when it comes to the quality, variety, and sheer quantity of its fly-fishing opportunities. For all our development and pollution problems (and they are enormous and ominous, so let us not pat our backs too hard), we've managed to preserve more fishing water than almost anyone else. It helps that we started with a lot more than most and that we've been at spoiling it for several centuries fewer than Europeans and Asians have. The opportunities are almost staggering, and we can't even begin to limn them here. Fortunately, they're relatively easy to discover: Just pick up one of the dozens of magazines or hundreds of books available. In the U.S. and Canada, a lot of good fly-fishing has been protected in our national parks and forests, and the states and provinces are anything but shy in promoting what they have to offer. I'm going to limit myself to skimming the cream and pointing out a few less well known places you might otherwise overlook.

CANADA

From Atlantic salmon and brook trout in the Maritimes to steelhead and Pacific salmon in British Columbia, Canada has more good fishing than almost any other country in the world (the United States being a possible exception). Much of the fishing in the middle of the country (for muskies, walleyes, lake trout, and smallmouth bass) has been developed for spin-fishermen, plug-casters, and trollers, but fly-rodders have an awful lot of water for pioneering.

Atlantic salmon fishermen already know about the wonderful waters in Nova Scotia, New Brunswick, Newfoundland, and Quebec. Newfoundland alone has 135 salmon rivers on its main island and 30 more in Labrador. A bit of Canada's salmon fishing is tied up in private clubs, but much of it is in public water, some which is surprisingly easy of access and inexpensive to fish. In New Brunswick, for example, it's possible to spend a week fly-fishing in the upper Miramichi watershed for less than you might spend trout or bass fishing almost anywhere in America. With a housekeeping cabin and a guide, a party of four might spend less than five grand, everything included, if they traveled by car. Even on Quebec's Gaspé Peninsula, waters formerly available only to clubby millionaires are now available to all at reasonable prices. If you want to fish the most famous waters, or the remote camps in northern Labrador or the Ungava Bay rivers far north in Quebec, expect to spend some heavy change on logistics alone.

Big, really big, **brook trout** are the main attraction in much of Labrador. Imagine catching dozens of fish in a week and their averaging more than five pounds. On rivers like the Eagle and the Minipi, it's what fly-fishing pilgrims have come to expect. Neighboring Quebec offers spectacular big-brookie fishing too, particularly in the many rivers flowing into and out of the wilderness Mistassini Provincial Park.

Alberta's Bow River offers some of the best, if often unpredictable, **trout** fishing (for both browns and rainbows) in Canada. What's most amazing is that the fishing is the product of an accidental stocking from a stock truck that broke down on its way to nearby Banff National Park, urban pollution that fertilized an otherwise inhospitable freestone stream, and the building of dams that ended the scouring of spring runoff.

Steelhead and British Columbia are almost synonymous. Like other Pacific salmon, steelhead are in serious trouble these days, from high-seas netting, watershed habitat destruction (largely by logging), and the construction of power dams, but B.C. still offers the finest steelheading on this side of the Pacific.

ALASKA

Fishing can be so good in the forty-ninth state it's almost boring. It also can be frustratingly difficult if you find yourself on the wrong river at the wrong time. Much of the best fly-fishing for **trout and Pacific salmon** is concentrated in the Bristol Bay watershed, but don't overlook the many wonderful opportunities in Southeast, the Alaska panhandle. Some of the small rivers near Misty Fiords also offer great **steelhead** fishing for pioneering sorts. Overshadowed by their larger, gaudier kissing cousins, **Arctic grayling and sheefish** (inconnu) can provide fast, fun fishing on a fly rod.

THE LOWER 48

You know about the trout edens in Pennsylvania, the Catskills, and the Rockies, the great flats fishing in the Florida Keys, the smallmouth bass fishing in New England and the Middle Atlantic, and the now-imperiled salmon and steelhead fishing in the Pacific Northwest. You also ought to know about the marvelous **trout** fishing barely more than an hour's drive from Manhattan in Long Island's Connetquot River, the rapidly developing fly-fishery for **striped bass, bluefish, and other inshore species** along the Atlantic Coast from Massachusetts to the Carolinas, and the really fine fly-rodding for both **trout and bass** in Missouri. Nor should you overlook the **largemouth bass** fishing in Lake Okeechobee and other lakes and inland rivers in Florida and the rest of the Southeast. Never mind that it's live-sucker, plastic-worm, and buzzbait country; those bass love big flies. And if the crowded conditions in the Yellowstone corner of Montana bother you, head north to the Flathead region and the Blackfeet Indian Reservation for some really great **trout** fishing.

Anywhere you can find flowing or standing water, you can probably find **sunfish,** great fun on a fly rod. Likewise the **saltwater panfish**—little snappers in south Florida, surf perch in northern California, cunners in the Northeast. **Pike** are completely underrated by fly-fishermen, and only a few anglers know how much fun it is to fly-fish for **gar** (as well as their saltwater equivalents, **needlefish**). Last, but definitely not least, consider the humble **carp.** In July and August on the Great Lakes, carp can be fly-fished on the flats as if they were bonefish—and the sporting similarities between the two species far outweigh the differences.

MEXICO

There may well be decent trout fishing here and there in the Sierra Madre, but Mexico's popularity among fly-fishermen stems from just two areas: Baja California and the Yucatan Peninsula.

Most of the fishing on either coast of the Baja peninsula is done by other means, but fly-rodders can find superb fishing for **sailfish, roosterfish, and other species.** The Yucatan is best known for its **bonefish and permit,** but **tarpon** can be found up and down the Gulf coast.

Caribbean and Bahamas

The Caribbean islands don't offer as much good fly-fishing as a quick glance at a map might suggest. Too many of the islands slope quickly into deep water without any flats or reefs, and too many of the reefs have been overfished.

LOS ROQUES

These Venezuelan islands out in the middle of the Caribbean blossomed as a major **bonefish** destination a few seasons ago but were zealously overbooked and lost ground to Christmas Island and the Bahamas. Still worth a look, though, now that the only established lodge is under new management. (If ever the Venezuelan military loosens its hold on Aves Island, the extensive flats look very promising for developing another bonefishing resort.)

VIRGIN ISLANDS AND
PUERTO RICO

Both have good fishing and well-developed tourist and sportfishing "infrastructures" (facilities, organization, guides, food, and so on), but they're mostly oriented toward diving and offshore trolling.

CUBA

Cuba used to have great fishing offshore for **billfish** and inland for **largemouth bass,** and its inshore waters look right for **tarpon, bonefish, and snook,** but the U.S. government's restrictions on traveling to Fidel's island are so stringent as to take the fun out of fishing. Canadian fly-fishers can explore Cuba's angling possibilities.

BAHAMAS

If anything, the fly-fishing opportunities here are better today than they were in the past. And that's saying a lot. Not that the fishing is as good—it probably isn't. But there are more and better lodges, more and better-trained guides. Research the options carefully, because some of those flats and reefs have been beat to hell, and others are just now coming into their own. Besides the vaunted **bonefish** flats, the islands also provide splendid opportunities for **tarpon, permit, blackfin and bluefin tunas, barracuda, sharks, various snappers,** and many other species.

Central America

On the Caribbean side, fly-fishermen can find great flats fishing for **bonefish** and fine lagoon fishing for **tarpon and snook.*** On the Pacific side, **sailfish and roosterfish,** as well as **marlin** for masochistic fly-fishermen, provide much of the action. Inland, several other species also provide fine fly-fishing, including **brown trout** in some mountainous regions. The **machaca** *(Brycon guatamalensis)* is an especially fine fish on a fly rod, taking flies like bluefish and fighting like rainbow trout. Lake Nicaragua used to be the hot spot, but you're probably better off these days looking for machacas on the edges of the big lakes in the Panama Canal or in the lagoons of Costa Rica.

BELIZE

Best known for its **bonefish,** the former British Honduras (English spoken here) also has excellent fly-fishing for **permit, tarpon, snook, barracuda, ladyfish, snappers, jacks,** and the usual assortment of saltwater sport species. You can find bigger fish of each species elsewhere, and more fish of a few, but few places can boast such a nice blend of size and numbers. Turneffe Island, Ambergris Cay, and the Belize River are the meccas. The season is long and is more dependent on weather and the vagaries of fish movements and behavior than anything else. The fishing infrastructure is highly developed.

---

*Over the past couple of years, quite a brouhaha has been raging in the pages of *The Angling Report* over the safety of skiff fishing outside the *bocas* (river mouths) on the Caribbean side. It's something you might want to look into rather closely before booking a trip to one of the tarpon camps.

COSTA RICA

The **tarpon** aren't as big or perhaps as plentiful as they are in, say, Key West Harbor, and the fishing is "blind" (as in most salmon fishing), but Costa Rica's jungle-lagoon fishing is a lot more peaceful and is sometimes faster. And the **snook** are bigger and more plentiful. Well-appointed camps at Barra del Colorado, Tortuguero, and Parismina have been in business for decades now and know the waters well. At Barra, the lagoons are also full of bull sharks, but I don't know if anyone has figured out how to tempt them with a fly. Big snook (twenty to thirty-five pounds) are in the lagoons in September to October, but they aren't easy to take on a fly; try big, white, flashy streamers and poppers. Tarpon high seasons are January to May and September to October, and the fish run consistently in the fifty- to ninety-pound range.

Among the indigenous species available to fly-rodders on the Caribbean side are the scrappy **machaca** described earlier, the large-mouthlike **guapote,** and the crappielike **mojarra.** Streamers, bass bugs, and poppers are the right flies.

On the Pacific side, Costa Rica has excellent offshore fly-fishing for **sailfish, marlin, and roosterfish.** Golfo de Papagayo is the place to be for fly-fishing, spring and summer.

Finally, consider Costa Rica's mountain fishing for **rainbow trout,** and you have the ingredients of an aerobatic grand slam: tarpon, rainbow, and sail. It takes a two-hour-plus jeep ride and lots of walking, but you just know that trout fishing among orchids, ferns, and other jungle plants has got to be worth the trouble. The Reventazon, Parita, and Cotton rivers generally are rated best for *gringos*, and spring is the best time for fly-fishing.

PANAMA

A well-traveled friend of mine once described Panama's Pacific coast as "the world's best fishing hole." Maybe catching and releasing half a dozen **sailfish and marlin** before lunch influenced his judgment. It's a late spring–early summer fishery, but weather vagaries are a factor. Other fly-rod targets include **dolphin, roosterfish, wahoo, jacks,** and (during the crab "hatch" when they come to the surface to feed) **cubera and other snappers.**

Lake Gatun in the canal offers fine fishing for **pavón** (a.k.a. **peacock bass**) **and machaca.** The Caribbean side probably fishes like Costa Rica, but there are no facilities.

South America

Besides sporting endemic species such as **pavón, payara, and dorado,** the continent offers world-class fishing for such transplanted exotics as **rainbow and brown trout, sea trout, coho and chinook salmon, and even landlocked Atlantic salmon.** The biggest fish are found in lakes (some of which can be fished from float tubes), but river fishing is more fun to my mind.

ARGENTINA

Argentina is justly famous for the size of its **brown and rainbow trout, and landlocked salmon,** and for the fishing lodges that have been developed, particularly in Patagonia. Depending on early-season snow melt and rains during the season, your best bet might be anywhere from January to April on such rivers as the Malléo, Trafúl, Chimehuín, Aluminé, Caleufu. Bring big, buggy flies as well as dries, because the freshwater *Aegla* crab (called *pancora*) is an important food item for these fish. In Tierra del Fuego, the fishing for **sea trout** (sea-run browns) is unexcelled anywhere, and rivaled only by southern Sweden. The Río Grande is regarded by many as the finest sea-trout river in the world. For **dorado,** head for the Parana River on the border with Paraguay and Brazil from August through October.

CHILE

Argentina gets most of the publicity, but the fishing in Patagonian Chile is on a par. Coyhaique seems to have emerged as the gateway to Chile's **trout and salmon** fishing. Almost everything that has been said about Argentina applies to Chile (including the need for *pancora*-imitating flies). Being less well known, Chilean fly-fishing offers more opportunities for bargains.

The offshore fly-fishing is almost certainly good (and in Peru as well), but it's hard finding charter boats, especially ones with experienced crews. And fly-fishing for **sailfish and billfish** is definitely a team effort. Wait for the development of a sportfishing infrastructure.

VENEZUELA

The best-developed jungle camps for **pavón, payara, and other endemic species** are in the Orinoco and Amazon basins of Venezuela. Other countries (Brazil, Ecuador, Colombia, Paraguay, and Uruguay, for example) have the fish, but not necessarily the fishing, lacking the accommodations and infrastructure. And those jungles can be downright dangerous, especially in Colombia and the gold-rich parts of Brazil and Ecuador. **Tarpon** fishing hasn't been fully developed along the northern coast, but look for it in the future. If the price is right, it might be worth the risk to book an exploratory Venezuelan tarpon trip.

Atlantic Ocean

BERMUDA

The island doesn't have the reputation it once had as a fishing destination. Part of the problem is self-inflicted—not so much from overdevelopment as from a shift in marketing strategies and a change in personnel. Until he retired several years ago, Pete Perinchieff kept Bermuda's fishing on the front burner. Now Bermuda lacks either the will or the competence to keep us abreast of the piscatorial possibilities. It's still worth a look, if fishing is part of a family vacation, but I wouldn't risk an out-and-out fishing-trip investment.

GREENLAND

It's not easy to get to or to get around in, but think of the cachet of going to Greenland to catch **sea-run Arctic char** and perhaps even an Atlantic salmon.

ICELAND

Until Russia's Kola Peninsula was opened up around 1990, this was *the* place to go catch large numbers of not particularly large **Atlantic**

salmon. In response to the Russian competition, Iceland has lowered its rates, keeping it in the front rank of salmon destinations. (Incidentally, Laxá simply means "salmon river" in Icelandic, and there are at least ten rivers so named. To properly identify one of the Laxás, you have to add a place name; for example, Laxá in Adaldal.)

AZORES, CANARY ISLANDS, AND MADEIRA

Most of the recent **marlin** action in these island groups has been in offshore trolling, but the adventurous fly-fisherman might give these places a try.

FALKLAND ISLANDS (ISLAS MALVINAS)

These British/Argentine islands in the South Atlantic were stocked with brown trout after World War II, but it wasn't until the mid-1950s that anyone realized the brownies hadn't disappeared, they'd just gone to sea. Inadvertently, the Brits had created a **sea trout** fishery. The biggest and best rivers, the San Carlos and the Malo, are on East Falkland. West Falkland has a number of smaller sea-trout rivers. Although the Malo has produced fish over twenty-three pounds, most of the returning trout weigh in at two to ten pounds. Two runs here: spring (October–November, when most of the big fish arrive) and fall (February–March). The best fishing is in brackish water close to the sea. (Upstream, the rivers hold resident **brown trout** that average about half a pound. The upland lakes also hold browns, up to a pound or two.) The good news is that there are fishing huts on some of the sea-trout rivers, and the Falklands are so lightly fished, you'd pretty much have the place to yourself. The bad news is that the weather is often nasty and the Falklands aren't easy to book—even Frontiers sends people there only as a two-day stop on its two-week Antarctica cruise.

Europe

World-class **brown trout** fishing can be found here and there all over Europe, from the British Isles and the Barents Sea coast of Russia to the Tyrolean Alps and the chalk streams of what used to be

Yugoslavia. (Time and again, my heart sank as I read or heard of military action around the great trout rivers of Bosnia: Neretva, Buna, Trebižat, Sturba, Šuica, Milac, Mrtvica, Drina, Drinjaca, Trebišnica.)

Most of the continental trout waters also hold **European grayling,** similar to ours, but larger and with a smaller dorsal fin. **Atlantic salmon** are best fished in Ireland, the United Kingdom, Scandinavia, and Russia, but there's also some salmon fishing in northern Spain. **Arctic char** occur in higher elevations and latitudes, but a lot of them live in deep lakes and aren't all that accessible to fly-rodders. Where they occur in rivers, char are great fun on a fly rod—if you can get them to take a fly. **Huchen** (also called Danube salmon and river charr) are found in the Danube system but are fairly rare and are easier to take with spinning tackle.

Europe's other popular sport species, the so-called **coarse fish**—pike, zander, perch, asp, carp, and numerous cyprinids—are usually taken on other tackle, but the adventurous fly-fisher will find plenty of targets in the British Isles and on the Continent. Your best bet is probably **pike** in the Baltic.

Fishing permits and regulations vary widely. On the Continent, many countries have national fishing licenses and some also require a local or private permit. In a few, you must join a fishing organization. If you are traveling on your own, the national tourist offices can steer you to the agencies that issue the permits and regulations.

UNITED KINGDOM

Where to begin? Here in the birthplace of fly-fishing, opportunities abound. The very names of the rivers are enough to give one goose flesh: Itchen, Test, Exe, Kennet, Ribble, Severn, Wye, Avon, Tweed, Tay, Spey, Thurso, Oykel, Dee, Usk, Dovey, Conway. One fishes the U.K. not so much for the quality of the fishing as to steep oneself in history and tradition, to fish in the shadow of Izaak Walton and Charles Cotton and Dame Juliana Berners. Be prepared to spend your Sundays sightseeing, for Sunday fishing isn't permitted in many places, and where it is the guides and gillies don't work on Sundays.

England

England can be a hard place to find quality fishing. So much of the good water is tied up by private clubs and in long-term leases. Some booking agents have good weeks reserved on some of the best waters, but be prepared to pay handsomely. If you want to explore English fishing on your own, the tourist boards can steer you to the hotels that own fishing access on many good rivers. English **salmon** fishing can be downright difficult, even if you manage to find a good beat on a good river in a good season. North American anglers are often amazed to discover that English salmon fishermen are not loath to use spinning and casting tackle in high water. The **sea trout** fishing is easier to find, and more reliable. Many hotels and clubs will sell visiting anglers day or week tickets. The best fishing is in West Country rivers that run into the Irish Sea. **Brown trout** are found throughout England, especially in hilly country, but the legendary chalk streams are in the south. Really top-drawer chalk-stream fishing is hard to come by, as most of it is private water. A dirty little secret: Trout caught in faster-flowing streams fight better than those taken in chalk streams. If you want to go really English, try fishing one of the reservoirs such as the Chew.

Scotland

Scotland's famous **salmon** fishing is quite variable, and the seasons vary from river to river. Some rivers have only one strong run of fish, others have two or even three. Costs vary from quite moderate to very dear. Salmon waters are controlled by clubs, hotels, private proprietors, and the Crown. You can count on the very best weeks on the very best rivers being booked solid, but access to decent fishing is good. Because of all the variables, study up carefully before investing in a Scottish salmon trip. The best **sea trout** fisheries are in the islands. The Orkneys fish best in spring and fall, the Inner and Outer Hebrides from late June into September, and the Shetlands in July through September. Because of the salmon and sea trout, **brown trout** get short shrift in Scotland's angling lore, but there is plenty of good trout fishing all across the country. Up in the highlands, an angler willing to walk across the peat moors can find plenty of tiny trout lochs that have seldom if ever seen a fly.

Wales

Americans seldom think of Wales when they think of British fishing, but the English do. In fishing terms, Wales is more or less a lilliputian England. Few American booking agents sell Welsh fishing trips, but it's relatively easy to gain access to good **salmon, trout, and sea trout** waters through hotels.

Ireland

Atlantic salmon fishing on the Emerald Isle is only so-so, despite the presence of the legendary Ballynahinch and thirty-some other salmon rivers. But the fishing is quite inexpensive compared to most *Salmo salar* venues, and it would be hard to top the beauty and charm of the setting. Most of the rivers have a spring (January to June) run of salmon and a summer (June to October) run of grilse, with a few large summer salmon here and there

Eire's **brown trout** fishing can be superb, if demanding, and Lough Corrib is reputed to be the best lake fishery in Europe (with nothing but wild, native trout). **Sea trout** can be found in most Irish rivers of any size and in some loughs that are connected to the sea. The best fishing occurs in the evening after a flood, when the water is a bit high, and on the west coast streams.

NORWAY

In a word, **salmon.** Norway has plenty of fishing, but Atlantic salmon is the name of the game. The best and most famous rivers—such as the Alta—are in the far north. Norwegians have done a good job of keeping salmon-fishing supply and demand in line, through pricing. Consequently, you can nearly always book a good week on a good river, if your pockets are deep enough. A week on a famous river in Norway costs more than twice or thrice what it costs to fish for salmon in Russia. Lesser streams are available at lower costs.

SWEDEN

Sweden has a few good **salmon** rivers from southern Sweden to the Finnish border, but most of its salmon streams have been spoiled by hydropower dams. The most productive streams are the Mörrum (late May–early June and August–September) and the Em (April–May and late August to mid-October). Swedish salmon tend to be large and the rivers relatively small: 8- to 10-weight, one-handed rods are in order. Sweden can't compare with Norway for salmon fishing, but to top Sweden's **sea trout** fishing (the Em and the Mörrum again), you pretty much have to go to Tierra del Fuego for bigger fish or the Barents Sea coast of Russia for faster fishing. April–May for *large*, holdover sea trout, late August to early October for bright fish fresh in from the Baltic.

Brown trout are everywhere (April to October in the south, June and July in Lappland), and the Swedish fly-fishermen I know all cite Jämtland—a forested montane region in the west-central part of the country—as their favorite trout habitat. Up in Lappland, **grayling** and **char** come into their own. Late June to early September for grayling. The Kaitum River is a particularly good grayling and trout stream. Most of the char fishing is done in high mountain tarns, difficult on a fly rod, high-speed, high-density sinking lines definitely required. Swedes prefer to jig for them through the ice.

In the Stockholm Archipelago of the Baltic Sea (the Norrtälje area being a hot spot), the **pike** fishing is nothing short of wonderful from April through the summer: huge fish, and plenty of them. A fifteen-pounder is considered borderline small.

Vidjajaura in Swedish Lappland. *(Jan Olsson)*

One trouble plagues Sweden's sportfishing: It isn't well organized for visiting anglers. Few lodges and fishing hotels exist, and guides are hard to find, so check with fly shops. In Stockholm: Karpens and Utters. If you're in Stockholm on business and want to get in a day or two of fishing, try the Stockholmström from the Royal Palace and Opera House all the way to the Baltic: **pike, zander** (European version of walleye), **sea trout,** even **salmon.**

FINLAND

Finland fishes a lot like Sweden, but its salmon fishing may be a bit better. Actually, there are just two or three **Atlantic salmon** rivers worth mentioning: the Tenojoki (Norway's Tana: it's a border river) for big fish, the Naatamojoki for large numbers of smaller fish, and perhaps the Tornio, a dammed stream that produces more sea trout than salmon. Salmon fishing peaks in late June through July, and sometimes there's a mid-August run. **Sea trout** abound in many rivers throughout the country, June through September. The Kuusamo peaks in late June to early July. **Trout** are fished mostly in spate streams, so dry flies don't work well. Many of Finland's streams are marshy—great habitat for both cloudberries and mosquitoes. In the Baltic, Finland's Ahvenanmaa (Åland Islands) rivals Sweden's Stockholm Archipelago for **pike.**

RUSSIA

European Russia probably has a lot more to offer, but so far only the **salmon** fishing on the Kola Peninsula has been adequately tested. And it has been found to be arguably the world's best. The north-coast rivers that flow into the Barents Sea (Rynda, Kharlovka, Eastern Litsa, Siderovka, Varzina, and so on) rival northern Norway for large fish but may produce greater numbers (and more grilse as well). The season gets going in mid-June and carries on into late August on some rivers. The rivers that drain south into the White Sea (Umba, Varzuga, Strelna, and the rest) fish like Icelandic rivers, but with even more fish, most of them grilse and smallish salmon (to twenty pounds). The largest river, the Ponoy, drains the peninsula to the east, and offers almost as many fish as the south-coast rivers, with more large fish in the mix. The Kola's salmon rivers, especially the north-coast rivers, also produce prodigious numbers of **trout and sea trout** as well. (Unfortunately, the Kola's salmon rivers are occasionally cursed with runs of the pink salmon the Russian fisheries people have stocked in the White Sea.) When you fish Russia, be prepared for delays, confusion, and screw-ups. The fishing is usually worth it.

AUSTRIA

For its size, Austria offers a lot of fine **trout** fishing, which is fly-only. Among the country's best rivers are the Traun, Enns, Alm, Mur, and Lammer. Wading usually is deep, so chest waders are a must. Small flies (sizes 14 to 22), fine tippets (6X and finer), and long leaders (12 feet and up) are the drill. Austrian trout fishing peaks when so much of ours goes flat: July and August. Besides the public and hotel waters listed in the excellent booklets available from the national tourist office, the Austrian Fishing Association and Austrian Workers Fishing Clubs control some fine waters throughout the country. Temporary permits can be obtained from both, which are headquartered in Vienna.

FRANCE

Hardly a major fly-fishing destination, but there's plenty of good **trout and grayling** fishing, mostly in Normandy, Brittany, and the mountains—Alps, Pyrenees, and the Massif Central. A. J. McClane considered the Loue, in Franche-Comté, the best trout river in France. **Salmon** fishing is but a shadow of its former self, but some technically remains in the Auvergne's Allier River and in the Pyrenean Gaves d'Olloron. Consider it as a minor diversion while sightseeing and wine-tasting. Most of the country's salmonid water is privately held, but fishing can sometimes be arranged through hotels and tackle shops.

SPAIN

Say "Spain" and most people think "bullfights," but "salmon, trout, and sea trout" would be almost as appropriate. Of the fifteen **salmon** streams in the country, McClane considered nine of them "above average." All these rivers flow north into the Bay of Biscay. The best months for salmon are March to June. **Trout** fishing (for native browns and some rainbows introduced long ago) runs from mid-May through September in the mountains (above 4,500 to 5,000 feet) and early March to mid-August in the rest of the country. It peaks in April and June–July. Spain has some 150 trout rivers, principally in the central mountains and northern-tier provinces (**sea-run trout** in the latter streams). The country's fishing infrastructure is well developed, with fishing huts, *paradores* (hotels), and *albergues de carretera* (wayside inns) located on or near all the major rivers.

SLOVENIA

This has got to be Europe's best-kept fly-fishing secret. This alpine country, formerly part of Yugoslavia, has some of the most beautiful and productive trout streams in the world, especially the Sava Bohinjka, Soča, Lepena, Krka, Sora, Unec, and Unica. Besides **brown and rainbow trout,** Slovenian rivers also produce **grayling** and the endemic **Soča trout** and *križanka* (a hybrid trout naturally occurring in the Soča and Lepena rivers). Because of the fighting in Bosnia and parts of Croatia, Slovenia has been given a bad rap. The war of independence lasted only a few days in Slovenia, and the country is perfectly safe and stable. And the trout fishing is incredible.

CROATIA

Because I haven't been able to get any accurate information out of Croatia, I can't recommend it just now. But the Gacka River is a chalk stream to put on your one-day-for-sure list.

Africa

There may be some fine trout fishing in the mountains of North Africa (the Atlas Mountains even have an endemic species, the now-rare Atlas trout), but you've got to be a real explorer to experience it. I don't know of any organized fishing in North Africa. Similarly, the heart of the Dark Continent also may hold some fine fly-fishing, once someone goes out and tests the waters and the species. (Nile perch, for example, have become popular sport species in several other places around the world where they've been introduced.) But much of the fishing that's likely to draw fly-fishers to Africa is for the rainbow trout that were introduced at the turn of the century and the brown trout the Brits seemed to introduce everywhere they could find cold water in the Empire. Where they planted tea and coffee, they planted trout.

A caveat: When fishing in Africa, you must be alert for snakes and potentially dangerous game animals—elephants, rhinos, lions, leopards—that may come to the stream for water. The good news is, crocodiles can't live in water cold enough for trout.

SOUTH AFRICA

Great trout fishing—for both **brown and rainbow trout**—is ready and waiting in Natal, the Transvaal, and Lesotho. The Natal streams are the easiest of access and are administered by the Natal Parks Board. Perhaps the best known are the Mooi and Bushmans rivers in the Drakensberg Range for brown trout and the Umzimkulu River system in the Underberg-Himeville District in southwestern Natal for rainbows. September–October and April–May are the best months, because summer rains may raise the rivers unfishably high.

If fly-fishing for bass is your métier, South Africa can supply that as well: for **largemouth, smallmouth, and spotted bass.** As in the U.S., early-morning and late-afternoon fishing pays off best, and so long as the water temperature doesn't get too low, the fishing runs almost 12 months, although largemouths can be hard to budge in winter (our summer). Bass are even more widely distributed than trout.

Among the widely distributed endemic sport fishes are three species of **yellowfish (*Barbus*), kurper (*Tilapia*), and freshwater snoek, or sawfin (another *Barbus*).**

ZIMBABWE, BOTSWANA, AND ZAMBIA

The **tigerfish** is widely distributed from the Lower Nile west to Ghana and south to the eastern Transvaal and Swaziland, but these are the right places, and March–April and September–October are the right times. Botswana's Okavanga Swamp and the Senyati Gorge at Zimbabwe's Lake Kariba on the Zambezi River are just two of the hot spots. If you haven't heard of tigerfish, try to imagine an overgrown bluefish that jumps like a tarpon. Zimbabwe also has good **trout** fishing in Chimanimani and Nyanga national parks.

KENYA

Along with South Africa, Kenya has the best trout fishing in Africa. Mount Kenya and the Aberdare Range support fine **rainbow trout** fishing at elevations above 5,000 feet, but the brown trout are now quite rare. The higher you go, the better dry flies work; by 10,000 feet, you can fish dries at midday. At such high altitudes, the rainbows will "take" year around, but avoid the March–April and October–November rainy seasons.

TANZANIA

As with the other African countries named, a very good place to combine fly-fishing with game viewing. Like Kenya's, Tanzania's trout fishery is a high-altitude **rainbow trout** fishery, above 5,000 feet. Mount Kilimanjaro has the best fishing as well as the country's only **brown-trout** stream, the Kikafu. Mount Meru's Teme and Nduruma rivers also offer good sport.

SIERRA LEONE

A lot of big, record-breaking **tarpon** have been taken on the coast of this West African nation, particularly the waters around Sherbro Island. Although the sportfishing infrastructure is still pretty rudimentary, the west coast of Africa may someday come to rival the east coast of Costa Rica as a tarpon-fishing destination. The fish are certainly much bigger. Bigger, even, than Florida's, some say.

Asia

Piscatorially speaking, most of the world's largest continent is a vast, uncharted wasteland. Turkey, Lebanon, Iran, Afghanistan, and the Pamir range in Kyrgyzstan and Tajikistan are all known to have supported trout species and subspecies, but there are too few left to even think about fishing for them. As for the remaining endemics, only Pacific salmon, steelhead, and the taimen, or Siberian salmon, seem to have much draw among traveling anglers.

RUSSIA (SIBERIA)

A few American and European outfitters mount occasional expeditions to Siberia or neighboring *Mongolia* in search of the elusive **taimen,** the largest of all salmonids, which may reach two hundred pounds. But they are solitary fish, so fishing for them is a moving crap shoot. With helicopter charter prices on the rise, enthusiasm for taimen fishing seems to be waning. You fish for them with huge flies— saltwater type streamers or life-size deer-hair mice—and they feed best late at night. The best locations seem to be east of the Lena River Basin. The other endemic Siberian salmonid, the **lenok** (two species), is a lot easier to find and catch. Lenok are strong, bulldogging fish, and they take surface flies avidly, but they seldom jump or fight spectacularly. Although they aren't all that closely related, they kind of resemble our bull trout.

On Kamchatka and a few other places in the Russian Far East, *kumzha* (steelhead) fishing is picking up in popularity among our West Coast fishermen who are on the verge of losing their own steel- heading.

INDIAN SUBCONTINENT

Can anything be as romantically remote, as positively nineteenth- century British Empire, as **trout** fishing in the Vale of Kashmir? Actu- ally, you can find trout all across the top of the subcontinent, from *Jammu and Kashmir* and *Uttar Pradesh* in the west to *Nepal, Sikkim, and Bhutan* in the east, and some trout fishing farther south in *India.* Thank the Raj. Trout fishing is also being developed in the Hindu Kush and the Karakoram in *Pakistan*'s North West Frontier Province and Northern Territories. Thank the Pakistani gov- ernment. The other piscatorial attraction in the region—in such rivers as Kashmir's Jhelum, Pakistan's Kunhar, and India's Cauvery— is the **mahseer,** a large (to one hundred pounds), predatory tooth- carp that makes largemouth bass look like tentative feeders. Thank Mother Nature. Fishing any of these areas, particularly Bhutan, requires lots of thoughtful planning, coordination, and paperwork. Lots of paperwork, thanks to border disagreements between India, Pakistan, and China. Best leave it to a good booking agent who knows the area well.

From what I can gather, best fly-fishing for trout in the snow-melt rivers is in April and August–September because monsoons turn them into raging torrents in May to July, but smaller, spring-fed streams fly-fish well across the season, mid-April to mid-October. Best mahseer fishing seems to be in January to March, at least in India's Cauvery.

JAPAN

The Land of the Rising Sun has plenty of salmonid fishing—for local species such as **yamame, amago, amemasu, illmemasu, sakuramasu, himemaru, iwana, ito** as well as **brown, rainbow, brook, and lake trout** introduced as early as 1892—and an estimated 20 million active anglers. But much of the fishing is controlled by local associations (which do sell daily permits), and it's hard to find English-speaking guides. Fishing hotels here and there make it easy to fish, but most of them are on lakes rather than flowing waters. Good trout streams with stocked browns and rainbows as well as wild *iwana* and *yamame* can be found in the gorges and narrow valleys in the Akika Keikoku district less than two hours outside Tokyo. Bring your own fly rod and reel, because most Japanese anglers are long-pole fishermen and fly tackle isn't easy to rent. Flies, fly lines, and leaders are readily available in tackle shops.

Australasia

When fly-fishermen think "Down Under," they almost invariably think of those big brown trout in New Zealand. Fair enough. But don't ignore the excellent trout fishing in Tasmania and the fishing for barramundi and more exotic species in Australia and Papua New Guinea.

NEW ZEALAND

The South Island's **brown trout** are big, live in thin, clear streams in profoundly beautiful settings, are wary as all get-out, and aren't easy

Far off and fine: trout fishing on New Zealand's South Island. (*Frontiers*)

to catch. It's quality, not quantity, fishing: sight-casting to maybe six to ten big fish a day. Many an American fly-fisher has been disappointed in New Zealand, mostly because he couldn't cast well enough or failed to heed the guide's good advice, which sometimes runs contrary to North American norms. If you are going to book a November to April trip to the South Island (and they are easy to come by, these days), plan to spend several weeks practicing your pinpoint casting, and leave your this-expert-needs-no-advice shoulder chip at home. If you want *easy* fishing for really big trout (**rainbows**) in virtually any month, try trolling flies in Taupo or one of the other trout lakes on the North Island.

Much of the excellent saltwater fishing in the Bay of Islands is oriented to big-game trolling, but saltwater fly-fishing is catching on.

TASMANIA

Because this Australian island state is so small (at 26,200 square miles, its area is between that of South Carolina and West Virginia), all of its **trout** fishing is within an easy drive of its main cities, Hobart and Launceton. Because of all the stocked lakes, Tasmanian trout fishing is a year-round proposition. Even the rivers are fishable most of the year, but they're a bit low by summer's end (March). The north-flowing streams (Brumby's Creek, and the Macquarie, North Esk, Meander, and Lake rivers) are generally considered the best for trout, but virtually all of the island's smaller rivers afford decent fly-fishing. Because Tasmania fronts on the Antarctic Ocean, the weather can be nasty in the early season (August–September), but the fishing is still good. The coolness keeps the caddises and mayflies hatching even in midsummer (January and February). To fish Tasmania, you must dress warm and be able to cast in the wind, because it's seldom calm the whole day long.

AUSTRALIA

There's some decent **trout** fishing in Australia (in the Snowy Mountains, for example), but is it worth the long, long trip? Probably not unless it's combined with other reasons—saltwater fishing, say, or diving on the Great Barrier Reef.

Barramundi (sort of a Down Under snook that takes to Lefty's Deceivers and other standard saltwater patterns) is the chief fly-rod target here. Much of the May–June and September–October fishing centers on the Coburg Peninsula and the Bathurst and Melville islands in Australia's Deep North. Among the other popular inshore species: **queenfish, trevally, threadfin salmon, tangigue, barracuda, mangrove jack.** Offshore fly-fishing (especially for **sailfish** in northern Queensland, from mid-May to August) is beginning to catch on in the Barrier Reef area, but trollers still dominate the fleet.

PAPUA NEW GUINEA

Freshwater **barramundi, niugini bass, and spottail bass**—big, tough brawlers, all—are the fish that bring increasing numbers of anglers to the jungle rivers of New Guinea. All can be taken on heavy fly tackle, but the preferred method is to tease them up with popping plugs, then cast a fly at them.

Pacific Ocean

The world's largest ocean is full of both fish and islands, and I suspect we've only begun to tap its sportfishing potential. For now, most of the fly-fishing opportunities can be counted on the fingers of one hand. Many islands and atolls have fish, even bonefish, in their lagoons and on their reefs, but heavy netting for food has so depleted the stocks as to make serious sportfishing futile.

HAWAII

The fiftieth state is primarily an offshore trolling destination, because the volcanic mountains slope away quickly into very deep water. However, some opportunities exist for offshore fly-rodding for such species as **dolphin, bonito, yellowfin and other tunas, and marlin.** Inshore, fly-fishing in the surf and the shallow waters around rocky points will produce **bonefish, crevalle jacks, and various smaller species.** Little fresh water occurs naturally on the islands, and gobies are the only native freshwater fish. Several reservoirs on Oahu, Hawaii, and Kauai have been stocked with **bass, carp, and channel catfish,** if reservoir fly-fishing is your cup of tea. Only one island, Kauai, has **trout** fishing during a short summer season at Kokee. I doubt anyone would want to travel all the way to Hawaii to go fly-fishing, but maybe it's worth carrying a travel rod and a box of trout or bonefish flies if you're going there anyway.

CHRISTMAS ISLAND

This island in the Republic of Kiribati is the piscatorial pearl of the Pacific. Extensive **bonefish** flats are the main attraction, but fly-fishing for *ulua* **(giant trevally), blue trevally, and striped trevally** (the South Pacific's answer to the Atlantic's permit) is a spectacular sidelight. Day trips offshore are possible, if you want to have a go at **blue or black marlin** (July and December), **sailfish** (November to

January), **dolphin, wahoo, yellowfin tuna, or giant trevally** (all year). You may lose your catch to sharks, though; they are least plentiful during the Kiribati winter (June to September).

KANTON ISLAND

This neighbor, also in Kiribati, is being added to the international fishing menu in 1995. Test-fishing in 1993–94 has people hoping that Kanton may be another Christmas Island.

Appendix B

THE VISUAL RECORD

Every fishing trip adds something to your repertoire of stories, your mental bank of memories. Your reputation as a raconteur probably rests as much on the stories of the hardships, fiascoes, and calamities endured as it does on those of the big fish you caught and the really fast fishing days when you released dozens of fish. Those memories and stories are perhaps the finest products of a fishing trip. For some, the memories are enough. For others, the memories are made more vivid, more abiding, when they are accompanied by photographs and videos.

If you don't like the pictures you bring back from your fishing trips, you're obviously doing something wrong. Get and read one of the many books on taking better pictures. (For point-and-shooters the thirty-three-page booklet *How to Take Great Photographs with a Compact Camera* is especially handy. It's available for $4.95 from Olympus Corporation, Crossways Park, Woodbury, NY 11791-2087; phone 1-800-221-3000, Dept. #042.) As I seldom bring back many photographic keepers from my trips, I decided to ask the following fishing photographers for advice:

▶ R. Valentine Atkinson of San Francisco, arguably the best fishing photographer at work today
▶ Tony Dawson of Anchorage, Alaska, a freelance photographer and outdoor writer, pilot, veterinarian, and natural-history lecturer

▶ David Hill, a senior producer at Alaska Video Postcards in Anchorage, whose videography is featured in the Sportfishing Alaska series

▶ Ron Spomer of Troy, Idaho, a freelance photographer and outdoor writer

Having digested their good advice and studied my own photographic failures, I've come up with the following bare-bones-minimum list of dos and don'ts:

▶ Carry a camera you will actually want to use. For most people that means an auto-everything, point-and-shoot camera that's easy to carry and will do most of the work for you.

▶ Start with a fresh set of batteries in the camera and carry some spares—at least one set for still cameras, half a dozen for video camcorders.

▶ Protect your camera from water. Get one that's weatherproof, if not waterproof, so you won't be afraid to get it wet. (At the very least, do what Leon Chandler does: carry your little point-and-shoot in a Ziploc plastic bag when you are wading. Leon, the long-time vice president of Cortland Line Company, now retired, is one of the best-traveled fly-fishermen around.)

▶ Buy and shoot a lot of *good* film—stick to Kodak, Fuji, Ilford, Polaroid, and other top-line films—and have it processed professionally. Don't trust the corner drugstore or the cheap mail-order labs.

▶ Keep your lenses clean and safe. Keep them covered with a skylight (1A) or UV haze filter. Remove dust, waterspots, and grime with lens tissues or a lean, dry, soft cotton handkerchief that's used only for your camera.

▶ Carry a lightweight tripod or monopod for long exposures and sharp pictures generally. Or steal a good idea from my friend Tony McCauley, president of Full Spectrum Productions in Mountain View, California. McCauley always carries a small, ringed tripod, with about six feet of sash cord tied to the O-ring. He steps on the cord and pulls up on the camera. "It's the cheapest investment you can make in sharp pictures," he says. "I've been using the same ninety-eight-cent tripod screw for more than twenty-five years."

▶ Work in close to your subject. The number one cause of dull, unexciting pictures is standing too far away.

▶ Steer clear of cluttered backgrounds. Squat or lie down to isolate your subject against the sky or a distant hillside; use a long lens and a wide aperture (f/4, f/5.6) to throw the background out of focus; put your subject in sunlight and use a dark, shaded background; get rid of cigarettes, beer cans, and extraneous clutter.

▶ Use color for contrast and interest. As Valentine Atkinson says, "If you can't make it good, at least make it red. Ask your friends to wear bright-colored clothing." Atkinson even carries a red windbreaker for this purpose. You might get by with a red or other brightly colored cap that you can put on drably dressed fishermen.

▶ Use fill-flash to eliminate the dark shadows under hat brims, in eye sockets, and under noses and chins that ruin portraits and candid shots of people on bright, sunny days. Most automatic cameras have this feature built in, so you don't have to learn anything other than how to switch it on. At the very least, ask your subjects to tilt their hats back and up and to look over your head rather than at the camera. "Try to use reflections off the water to fill in the shadows," Ron Spomer suggests. "Have your subject turn both ways until you see that the water is bouncing light up into his face." Tony Dawson reminds us that "you can also use fill-flash to brighten back-lit subjects or gray-day portraits."

▶ White-balance video cameras often, David Hill says—every hour in high latitudes—to compensate for color-balance shift as the sun moves across the sky.

▶ Don't overdo the panning and zooming. I've seen fishing videos that almost made me seasick, with all their rapid panning from side to side and their zooming in and out.

▶ Do your friends a big favor by editing mercilessly. Don't show seven or eight shots of the same thing when one or two will do. Don't show your fuzzy, over- or underexposed pictures.

▶ Think like a storyteller. Look for humor, drama, telling details. Shoot the food on the table, your guide resting on the bank, the woman who does the laundry and changes the sheets. They're all part of the fishing experience you had, part of the story you want to tell.

▶ Don't keep your eye glued to the viewfinder. You'll see and remember a lot more with the naked eye.

Film Security

Before you get into a knock-down-drag-out with airport security over X-raying your film, know that a study conducted in 1993 by the National Association of Film Manufacturers (NAPM) tested nearly five hundred rolls of black-and-white and color (both slide and transparency) film. The films tested ranged in speed from ISO (ASA) 50 to 1600 (with some black-and-white rolls "pushed" to 3200) and were divided into four groups and exposed to X-ray inspection one, four, sixteen, or a hundred times. The films were then processed and compared to a control group of films that hadn't been exposed to X-radiation. Here's what the test showed:

▶ Effects are virtually undetectable, even on the fastest films, after sixteen X-ray exposures.
▶ Even after one hundred exposures, it takes a "discriminating viewer" to notice the effects.
▶ Black-and-white film is more tolerant of X-ray exposure than is color-negative film, and color-reversal (transparency) film is "the least susceptible to X-ray effects."

In other words, your snapshots are reasonably safe. However, the film manufacturers befogged the rosy picture a bit by hedging their bets: "The NAPM continues to recommend that consumers avoid X-ray inspection of films faster than ISO 400 speed."

It must be noted that the NAPM test used properly maintained X-ray machines calibrated to FAA regulations. At airports overseas, your guess is as good as mine.

In its "Current Information Summary on X-Ray Fog," Eastman Kodak says, "The most common cause is X-ray inspection equipment used in foreign countries that emits a higher level of radiation than equipment used in the United States." Kodak's recommendation: "At airport inspection stations, request visual inspection of photographic materials." The operative word here is *request.* Don't demand, and don't argue. Otherwise, you may wind up in the back room (as I once did in Stockholm), having a tense little tête-à-tête with the airport security gestapo. If you want to try to avoid X-raying your film, remove

35mm film cassettes from their cans and put them in clear plastic bags for easy inspection. Ask politely, and hope for the best.

Two last points:

▶ Never put film in checked baggage, which is inspected using much stronger X rays. And don't try to put film in those "X ray–proof" lead-foil film bags and then pack them in your checked baggage. They will show up on the screen as a suspicious void and may result in your bags being delayed and broken into, while you are sipping a cocktail at thirty-five-thousand feet, blissfully unaware that your bags are still back at JFK or LAX.

▶ As for videocassettes, you needn't worry about X-ray inspection, but it's probably not a good idea to carry them through a metal detector. On international flights, don't put them in your checked baggage, either. According to Sony Electronic's Recording Media Products Group, "The baggage conveyors on international flights often have large electric motors that generate strong electromagnetic fields that might cause problems on videotapes. You should carry your videocassettes with you while traveling abroad, and hand them off before you go through the metal detectors." Ditto for audiocassettes.

Appendix C

TRIP LISTS

As Tony Dawson observed in Chapter 2, you can't properly plan for a fishing trip without making lists. You will need at least two: a to-do list of things that must be done before you leave home and a packing list of things you will need to bring. Eventually, if not sooner, you will want to make your own, custom-tailored lists. In the meantime, you may want to use the generic lists on the following pages,* which have been adapted from the lists I use.

The lists are intended to cover every conceivable type of trip, so don't think you should carry everything listed. Just cross off the items that don't apply to you (or to the particular trip). The blank lines are there so you can add things you need that I don't. The bracketed spaces are for noting the number of such items you need to pack. And there's plenty of space for you to list the particular rods, reels, spare spools, lines, leaders, and flies you wish to carry on the trip.

---

*You are hereby granted permission to copy and reproduce the to-do and packing lists on the following pages for your personal, noncommercial use.

TO-DO LIST

Six to Eight Weeks Prior to Departure

☐ Obtain/renew passport
☐ Apply for necessary visa(s)
☐ Consult doctor, begin daily conditioning exercises
☐ Make appointment with doctor for a checkup
☐ Make appointment with dentist for a checkup
☐ Start reading up on the area you'll be visiting, the fish you'll be fishing for
☐ _____
☐ _____

Three to Four Weeks Prior to Departure

☐ Check insurance coverage abroad
    ☐ Medical coverage
    ☐ Air-evacuation coverage
    ☐ Auto coverage
☐ Look into trip insurance
☐ _____
☐ _____

Two to Three Weeks Prior to Departure

☐ Call CDC International Travelers Hotline (1-404-332-4559)
☐ See doctor for checkup
☐ Get letter from doctor
☐ See dentist for checkup
☐ Buy trip insurance, if needed
☐ Begin daily casting practice with trip tackle
☐ Get references from booking agent, outfitter, or guide of at least two anglers who booked the same trip the year before
☐ Call angler references
☐ Buy/tie recommended flies
☐ Buy other recommended tackle and gear
☐ Buy traveler's phrase book

☐ Buy pocket dictionary
☐ Start practicing your Hellos, Pleases, Thank-yous, and other phrases
☐ _____
☐ _____

Two Weeks Prior to Departure

☐ Lay out tackle for trip
☐ Clean, lubricate reels
☐ Clean fly lines
☐ Check over rest of tackle, gear; replace, repair, overhaul as necessary
☐ Check, replenish contents of fishing vest/tackle bag
☐ Replenish toilet articles, first-aid kit, etc.
☐ Check accuracy of dates, other data on visa(s)
☐ Consult Consular Information Sheets, Travel Warnings (Consular Affairs Bulletin Board, phone 1-202-647-5225, fax 1-202-647-3000, modem 1-202-647-9225)
☐ Confirm reservations
    ☐ Airline
    ☐ Rail, other transport
    ☐ Car rental
    ☐ Hotel

Last Week Prior to Departure

☐ Lay out clothing, other gear
☐ Fill prescriptions
☐ Buy over-the-counter medications
☐ Buy snacks
☐ Buy small gifts for guides, camp staff
☐ Get money [$_____], including small bills
☐ Buy traveler's checks [$_____]
☐ Convert a little currency [$_____]
☐ Make list of contacts abroad and phone, fax, account, policy numbers to carry with you
☐ Make list of itinerary, contact numbers to leave behind
☐ Leave list(s) with relative, friend, neighbor

- [ ] Make photocopies of
    - [ ] Passport
    - [ ] Visa(s)
    - [ ] Airline, other tickets
    - [ ] Traveler's check serial numbers
- [ ] Mow lawn
- [ ] Pay bills
- [ ] Stop newspaper delivery
- [ ] Hold/redirect mail
- [ ] Notify police
- [ ] Notify neighbors
- [ ] Get haircut
- [ ] _____
- [ ] _____
- [ ] _____
- [ ] _____

TRIP PACKING LIST

- [ ] Passport
- [ ] Visa/tourist card
- [ ] Airline tickets
- [ ] Hotel reservation info (including confirmation #)
- [ ] Rental car reservation info
- [ ] Cash (including small bills) [$_____]
- [ ] Traveler's checks [$_____]
- [ ] Credit card(s)
- [ ] Money pouch/holster
- [ ] Contact lists for destination
- [ ] Phone/fax/account/policy #s back home
- [ ] Prescriptions for medicines, eyeglasses
- [ ] Letter from doctor
- [ ] Photocopies of important papers
- [ ] Customs registration for cameras
- [ ] Extra eyeglasses
- [ ] Polarized sunglasses
- [ ] Eyeglass cleaner

- [ ] Prescription medicines
- [ ] Prescriptions
- [ ] Letter from doctor
- [ ] First-aid kit (see pp. 164–65)
- [ ] Over-the-counter medications
- [ ] Special foods (decaffeinated coffee or tea; sugar or salt substitutes; lactase tablets; etc.)
- [ ] Toilet articles kit
- [ ] Toilet paper
- [ ] Skin lotion
- [ ] ChapStick or similar lip moisturizer
- [ ] Insect repellent
- [ ] Head net
- [ ] Bug jacket
- [ ] Sunscreen
- [ ] Sunblock
- [ ] Candy/snacks
- [ ] Booze
- [ ] Business cards
- [ ] Notebook
- [ ] Pens/pencils
- [ ] Electric converter set
- [ ] Reading material
- [ ] Fishing trip log
- [ ] Phrase book
- [ ] Pocket dictionary
- [ ] Area/country guide book
- [ ] Underwear [_____] shirts
- [ ] Underwear [_____] shorts
- [ ] Shoes for plane/city
- [ ] Socks for city shoes
- [ ] City slacks [_____]
- [ ] Blazer/sport coat
- [ ] Dress shirt(s) [_____]
- [ ] Tie
- [ ] Photojournalist vest
- [ ] Umbrella/raincoat
- [ ] Belt

- [ ] Pajamas
- [ ] Bathrobe
- [ ] Slippers
- [ ] Travel alarm clock
- [ ] Fishing hat/cap
- [ ] Fishing shirts [_____]
- [ ] Fishing pants [_____]
- [ ] Rain gear
- [ ] Windbreaker
- [ ] Hiking shoes/camp boots
- [ ] Camp socks [_____]
- [ ] Towel
- [ ] Swim trunks/suit
- [ ] Shoe/boot laces
- [ ] PFD/inflatable vest
- [ ] Fishing vest
- [ ] Shoulder tackle bag
- [ ] Day pack
- [ ] Fanny pack
- [ ] Camera
- [ ] Camcorder
- [ ] Extra batteries [_____]
- [ ] Film [_____] rolls
- [ ] Videotape [_____] cassettes
- [ ] Camera/camcorder case (padded, and preferably waterproof)
- [ ] Tripod/monopod
- [ ] Binoculars
- [ ] Bird book
- [ ] Other field guides _____

  _____

- [ ] Plastic garbage bags [_____]
- [ ] Zip-locked plastic bags [_____]
- [ ] Canteen/flask for water
- [ ] Flashlight
- [ ] Rods, including spare(s) [_____]: _____

  _____

  _____

- [ ] Rod cases [_____]

- [ ] Rod repair kit
- [ ] Reels, including spare(s) [_____]: _____
  _____
  _____
- [ ] Spare spool(s) [_____]: _____
  _____
  _____
- [ ] Reel repair kit
- [ ] Fly lines, including spare(s) [_____]: _____
  _____
- [ ] Fly-line dressing
- [ ] Leaders, including spare(s) [_____]: _____
  _____
  _____
- [ ] Leader/tippet spools [_____]: _____
  _____
  _____
- [ ] Stripping basket
- [ ] Flies
  - [ ] Dry flies: _____
  - [ ] Wet flies: _____
  - [ ] Streamers: _____
  - [ ] Nymphs: _____
  - [ ] Terrestrials: _____
  - [ ] _____
  - [ ] _____
  - [ ] _____
- [ ] Fly-tying tools and materials
- [ ] Hook file
- [ ] Hemostat
- [ ] Pocketknife
- [ ] Side-cutting pliers
- [ ] Nail clipper/line nipper
- [ ] Stream thermometer
- [ ] Glue (epoxy, Pliobond, Super Glue, Zap-a-Gap)
- [ ] Duct tape
- [ ] Compass

- ☐ Map(s)
- ☐ Signal mirror
- ☐ Whistle
- ☐ Matches
- ☐ Tape measure
- ☐ Weight scale
- ☐ Reasonable expectations and a sense of humor
- ☐ _____
- ☐ _____
- ☐ _____
- ☐ _____

For Temperate and High-Latitude Trips

- ☐ Warm wool trousers [_____]
- ☐ Shorts/swim trunks for sauna (if available)
- ☐ Long underwear [_____]
- ☐ Insulated underwear [_____]
- ☐ Fleece wader pants
- ☐ Warm shirts [_____]
- ☐ Heavy wool sweater/fleece pullover
- ☐ Warm-up/sweat suit
- ☐ Warm hat/watch cap
- ☐ Fingerless insulated gloves (wool, neoprene, polyfleece)
- ☐ Warm gloves
- ☐ Insulated vest
- ☐ Insulated parka
- ☐ Hip waders/boots
- ☐ Chest waders/boots
- ☐ Wader suspenders
- ☐ Wader belt
- ☐ Wading staff
- ☐ Wader repair kit
- ☐ Wading chains
- ☐ Wading boot laces
- ☐ Heavy socks [_____]
- ☐ Inner socks/sock liners [_____]
- ☐ Emergency/Space blanket

☐ Eye shades (for sleeping under the midnight sun)
☐ _____
☐ _____
☐ _____
☐ _____

For Tropical and Saltwater Trips

☐ Light cool pants [_____]
☐ Fishing shorts [_____]
☐ Light sweater
☐ Deck shoes
☐ Wading shoes/sandals
☐ Waterproof boat bag
☐ Waterproof lubricant spray for reels, reel seats
☐ Snorkeling gear (mask, fins, snorkel tube)
☐ Golf glove
☐ _____
☐ _____
☐ _____
☐ _____

Appendix D

FISHING TRIP LOGS

Even if you don't normally keep a fishing log when you fish around home, keep one when you travel far afield. Your log will be as important as your photographs in jogging your memory and making your memories come alive.*

Numerous logs are available in fly shops and from mail-order catalogs. If you can find one that suits your needs, buy it. Otherwise, feel free to borrow mine. The logs on the following pages are reduced copies of the ones I carry in a three-ring binder—printed or photocopied on heavy (67 lb. basis), 8½-by-11 Bristol Vellum. If you'd like, you can photocopy† these blank logs, or you can use them as guides for developing your own. (If you decide to photocopy them as is, keep them in a smaller binder; or enlarge them by 130 percent so they will fit on 8½ × 11 paper.)

---

*If you'd like to see how wonderful a fishing log can be, try to find a copy of *Muriel Foster's Fishing Diary*, published in 1980 by The Viking Press. It's a lavishly reproduced copy of an utterly charming fishing diary (complete with watercolor and ink sketches) kept from 1913 to 1949 by a Scottish angler of no mean skill and talent. The book is out of print, but it's certainly worth looking for. If you can't find it in your secondhand book shops, try Judith Bowman Books, Pound Ridge Road, Bedford, NY 10506, phone 1-914-234-7543; The Anglers Art, P.O. Box 148, Plainfield, PA 17081, phone 1-800-848-1020; or a rare book dealer. Expect to pay $40 to $60 for a mint copy, $20 or so for one that's seen some wear. Worth it and then some.

†You are hereby granted permission to copy and reproduce the blank logs on the following pages for your own personal, noncommercial use.

I keep my logs on a computer disk, so I print them out as needed. The computer also allows me to revise and otherwise tinker with them from time to time. Sometimes I even make trip-specific logs.

The little arrows on the first pages of the logs indicate that information can be carried over to the log's "Notes" section.

Besides angling information, use the "Notes" section to record such other details as the names of your fellow fly-fishers, your impressions of the camp or lodge, comments on the facilities and equipment, the manager's name, the shore-lunch menus, the skill of your guide, colorful quotes, anything else that might be useful in show-and-tell sessions back home.

FLY-FISHING LOG

PLACE:

DATE: _____

TIME: _____

WATER
TEMP:
LEVEL:
CLARITY:

WEATHER
TEMP:
WIND:
BAR: R–S–F
SKY:
PRECIP:
HUMIDITY:

FEEDING ACTIVITY

HATCHES

STOMACH CONTENTS, ETC.

NOTES

TIME	SPECIES	SIZE	FLY	LOCATION	REMARKS

SALMON FISHING LOG

PLACE:

DATE: _____

TIME: _____

WATER	
TEMP:	
LEVEL:	
CLARITY:	
TIDE	H L

GUIDE:

NOTES: _____

_____

_____

_____

_____

_____

_____

_____

_____

_____

_____

WEATHER	
TEMP:	
WIND:	N / W–E / S
BAR:	R–S–F
SKY:	
PRECIP:	
HUMIDITY:	

_____

_____

_____

_____

_____

_____

_____

_____

_____

_____

_____

_____

_____

TIME	♂ \ ♀	SIZE	FLY	LOCATION	REMARKS

SALTWATER FLY-FISHING LOG

PLACE:

DATE: _____

TIME: _____

WATER

TEMP:

WAVES:

COLOR:

WEEDS:

TIDE   H   L

WEATHER

TEMP:

WIND:

BAR: R–S–F

SKY:

PRECIP:

HUMIDITY:

GUIDE:

BIRD ACTIVITY AND FISH SIGN

NOTES

TIME	SPECIES	SIZE	FLY	LOCATION	REMARKS

INDEX

About the Author

Gary Soucie is a zealous fly-fisher who spends far too much time at the word processor writing and too little time at the vise tying pretty little flies. He met his wife, Marina Brodskaya, on his most recent trip to the salmon rivers of Russia's Kola Peninsula.

A Woodrow Wilson fellow at the University of Indiana, Soucie graduated from the University of North Carolina at Chapel Hill with a bachelor's degree in comparative literature.

Soucie was the executive editor of *Audubon* magazine for twelve years and a senior staff member of *National Geographic*. He has written hundreds of articles for magazines such as *Fly Rod & Reel*, *Atlantic Salmon Journal*, and *Outdoor Life*, and his books include *Hook, Line, and Sinker: The Complete Angler's Guide to Terminal Tackle* and *Soucie's Field Guide of Fishing Facts*.